Media Business Models

This book is part of the Peter Lang Media and Communication list.
Every volume is peer reviewed and meets
the highest quality standards for content and production.

PETER LANG
New York • Bern • Frankfurt • Berlin
Brussels • Vienna • Oxford • Warsaw

Media Business Models

Breaking the Traditional Value Chain

Edited by Klaus Zilles and Joan Cuenca

PETER LANG
New York • Bern • Frankfurt • Berlin
Brussels • Vienna • Oxford • Warsaw

Library of Congress Cataloging-in-Publication Data

Names: Zilles, Klaus, editor. | Cuenca, Joan, editor.
Title: Media business models: breaking the traditional value chain /
edited by Klaus Zilles, Joan Cuenca.
Description: New York: Peter Lang, 2016.
Includes bibliographical references and index.
Identifiers: LCCN 2015038795 | ISBN 978-1-4331-3179-0 (hardcover: alk. paper)
ISBN 978-1-4331-3178-3 (paperback: alk. paper) | ISBN 978-1-4539-1700-8 (e-book)
Subjects: LCSH: Social media—Marketing. | Social marketing.
Classification: LCC HF5414.M43 2016 | DDC 658.8/72—dc23
LC record available at http://lccn.loc.gov/2015038795

Bibliographic information published by **Die Deutsche Nationalbibliothek.**
Die Deutsche Nationalbibliothek lists this publication in the "Deutsche
Nationalbibliografie"; detailed bibliographic data are available
on the Internet at http://dnb.d-nb.de/.

29 Broadway, 18th floor, New York, NY 10006
www.peterlang.com

Table of Contents

Media Business Models: Breaking THE Traditional Value Chain

BY JOSEP MARÍA CARBONELL, KLAUS ZILLES, AND JOAN CUENCA

The technological revolution we have been experiencing over the past two decades has profoundly altered the world of communication and the way in which we experience communication. The Information Age[1] represents the beginning of a world built around information technologies, which in terms of generating, processing, and transmitting information are the fundamental sources of power and means of production in most contemporary societies. The information technologies do not only shape the economic structures but they also impinge on cultural, social, and political conditions. Communication and media are permanently altered by the technological changes and the influence of electronic communication networks in their development, and one of the core elements in this scenario is the "media value chain" paradigm. This paradigm is based on the numbers of readers, viewers, and users which the mass media can "sell" in exchange for advertising revenue. This value chain has now entered a critical phase owing to the advent of the social media, digitization, and horizontal mass communication.

The flows of information in the new digital communications networks have found unsuspected conduits to disseminate a wealth of information around the world which, along with the digitization of information, has allowed content and information to circulate in every which direction, from peer-to-peer—or point-to-multipoint. Historically, much of this content and information was mostly created, managed, and spread by the communication media and audiovisual culture.

For Manuel Castells, "electronic communication networks will constitute the backbone of our lives" (2000a, p. 384). At the same time, "in a broader historical perspective, the network society represents a qualitative change in the human experience" (2000b, p. 508), in which "information is the key ingredient of our social organization and why flows of messages and images between networks constitute the basic thread of our social structure" (2000b, p. 508). In his 2009 study, *Communication Power*, Castells avers that "all networks of power exercise their power by influencing the human mind predominantly (but not solely) through multimedia networks of mass communication. Thus, communication networks are the fundamental networks of power-making in society" (2009, p. 426).

As a matter of fact, the term "informational capitalism" discussed by Christian Fuchs in his book, *Internet and Society: Social Theory in the Information Age* (2008, p. 102), conveys clearly and boldly the historical, economic, and social context in which the world of mass communication now resides. As for the term "capitalism," Fuchs clarifies that "the historically novel quality is that in more and more systems, such as the economy, polity, and the Internet, we find transnational actors that operate on a global scale; they are transnational/global networks. Hence, it is more appropriate to speak of transnational/global capitalism, transnational/global network capitalism, or transnational/global informational capitalism in order to stress the dialectic of continuity and discontinuity and the role of information and new information and communication technologies (TNCs) in society" (2008, p. 101).

The technological revolution and global, transnational capitalism—up until now discrete movements—have undergone a process of convergence affecting the realms of information, communication, and culture. In his book, *Convergence Culture* (2006), Henry Jenkins provides an in-depth analysis of the effects this convergence process has on the development, creation, and dissemination of culture. He draws attention to the fact that as early as 1983, Ithiel de Sola Pool, a professor at MIT, became, as it were, the first 'prophet of media convergence.' In his book, *Technologies of Freedom*, de Sola Pool emphasizes the process of convergence of contents and networks. Indeed, he states that "a process called the 'convergence of modes' is blurring the lines between media, even between point-to-point communications, such as the post, telephone, and telegraph, and mass communications, such as the press, radio, and television" (De Sola Pool, 1983, p. 23).

Over the last fifteen years there have been three parallel processes of great significance in this sector: the first, which always occurs as a result of technological change, is a process of technological convergence in the field of microelectronics which has affected, in one way or another, all sectors of the audiovisual industry (see Grant & Wilkinson, 2009). In this technological process, digital communication has proven decisive. Secondly, and as an obvious result of the first process, this technological convergence represents a coming together of all stakeholders in different areas of the industry—producers and providers of content, distributors, and Internet and telecommunication providers. Thirdly, there has been a converging of businesses, with wide-reaching international alliances, and the emergence of large corporations that run the communication networks and multimedia, thus controlling the entire process of media production. Technological convergence, convergence of providers, and business convergence: the three key processes that have shaped the nature of media communication in recent years, and which will do so even more in the years to come.

In this same time span, the digitization of information has compelled the print media to reorganize their newsrooms and editorial staff and the way in which they handle news coverage in general. Even the division into printed news and online news has gradually been eradicated and given way to multimedia newsrooms. Digitization and streamlining of information processing has made news coverage much more cost effective and has led to severe cutbacks in personnel while at the same time opening up a range of channels and devices through which media outlets connect with their users. The traditional media have had to go with the times. Their position of hegemony in the area of news coverage has been challenged.

In television, the technological benefits of digitization have resulted in an explosion of TV channels in many countries, with some countries boasting five times as many channels as before the advent of digital TV. Surprisingly, this trend has not affected radio broadcasting. It appears that national regulations and standards are too diverse to establish an international model for digital radio, and although there are stations in the UK, France, Korea, and the US, for instance, the trend of digital radio is lagging far behind other types of media. Almost certainly, though, the one media industry which has been subjected to the most significant changes is the daily newspaper in its printed form, to the extent that this industry is facing an uncertain future.

Through multiple window screens, media outlets strive to find communication strategies to create the necessary synergies to reach their diverse publics. Even so, the traditional media have struggled to find their footing in this new media landscape. Many undoubtedly were weighted down by burdensome managing structures, but all of them have had to face the vital need for reform (Stone & Bierhoff, 2002). Journalists witnessed how their papers' digital editions reached wider audiences than their print editions. Consequently, the media conglomerates, caught up in a fierce contest for audiences, had no choice but to find ways to reach the multimedia consumer with newspapers encroaching on radio and TV, while the audiovisual media, in turn, set about invading the terrain of the printed press. This process reached its culmination with all stakeholders developing their respective web-based media projects.

Another aspect of the deep impact the technological transformation has had on the traditional and the new media is the phenomenon of "mass self-communication".

In his book, *Communication Power*, Manuel Castells describes how the proliferation of horizontal networks, mainly the social media, facilitated the new phenomenon of mass self-communication, which is marked by the communicating individuals' independence from the large communications companies, and by the fact that users both send and receive messages (2009, p. 4). Castells posits that,

> with the diffusion of the Internet, a new form of interactive communication has emerged, characterized by the capacity of sending messages from many to many, in real time or chosen time, and with the possibility of using point-to-point communication, narrowcasting or broadcasting, depending on the purpose and characteristics of the intended communication practice [...] The three forms of communication (interpersonal, mass communication, and mass self-communication) coexist, interact, and complement each other rather than substituting for one another. What is historically novel, with considerable consequences for social organization and cultural change, is the articulation of all forms of communication into a composite, interactive, digital hypertext that includes, mixes, and recombines in their diversity the whole range of cultural expressions conveyed by human interaction. (2009, p. 55)

This new concept perfectly conveys the import of the radical transformation which all web-based media are undergoing. It designates the rupture of a media paradigm marked by a sense of control over the flows of media circulation. With the advent of the Internet, and the vast repercussions it had on the management, production, and distribution —but above all the cost-cutting effect— it seems that we are witnessing a factual breaking of the core elements of the media paradigm and its time-honored value chain dynamics, which were mediated and managed by a few, and within a well-defined cultural context.

Mass self-communication is here to stay—a phenomenon with certain limitations, and many challenging and perhaps even daunting qualities. Nonetheless, it is one of the transformations that are going to shape the media landscape throughout the new millennium. Ironically though, this process is taking place at the same time we are witnessing a process of convergence of media ownership on a global scale.

The simultaneity of these two processes is contradictory and paradoxical: concurrent and parallel to the emergence of mass self-communication, the means of production of audiovisual commodities—both in the news and entertainment industries—wind up in the hands of fewer and fewer owners, all great global players in the world of communication with a strong influence in the televised prime-time sector, in the print media with the largest readerships, and the Internet sites that get the largest share of hits.

The discussion of these major transformations in the media landscape culminates in the subsequent chapters of *Media Business Models: Breaking the Traditional Value Chain* which address a series of key ideas in a thoughtful and insightful fashion:

Firstly, the alteration and apparent rupture of the Media Value Chain, which hinges on the funding of information and entertainment media through advertising revenue, affect the communication industries in their entirety, in all their facets, on the entire globe. Nothing will be the same.

Secondly, no doubt the traditional business models are taking the brunt of the impact the electronic communication has dealt the Media Value Chain. In fact, the end of the media landscape as we know it is taking its toll on the public broadcasting services which until recently have managed the communication media, and which are accustomed to operating in a nation-state environment and within a specific cultural context. This outmoded model is at least in part responsible for the current crisis in the media industries.

And thirdly, we are witnessing a breaking of the cultural and democratic value chain. The process of mediation performed by the traditional media, the press, TV, and radio, is no longer required. The social media are increasingly functioning as a public space for organic interaction and exchange, participation and learning, structuring and gathering which is used by a wide range of communities.

From the situation we have so far outlined arises the dilemma between the participative nature of the new media on the one hand, and their corporative character on the other. The business link between the communication media and advertising is in a moment of crisis as the number of users who are willing to pay for a service is plummeting. As a result, we are now hearing some voices who advocate new business models without commercials as well as those who propose to rethink the transaction between advertisers and agencies. They support innovative approaches to the value chain concept through new ways of segmenting the target, narrowing the demographic, and offering attractive, more specialized brand substances.

The present volume aims to make a significant contribution to pointing the way out of the general bewilderment, supplying answers to frequently asked questions, and ideas for new guidelines and solutions. Is there going to be business for the media in a post-Internet era? What are the best mechanisms to ensure a greater degree of freedom for the individuals who use the World Wide Web, regardless of their economic and technological backgrounds? What are the new alliances and partnerships media and advertisers have to forge in the area of social networks? Which contents are users willing to pay for?

Thus, **Part One** of our volume is entitled "U.S. and European Perspectives of the Changing Media Value Chain Paradigm in Social Networks and Blogs". In the opening chapter, entitled "Face and the Ethics of Social Networks", Polish researchers Nika Bogdanowska and Ewa Bogdanowska-Jakubowska explore Facebook, the new media business model *par excellence*, in terms of users' self-presentations. In particular, they examine the way in which the depiction of one's own face speaks to a specific code of norms and ethics touted by Facebook's makers in the users' respective cultural context.

In chapter two, "Mom 2.0: Mothering in the Blogosphere", US scholars Jennifer Raymond and Jodi Cohen, home in on the blogosphere as a new business model which offers an alternative to published information, which previously resided with the wealthy and influential, in a domain where women remain underrepresented but are now increasingly staking their claim on the public discourse.

Ilona Biernacka-Ligieza, on the other hand, focuses not so much on new business models, but instead on the socio-political contexts in which new business models can flourish. In her chapter, "Virtual Local Public Sphere: The Role of New Media in Creating a Contemporary Local Democracy", she delves into the phenomenon of "glocalization", i.e., new forms of highly localized political organization employing communication technologies in e-government and e-participation. Biernacka-Ligieza illustrates that the use of ICT in local communities is more likely to help advance political and commercial endeavors, tailoring them to specific regional conditions in an economically diverse country such as Poland.

In **Part Two**, "Momentous Challenges in Uncharted Territory: Advertising and Public Relations", we shift focus from socio-political phenomena to the context of Advertising and Public Relations. Thus, chapter four, "Effects of Communication in Public and Media Rationale: Result Measures of Public Relations", brings a pragmatic approach to the question of how to ensure dependability of data when measuring results in Public Relations. Spanish researchers Guillem Marca, Kathy Matilla, and Andréa Oliveira pinpoint the most pressing challenge as the need to adapt to the recent paradigm shift without relinquishing the credibility still associated with the traditional media.

Both PR and advertising currently face a momentous contest arising from the need to procure new business models and ways to engage their various target demographics. In her article, "Hot Brands Are Cool: The Temperature Scale as a Tool for Branding in a Digital Society", Patrícia Dias explores the semiotic and cognitive aspects of the current information-cluttered and stimuli-overloaded media environment. In an empirical, qualitative research project she has analyzed 15 cases of rebranding on the Portuguese market. Cases range from retail marketers, banks, and publishing houses, to TV networks, all of which were positioned on a temperature scale designed to gauge the intensity in which they generate involvement, engagement, and participation.

Whereas Dias focuses on challenges for new business models arising from the difficulty of correctly gauging the appeal of specific rebranded businesses, Araceli Castelló-Martínez and Juan Monserrat-Gauchi see the challenge in the drastic changes affecting the relations and work processes between different stakeholders: the advertiser, the advertising and media agency, the media and, of course, the audience. They profess the need to incessantly conduct research to find better ways to engage and empathize with their target demographic. In their chapter, "The Advertising Offer in the New Media Landscape", they submit a series of frameworks, all using different approaches, that are designed to deploy new strategies for measuring the success of complex social media marketing campaigns.

Felip Vidal, in his chapter entitled, "Media and the Creation of Brand Value in Signification Advertising", paints a picture of a media environment in which traditional media no longer hold the advertising monopoly. Instead, he submits "'signification advertising'" as a term used to describe recent innovations in brand value creation. Three case studies, *Muji*, *Moleskine*, and *Bench*, are used to illustrate the advertising professionals' struggle to generate a renewed semiotic production by reshuffling different industries and media, by narrativizing the brand and thus engendering an "embodiment of the brand in the activity of the consumer".

Elisenda Estanyol, Mireia Montaña, and Ferran Lalueza's chapter on gamification ("Engagement Is the Name of the Game") concludes this volume's advertising and PR section on the metamorphosis of the time-honored media chain paradigm. Gamification constitutes "the use of game design elements in non-game contexts". Using a three-pronged approach, the researchers present data obtained from 1,600 interviews with Spanish Internet users, in-depth interviews with marketing and communication directors, and analyses of various communication campaigns with gamification components.

Part Three, "Traditional Television Teams Up With the Social Networks", features a section especially dedicated to the ways in which the changes of the value chain paradigm have impacted one of its strongholds—network television. In the opening chapter, "Value Changes in Television Audiences: From the Traditional Audience to the Social Audience", Ana González-Neira and Natalia Quintas-Froufe explore phenomena such as "the social audience", "the second screen", and "prosumers", thereby showing how TV content can be complemented and enhanced by social networks campaigns which allow audiences to engage by interacting and participating in the development of a program. Conversely, Boris Ružić's "Towards a History of Media Conjuncture: *The Daily Show*, Audience and the 'Revolution'" zooms in on one particular US TV format, namely Jon Stewart's *The Daily Show*, which he juxtaposes with the mediatization of the 2014 revolution in Ukraine. Ružić proposes to relinquish the notion of "breaking the media value chain" in favor of the concept of media "conjuncture", a term used by Antonio Gramsci and subsequently Stuart Hall, and which according to Ružić continues to speak to the dynamics of ideological struggles in countries like Ružić native Croatia.

The concluding **Part Four** of the present volume, entitled "Inter-Continental Corollaries of Breaking the Media Value Chain in Journalism", turns the spotlight on intercontinental phenomena that illustrate the transformations the media value chain model has been subjected to since the advent of digital communication media. Thus, in chapter eleven, "The Disruption of the Portuguese Media Democracy? Economic Crisis and Media Ownership", Portuguese scholars, Rita

Figueiras and Nelson Costa Ribeiro, analyze instances of media outlets being acquired by new investors that were not traditionally involved in the media and communication business. Many of these acquisitions were made possible by the weakened economic circumstances of traditional media outlets (such as the *Washington Post* purchased by Jeff Bezos in 2013), which in turn must be attributed to the breaking of the media value chain. Plummeting readerships and the ensuing decline in press advertising resulting from the trend toward accessing information gratis on portable devices have made many long-standing media institutions easy prey for investors. The researchers briefly sketch out internationally notorious cases and then move on to pinpoint similar cases in their native Portugal. They particularly observe the rapidly growing Portuguese assets that are now in the hands of Angolan investors, thereby not only disrupting traditional business models, but also creating alarming dynamics and irregularities regarding the freedom of the press and its role as watchdog, both in Portugal and in its former colony.

Bringing up the rear of our book, a different intercontinental view is taken by Luis Concepción Sepúlveda and Alfons Medina, who scrutinize the portrayal of "Africa in Spanish Newspapers: From Indifference to Irrelevance". They show how the coverage of immigration attempts from Sub-Saharan Africa in Spanish online versions of traditional quality newspapers such as *El País* and *El Mundo* took on increasingly detrimental forms of reporting until the financial crisis eventually overshadowed immigration. By using a three-pronged, analytical framework consisting of journalistic analysis, semantic analysis, and formal pragmatic analysis, they conclude that the breaking of the media value chain compelled these newspapers to a more sensationalist style of news coverage in their online versions. Concepción and Medina deplore that this type of reporting has reinforced a negative construction of the image of Africa, which ultimately is symbolic rather than textual, and social rather than journalistic.

The inevitable conclusion the contributors of this volume arrive at is that media outlets must learn unprecedented, groundbreaking methods of distributing, delivering, and monetizing their contents. Users expect access to their preferred content whenever and wherever they are, on a wide range of media devices that are incessantly being modernized, innovated, expanded, and made more affordable. Formerly stable models of the media value chain are now in perpetual flux, requiring adaptation to the rapid progress of technology and the volatility of user preferences. Can media companies cope with these new circumstances and at the same time fulfill their traditional roles?

It is also becoming apparent that new power relations and the exercising of control and regulation are increasingly taking center stage in the debate surrounding the social networks. The Internet abounds with influential intermediaries and gatekeepers who shape and govern the degree of tolerance, plurality, and freedom of the Internet. They also determine the conditions of the information flow, and the nature of the contents which will ultimately influence our behavior, interrelationships, and the evolution of society at large.

REFERENCES

Castells, M. (2000a). *End of millennium* (2nd ed.). Malden, MA: Blackwell.

Castells, M. (2000b). *The rise of the network society* (2nd ed.). Malden, MA: Blackwell.

Castells, M. (2004). *The power of identity* (2nd ed.). Malden, MA: Blackwell.

Castells, M. (2009). *Communication power*. New York, NY: Oxford University Press.

De Sola Pool, I. (1983). *Technologies of freedom: On free speech in an electronic age*. Cambridge, MA: Harvard University Press.

Duff, A. (2000). *Information society studies*. London, UK: Routledge.

Fuchs, C. (2008). *Internet and society: Social theory in the information age*. London, UK: Routledge.

Grant, A. E., & Wilkinson, J. S. (Eds.). (2009). *Understanding media convergence: The state of the field*. Oxford, UK: Oxford University Press.

Jenkins, H. (2006). *Convergence culture: Where old and new media collide*. New York, NY: New York University Press.

Stone, M., & Bierhoff, J. (2002). The state of multimedia newsrooms in Europe. In *The European multimedia landscape*. Heerlen, The Netherlands: International Institute of Infonomics, European Center for Digital Communication.

Webster, F. (2002). *Theories of the information society*. London, UK: Routledge.

NOTE

1. See for example, Castells (2000a, 2000b, 2004, 2009); Duff (2000); Fuchs (2008); and Webster (2002).

Part One: U.S. and European Perspectives of the Changing Media Value Chain Paradigm in Social Networks and Blogs

CHAPTER ONE

Face AND THE Ethics OF Social Networks

NIKA BOGDANOWSKA AND EWA BOGDANOWSKA-JAKUBOWSKA

INTRODUCTION

The main function of social networks is to bring people together and provide them with a platform on which they can interact and exchange information. Like in face-to-face interaction, participants joining a social network establish and maintain relationships with their real friends and "friends" (the individuals they have invited, or the ones they have been invited by to their network circle), and through interacting with them they create their self-image (face) (Goffman, 1967). Upon entering the reality of a social network, people comply with the code of ethics and the generally understood norms of politeness which reflect the codes of ethics and norms of politeness specific to their culture.

The aims of the study are:

- to analyze face-management patterns in social network interactions, and
- to look for self-presentation strategies used in this context.

Erving Goffman's theory of social interaction and face, together with *the extended model of face* (Bogdanowska-Jakubowska, 2013a) constitute the theoretical framework of our analysis.

The data used in the study come from Facebook. On Facebook, people can find their friends and identify them by their names and faces, fulfilling a function similar to the books given to freshmen students at the start of the academic year by university administrations with the intention of helping them get to know each other better, and from which Facebook derives its name. Thus, 'face' is the focus of people's attention, like in face-to-face interaction. On Facebook, exchanges of posts and other actions (e.g., inviting friends, liking, sharing pictures and information, creating groups, and inviting friends to an event) strongly resemble acts performed during face-to-face interactions. In both situations, maintaining 'face' is the basic condition of interaction (Goffman, 1967).

COMPUTER-MEDIATED INTERACTION

During their lifetime people strive to satisfy different kinds of needs. As Abraham H. Maslow (1970) claims, the basic human needs are the key to understanding their behaviour. Apart from physiological and safety needs, people have *belongingness and love needs,* and *esteem needs.* They want to have a place in their group or family, they want to be loved and cherished, or at least accepted by their loved ones. But apart from relationships, they crave achievement, for mastery and competence, and for independence and freedom. They also have "what we may call the desire for reputation or prestige (defining it as respect or esteem from other people), status, fame and glory, dominance, recognition, attention, importance, dignity, or appreciation" (Maslow, 1970, p. 45). Satisfaction of these needs leads to feelings of self-confidence and self-worth.

Invariably, these needs may only be satisfied when people are among other people. Being in proximity to others who approve of them is what individuals need in order to feel good. This is possible in face-to-face encounters, and the founders of the social networks claim that this also holds true in virtual reality.

Facebook as a social networking site is said to provide us with the opportunity to meet people in virtual reality and make friends, to establish and maintain relationships, to interact and communicate with others.

> Facebook's mission has always been to make the world more open and *connected.* We seek to provide a platform where people can *share* and surface content, messages and ideas freely, while still *respecting the rights of others.* When people can engage in meaningful conversations and exchanges with their friends, family and communities online, amazingly positive things can happen. To facilitate this goal, we also work hard to make our platform *a safe and respectful place for sharing and connection.* This requires us to make difficult decisions and balance concerns about free expression and community respect. (https://www.facebook.com/notes/) (the emphasis is mine)

In order to satisfy the belongingness and love needs, as well as the esteem needs, on Facebook users can engage in the following activities:

- finding friends (and inviting them to their own circle, or accepting their invitations);
- liking—unliking (their friends' posts);
- commenting (e.g., on real-life events or on other people's posts);
- sharing (e.g., a picture or some information);
- creating a group or an event;
- inviting friends to an event;
- recommending a page or a friend to other friends.

The activities are highly interactive; we need others to add them as friends or to send a message. Paradoxically, however, while we are sharing interests, photos, or information with them, we are alone, isolated, sitting at our own desk.

On Facebook, people may express their opinions (*What's on your mind?*) and show emotions, using the "like/unlike" button, or they can unfriend someone. The verb *unfriend* can already be found in *The New Oxford American Dictionary* (2010), and it means to "remove (someone) from a list of friends or contacts on a social networking website" (e.g., *She broke up with her boyfriend, but she hasn't unfriended him).*

FACE: A SELF-IMAGE AND A PART OF THE BODY

To be able to interact with others, one needs a face, both in the literal and metaphorical sense. It is true that "the face is an identity card" (Kępiński, 1998b, p. 196). The identification of a person is almost impossible when his/her face is hidden or covered up. 'Almost' impossible, because there are other marks which can help identify him or her. Kępiński (1998a, 1998b; cf. Ciechowicz, 2000) claims that legs and hands can also have an identification function. However, it was the face that was used by Alphonse Bertillon (1853–1914), a French physiognomic anthropologist and criminologist, who in 1883 developed the photographic identification system. These were photographs of the head, taken in profile and in full face, printed on a card providing pertinent information for the purposes of identification (e.g., date of birth, height, or hair colour) (Kemp, 2004). Known as *mug shots*, these photographs have been used for many decades by the police to identify criminals. Later, however, the full-face identification photograph has become the international method for identifying individuals on passports, driving licences, and identity cards (Kemp, 2004). So, unlike any other part of the body, the face functions as an identification mark for a particular person. The metonymy THE FACE FOR THE PERSON has been used also in the name Facebook.

Face as a scholarly concept was introduced to academic discourse by Erving Goffman (1955, 1967). He created the theoretical construct, and based it on the

Chinese concept of face, presented by Hsien Chin Hu (1944), and on some sociological theories (e.g., Emile Durkheim, 1915). Goffman's ideas about face and facework became an inspiration for scholars in many areas of social sciences. Their traces can be found both in social psychology and linguistic research.

The necessary condition of social interaction is maintaining face, defined by Erving Goffman (1967, p. 6) as "the positive social value a person effectively claims for himself by the line others assume he has taken during a particular contact" or "an image of self delineated in terms of approved social attributes". However, face-sensitive issues go far beyond the self understood as "the inner psychological entity that is the centre or subject of a person's experience", perceptions, thoughts, feelings, and beliefs about oneself (Leary & Tangney, 2003, pp. 6–8).

Face in its structure can be compared to lettuce, a leafy vegetable whose leaves get softer towards its centre. Similarly, some aspects of face, the central (internal) ones, are most sensitive and vulnerable to attack or damage; for other aspects (external), the more distant from the centre they are, the less vulnerable to face-threats they become (for a similar conceptualization of face, see Liu (1986)). *The extended model of face* consists of elements which belong to six main categories (Bogdanowska-Jakubowska, 2013a):

1. Personhood (character, behaviour, moral integrity, biography, independence, appearance);
2. Prestige (social status, education, job, achievements);
3. Competence (abilities, knowledge, skills);
4. Family (parents, children, husband/wife, relatives);
5. Affiliation (nationality/ethnicity, world-view, religion, sexual orientation, social group, profession, beliefs);
6. Background (place of birth, place of residence, schools, friends, interests, property).

The first three categories of face-elements refer to the self as an individual, the other three categories refer to the self as a group member and the self in relationship with the outer world (people and things) (cf. Spencer-Oatey, 2009).

The elements belonging to the category *Personhood* constitute the most sensitive area of face. However, they are not of equal importance across cultures. Different social attributes are valued in different cultures. The desire for proximity and approval, and the desire for distance and independence, are inherently present in every individual and in every culture (cf. Brown & Levinson's (1987) positive and negative face), but they differ in intensity. The category *Prestige* involves various social status indicators based on personal effort and achievement, such as educational attainment, occupational status, and income (cf. Ho, 1994). High social status often results from the individual's competence and expertise. So there is a strong connection between these two categories of face-elements. In the category *Competence*, educational attainment is the main social status indicator based on personal effort and achievement. The three categories constitute the central elements of the individual's self-image, which are also those most sensitive to threat.

The other three categories are also relevant because they make the self-image complete, providing the details and facts which help others understand the self. The category *Family* matters in many cultures, but it is especially important in collectivistic cultures, where individuals are bound together by in-group solidarity, and mutual role obligations and duties (Ting-Toomey & Kurogi, 1998). Belonging to a particular family may also have an impact on the individual's social status (and the Prestige category). The *Affiliation* category, which locates the individual in a broader sociocultural context, can also be characterized by in-group solidarity. This time, however, it is not connected with kinship, but with common goals, interests, ideology, or beliefs (cf. Spencer-Oatey, 2009). The *Background* category completes the image of the self, providing the details which may have an explanatory function and justify the individual's face expectations.

To maintain face, participants engage in *facework*, actions in which individuals engage to maintain their own face and the face of the other. There can be observed two types of facework (Bogdanowska-Jakubowska, 2013a):

- *Unmarked facework*, involving actions intended to maintain or enhance self and/or other face, behaviour aimed at establishing a good relationship or at sustaining the current state of a relationship—appropriate behaviour:
  - (a) ethical behaviour,
  - (b) polite/politic behaviour (cf. Watts, 2003; Locher, 2006);s
- *Marked facework*, involving actions which do not meet the addressee's expectations—inappropriate behaviour:
  - (a) unethical behaviour,
  - (b) marked (im)polite behaviour:
    - overpolite behaviour,
    - impolite or rude behaviour.

Thus interacting with others, individuals engage in actions whose appropriateness may be interpreted both in terms of ethics and politeness.

ETHICS OF EVERYDAY LIFE

As Paul Ricoeur (1992, p. 172) claims, ethics involves "aiming at the 'good life' with and for others". Understood as "a set of standards by which a particular group or community decides to regulate its behavior", it distinguishes "what is legitimate or acceptable in pursuit of their aims from what is not" (Flew, 1979, p. 112). Thus, ethics refers to standards of morality that apply to men in relation to other men, and in addition can be associated with a specific activity or profession. It can be associated with values significant for good social relations, such as interdependency, freedom, honesty, dignity, uprightness, sincerity, and respect for the other.

Ethical action is situated "explicitly in relationship" (Austin, 2008, p. 748). Rules of ethics imply responsibility for the other and for his/her well-being. Emmanuel Levinas (1985), who writes about the ethical aspects of face-to-face relations, argues that entering into a relationship with the other we create the image of his body (face), which makes us serve him (cf. Levinas, 1969). This is a moral relationship:

> The Other is higher, he gives us an order, "you shall not commit murder." It is a commandment in the appearance of the face, as if a master spoke to me. (Levinas, 1985, p. 89)

This responsibility for the other makes the individual turn into a fully fledged human being and restricts his freedom of action. This is "the ethical challenge to which humans are exposed by the very presence of others, by the 'silent appeal of the Face'" (Bauman, 2008, p. 48).

As a consequence, all social activities in which the individual is engaged are highly ethical. Since each participant has to do everything both to save his own face and to protect the face of the other, every social interaction can be treated as an undertaking requiring "tacit cooperation in face-saving" (Goffman, 1967, p. 29). Ethics is an indispensable element of the constant redefinition of individuals' face and the interaction in which they participate with others. It is situated in relationship and can be characterized by reciprocity which dominates in face-to-face encounters and makes interaction between people possible:

> Just as the member of any group is expected to have self-respect, so also he is expected to sustain a standard of considerateness; he is expected to go to certain lengths to save the feelings and the face of others present. (Goffman, 1967, p. 10)

However, setting standards of behaviour does not have to lead to adherence to them. Nowadays, responsibility for the other and his well-being are neglected. Zygmunt Bauman (2008, pp. 52–53) describes modern ethical relations in the following way:

> The concepts of responsibility and responsible choice, which used to reside in the semantic field of ethical duty and moral concern for the Other, have moved or have been shifted to the realm of self-fulfillment and calculation of risks. In the process, the Other as the trigger, the target, and the yardstick for a responsibility accepted, assumed, and fulfilled has all but disappeared from view, having been elbowed out or overshadowed by the actor's own self. "Responsibility" means now, first and last, responsibility to oneself ("You owe this to

yourself," as the outspoken traders in relief from responsibility indefatigably repeat), while "responsible choices" are, first and last, such moves as serve well the interests and satisfy the desires of the actor and stave off the need to compromise.

AN ANALYSIS OF FACEBOOK USERS' FACES AND ETHICS

To investigate face-management patterns and self-presentation strategies used in social network interactions, we have conducted an analysis of the contents of selected Facebook accounts. Using the theoretical framework of the extended model of face, we have analysed:

- how people present themselves, and what social attributes are foregrounded;
- how they manage to present their "desired identity";
- how everyday ethics is applied in social network interactions;
- what role Facebook "friends" have in face-creation;
- how the "like" button is used in ratificatory rituals.

The analysis consists of two parts, the first one focusing on self-image (face) creation in a Facebook account, the second focusing on the use of self-presentation strategies made available by the Facebook authors.

CREATING A SELF-IMAGE IN A SOCIAL NETWORK

The analysis of the selected Facebook accounts has shown that the self-images created by the participants reflect the structure of face presented in the extended model of face.

As has already been said, the elements belonging to the category *Personhood* constitute the most sensitive area of face. While the person's character and behaviour can best be gauged by his/her activity on the wall (i.e., its intensity and the content of the posts and shares), his/her moral integrity usually cannot be determined so easily, as people try hard to show high moral standards, and their self-presentation is often exaggerated and results in an idealized image. The most important manifestation of the person's personhood is his/her picture, as it is to help identify the account owner.

To create the *Prestige* aspect of face, participants provide detailed information concerning their education and work, sometimes mentioning the positions they hold (see Example 1). They enhance this aspect of their face by means of the posts put on their timeline, on their professional activities (see Example 2), pastime activities (e.g., scuba diving, eating in expensive restaurants, visiting many beautiful and/or distant places abroad), and achievements (see Examples 3, 4, and 5; all posts are quoted verbatim, respecting the users' linguistic idiosyncrasies.)

Example 1

Associate Professor at University of Iceland
Director at Commonside Community Development Trust
Professeur at DIP - Genève
Poseł na Sejm RP at Sejm Rzeczypospolitej Polskiej (Member of the Polish Parliament)
redaktor naczelna, dyrektor programowa at RDC (editor-in-chief, director of programmes at RDC)
Właściciel at Instytut Wydawniczy Latarnik (Owner at the Publishing Institute *Latarnik*)
Owner at Transla Project.
Works at Ukrainian section Association of European Journalists - AEJ
Worked at Polskie Radio
Works at Morgan Stanley
Former Number one at San Graal

Example 2

Having a guest lecture at the University of Stockholm, Frescati, tomorrow afternoon; beautiful spring weather, clever students, comfortable library with a weird cataloguing system and a (suprisingly nice) Thainese food at a university canteen.

Example 3

Wszystkich językoznawców przeszłych, obecnych i przyszłych, a także studentów, których zaintrygowały choć trochę moje opowiadania o metonimii, informuję, że ukazała się w końcu (po trzech latach) moja książka "Metonymy in Language, Thought and Brain" w brytyjskim wydawnictwie Equinox Publishing. Z kupnem będzie chyba ciężko, bo to UK, a poza tym cena 367zł lub 175$, ale robię darowizny dla bibliotek UŚl w Sosnowcu i AJD w Częstochowie.

(To all linguists, past, future and present, as well as to students who were at least slightly intrigued by my talks about metonymy, I would like to inform you that finally (after three years) my book *Metonymy in Language, Thought and Brain* has been published by the British publisher Equinox Publishing. Buying may be difficult, as it is (available in) the UK, and besides the price is PLN367 or $175, but I have sent complimentary copies to the libraries of the University of Silesia in Sosnowiec and AJD in Częstochowa.)

Example 4

Odebrałam dziś w Pałacu Prezydenckim Złoty Krzyż Zasługi za wkład w niepodległość, demokrację i tak dalej:)) [...] A tu w klapie. Uściślając - (bo tak było w uzasadnieniu KRRiTV) - to jest za "wkład w rozwój wolnych mediów w Polsce". I już kończę ten temat :)

(Today in the Presidential Palace, I have received the Gold Cross of Merit for the contribution to independence, democracy and so on :) [...] And here in my (jacket) lapel. To be more specific – (it was the justification provided by the National Broadcasting Council) – it is a medal for "the contribution to the development of free mass media in Poland". An that's the end of the topic :)

Example 5

Got a thank you letter from Dave (Cameron) yesterday - for my role at the 2012 Olympics. I chose to do it to make my kids proud, not for a thank you letter from the PM.

Participants create the *Competence* aspect of their face by means of the information provided in their profile (see Example 6) and the information posted on their timeline (see Examples 7 and 8), highlighting the skills and abilities they possess.

Example 6

Works at Pisanie (Works at "Writing")

Example 7

Gdyby ktoś się jeszcze wahał, co zrobić z tak wrednym sobotnim wieczorem, to przypominam, że gram dziś w towarzystwie samego Krzysztofa Gawlasa w Bielsku Pod Sceną. Zaczynamy o 20.00. Boski Balance: godzina+ intelektualno-estetycznych pobudzeń, czyli koncert.

(If you still couldn't make up your mind what to do with such a beastly Saturday evening, I remind you that today I am playing with Krzysztof Gawlas himself in Bielsko, in the theatre café *Pod Sceną*. We start at 8.00 p.m. Divine Balance: an hour+ of intellectual and esthetic excitement, that is concert.)

Example 8

the photo for January is mine! :) Kalendarz Instytutu Języka Angielskiego na rok 2013 dostępny w Księgarni Akademickiej ŻAK (Tył hallu w budynku Filologii)

(the photo for January is mine! :) The Institute of English calendar for 2013 is available at the Academic Bookshop *Żak* (at the back of the hall of the Philology building))

Sometimes self-image creation goes far beyond positive self-presentation, and acquires features specific to marketing and advertising (see Examples 3, 7, and 8). Apart from the written information, the face-enhancing function may be performed by photos depicting the person engaged in activities, or in situations and places which attest to his/her possession of certain abilities, skills, and achievements. The function can be performed also by certificates, posters, book covers, or conference programmes in which the person's name is mentioned.

In the Facebook context, the category *Family* is of secondary importance. As in any social network, here the focus is on friends. Thus, in the Facebook culture, stressing family bonds is optional. Some do so, although the majority of KINSHIP-RELATED POSTS are mainly AIMED at other than family relations. People may be divided into:

- those who present themselves as individuals, without any openly stated family responsibilities;

- those who rarely admit to having husband/wife/children and/or describe other Facebook participants as family members;
- those who frequently comment on family matters (see Example 9) and engage in post-exchange with their family members (see Example 10).

Example 9

Tammy got an A in her photography assignment! Whoop!

So.......today Claudia gets the news that she has passed GCSE Science with a B and Mark wins Book Day in his class....a good one for our kids. Pleased for them and proud of them!

Omg my sister just found Huddersfield. This is the house I grew up in!

My sister Helen is the only person I know who would send a text saying "when are you going to see Mum and Dad in Devon - could you pick up a sousaphone I bought on eBay?".

Yikes, my 80-something year old parents just got a skype account. Worried now - what if my mum gets a facebook account and starts checking up on what I'm doing!

Great weekend! Family wedding, time spent with lovely sisters and nieces/nephews yesterday and a lazy day today with a spot of Poirot in the middle!

Example 10

Daughter: *Love you so much momma! Thank you for everything you have done for me, Im greatful for everything you have given me in this great life of mine. I hope youre enjoying your time in Europe and can't wait to see you when I get home. Love you and the family very much! te amo mucho mommita! nos vemos muy pronto lindaa*
Mother: *YES! I "LIKE" IT!!!! (notice all in caps)*
Daughter: *you're so weird*
Mother: *My life would be void without your life in mine, Hija!*

The *Affiliation* category, like the *Family* category of face, can be characterized by in-group solidarity. In the Facebook context, affiliation can be manifested by stating one's own religious and political views, by declaring one's sexual orientation, and providing information on groups one belongs to (see Examples 11–13).

Example 11

Religious views	*Buddysta ateista* (Buddhist atheist)
Political Views	*liberalno-lewicowe* (liberal-leftist)
Gender	*male*
Interested in	*women*
Relationship Status	*in a relationship*

Religious views	*Blend of Christian and Buddhist*
Political Views	*Civic Platform*
Gender	*male*

Interested in	*women*
Relationship Status	

Religious views	*Born and Raised Catholic* *"I'd rather live my life as if there's God and die to find out there isn't than live as if there isn't and die to find out that there is." Albert Camus*
Political Views	*Never trust politicians*
Interested in	*men and women*
Relationship Status	*in a relationship with Michał Nowak*

Example 12

Wiecie co "anarchiści"? Puknijcie się w swoje puste łby
(Anarchists, you know? Knock on your own empty heads)

Example 13

A message on X's own timeline:
X is a proud Icelander today. Majority of the Icelandic parliament voted for an independent and sovereign Palestine! Iceland is the first country to do so in western Europe. Fantastic news on this International Day of Solidarity with the Palestinian Nation.

The *Background* category includes everything that the person is face-sensitive to, but which is relatively distant from the self. These are elements concerning his/her everyday life, such as place of birth and residence, "friends" (real friends or persons one wants to be identified with), groups he/she belongs to (e.g., *Kraków Photography Group, Second Life for Educators, CRITICAL DISCOURSE ANALYSIS (CDA), Prog Rock, Swords & Wizardry, bird lovers and breeders!*), and interests one really has or wants to be identified with.

Reflecting the structure suggested by the extended model of face, the self-image presented by Facebook users on their accounts and available to selected viewers contributes to the creation of their face (see Table 1.1).

Table 1.1. The Person's Face on Their Facebook Account.

The person's face	The person's account content
Personhood (character, behaviour, moral integrity, biography, independence, appearance)	The profile picture The truthfulness of the personal information The category and number of "friends"
Prestige (social status, education, job, achievements)	Information on work and education Information on the person's professional and pastime activities Posts on the person's achievements
Competence (abilities, knowledge, skills)	Posts on the person's skills and abilities

The person's face	The person's account content
Family (parents, children, spouse, relatives)	Family members among "friends" Relationship status Posts on family matters Post-exchange with family members Family pictures
Affiliation (nationality/ethnicity, world-view, religion, sexual orientation, social group, profession, beliefs)	Religious views, political views "Interested in women/men"
Background (place of birth, place of living, schools, friends, interests, property)	Living, education "Friends" (i.e., close friends, family members, classmates, colleagues, acquaintances, students, public figures, celebrities, historical figures, dead scholars and artists) Groups the person belongs to "Likes" (e.g., music, films, TV programmes, books, events, public figures) Life events (e.g., a new hobby, tattoo, piercing, the first word, kiss, and religious rites of passage)

However, not all participants are ready to provide all the necessary information, and as a consequence their self-image appears to be incomplete, and sometimes they can be difficult to identify (especially, when no profile photo is available). Usually, the main reason for withholding personal information is the individual's sense of privacy. People with a strong sense of privacy value security over self-promotion and prefer to reveal themselves selectively. Protection of some face-sensitive personal data makes them less prone to face threats, but at the same time it makes their face enhancement less likely. People with a weak sense of privacy easily expose and voluntarily share information about themselves, which makes their Facebook face complete and more attractive to viewers, albeit more susceptible to face threats.

SELF-PRESENTATION STRATEGIES EMPLOYED BY FACEBOOK USERS

Boasting and a desired identity

On Facebook, people concentrate on self-presentation and self-promotion, stressing those aspects of their self-image (face) to which they are most sensitive. The vast majority aim at "constructing a desired identity", i.e., a positive self-image, resulting from the two desires for having positive, socially desirable, qualities, and for the approval of others (Schlenker, 2003). *Desired identity* and *socially desirable qualities* have different meanings in different situations and in the presence of different others. Thus, different attributes can be highlighted, and some attributes can be evaluated differently by different people. As in everyday interaction in real life, on Facebook people try to keep a balance between the need to boast and a sense of modesty (see Example 14). Sometimes, the desire for the approval of others makes them boast (see Example 15). Sometimes, they jokingly praise themselves (see Example 16).

Example 14

My presentation in Tallinn for those who can be bothered! I am not going to listen to myself. I always find it embarrassing.

Example 15

book proposal had the most fantastic review and acceptance from publisher.

Example 16

Sometimes I think that I deserve a medal for getting both children to school on time with their right stuff, with something half-way healthy inside their tummies for breakfast and school uniform on that is clean…

ETHICAL ASPECTS OF LYING ON FACEBOOK

"Principles, established as the foundation of the rights and responsibilities of those within the Facebook Service" provide users with norms of behaviour which have to be adhered to in interaction with other users (https://www.facebook.com/principles.php). However, setting standards of behaviour, or formulating norms does not have to lead to adherence to them. The act of lying is generally perceived as morally wrong. According to Coleman and Kay (1981, p. 28), one can talk about a lie, when

> the speaker (S) asserts some proposition (P) to an addressee (A):
> a. P is false.
> b. S believes P to be false.
> c. In uttering P, S intends to deceive A.
> The prototypical lie, then, is characterized by (a) falsehood, which is (b) deliberate and (c) intended to deceive.

When a person lies, he/she does harm to the other whom he/she deceives, but at the same time he/she undermines a valuable social practice—the use of language to convey information (Kant, 1991; Owens, 2006).

On Facebook, one can observe false information concerning the self, and false information concerning the other. This fictitious information concerning the self is usually included in the person's profile and timeline on purpose with the intention to deceive others. Providing a wrong name and false personal data constitutes a prototypical lie, which is a breach of Facebook's requirement that users should give their true identity. Deception can also involve the use of a profile photo that does not represent the account owner. In some cases, however, when there is no profile photo at all, or when the photo makes the person impossible to recognize, or the falsity of the representation is evident (e.g., a photo of Marilyn Monroe, James Dean, or a cat), the person's intention may not be to lie but to protect his/her privacy and avoid recognition (which is also against Facebook's policy).

To enhance their self-image, people often post false information on their timeline; such deception is to make them more attractive to others and more worthy of respect. Sometimes they deceive others indirectly, e.g., by way of false implicatures, deliberate ambiguity, or by casually leaving misleading evidence (e.g., showing pictures from holidays in places they have never been, or pictures featuring the user at the wheel of a car he/she does not own).

Generally speaking, one of the main reasons for lying and deceiving on Facebook is to make one's self-image more positive and to appear to have desired attributes.

FACEBOOK "FRIENDS"

The concept of friend has different interpretations in different cultures. The English word *friend* can be defined as "person, not a relation, whom one knows and likes well" (Hornby, Cowie, & Gimson, 1980), or "a person who shares the same feelings of natural liking and understanding, the same interests, but is not a member of the same family" (*Longman Dictionary of Contemporary English*, 1987). Although the definitions are quite broad, they do not include all the possible meanings of the Facebook meaning of *friend*. This results from the devaluation of the concept of friendship which has been triggered by social networking sites.

In Facebook reality, friendship, resembling rather superficial friendliness, is based on spontaneity (cf. Naylor, 1998, p. 61; Althen, 1988). The individual's success on Facebook can be measured by the number of his/her "friends".

> [Facebook] encourages a disturbing competitiveness around friendship: it seems that with friends today, quality counts for nothing and quantity is king. The more friends you have, the better you are. (http://www.theage.com.au)

That is why people "send a friend request" to others they barely know, to total strangers, friends of friends, public figures, celebrities, dead scholars and artists (e.g., Erving

Goffman, Pierre Bourdieu, Karol Szymanowski), or institutions (e.g., Uniwersytet Śląski, Stowarzyszenie *Help Animals* (The Society *Help Animals*), Stowarzyszenie Antropologów Kultury Etnosfera (The Society of Cultural Anthropologists *Etnosfera*)). Some "friends" may attest to the person's high social status, others to his/her power, relational skills, or attractiveness.

Quantity also matters to those who accept invitations irrespective of who invites them. Such behaviour can be interpreted as a kind of deception (one calls someone a friend one barely knows, or doesn't know at all), aimed at enhancing the person's face.

THE APPROVING AND RATIFICATORY FUNCTION OF THE "LIKE" BUTTON

As has already been mentioned, one of the most important human desires is that one's self-image be appreciated and approved of. The face in its broad sense, presented in the extended model of face, needs appreciation, or at least acceptance from others.

Changes in an individual's status have a strong impact on his/her life, whether they involve his/her relationships, appearance, or rank, in general, or his/her prospects and social position. These changes cannot be ignored by people with whom the individual is in a certain relationship, and require a ritual action on the part of the others. These actions, which Erving Goffman (1971) calls *rituals of ratification*, serve to symbolically ratify the change, and in this way express respect and support for the individual. They are "provided him, not so much to establish a link between the new and the old as to confirm that the new presentation of self is accepted and approved" (Goffman, 1971, pp. 67–68). Rituals of ratification are "performed for and to an individual who has altered his status in some way—his relationships, appearance, rank, certification, in short, his prospects and direction in life" (Goffman, 1971, p. 67). Being part of social convention and routine, they constitute an indispensable element of facework.

The "like" button is a social networking feature which allows users to express their appreciation of content such as status updates, comments, and photos (cf. Bogdanowska, 2003). It performs the same function as rituals of ratification. A new profile picture, notification of success or achievement in the person's professional or private life can be approved of and symbolically ratified by clicking the "like" button, which constitutes a face-enhancing act (or, as Kerbrat-Orecchioni (2005) calls it, a *face-flattering* act). Clicking the "like" button stands for or is accompanied by other-face-enhancing acts, such as compliments and congratulations, and by emoticons with appreciative meaning (see Example 17).

Example 17 Comments on a person's new profile photo
You and 50 others like this.
VS: *sexy*
KŁ: *Muuuuy guapa!*
AT: *breath-taking…*
SK: *¡qué guapa!*
PW: :)
MPC: *¡¡Olé las polacas bien guapas!!*
ATS: *quite pretty!*
KF: *Piękna jak zwykle* (Beautiful as usual)
MB: *Nie wiem co powiedzieć brak mi słów.*
(I don't know what to say, I have no words [to express what I feel])
JAM: *Iwona jak pieknie wyglądasz, dawno Cię nie widziałam usciski serdeczne.*
(Iwona, how beautiful you look, long time no see, hugs)

The "like" button allows Facebook users to show their support and appreciation for other persons' comments, pictures, and wall posts. The "like" can be interpreted as a nonverbal positive comment or a nonverbal compliment.

The "like" button is also used to reciprocate a similar action taken by a "friend" (e.g., you like my music, and I like yours). The "like" can mean "I appreciate your comment", "I like your idea", or "I agree", and then it serves as a response. As a response to a compliment, it means "Thank you".

What does it mean when the "like" button is not used? Does it mean that the person does not like the other's comment or idea, or he/she does not want to ratify the change in the other person's life? The character of interaction on social network sites differs from the interaction in face-to-face encounters, where non-performance of a ritual is treated as inappropriate behaviour. The lack of "like" in a situation when it is expected may be interpreted as inappropriate behaviour only if the person in question is engaged in some other activity on Facebook at that time. Otherwise, the reason for non-performance of a ritual may be the person's absence on the site.

Apart from the other-face-enhancing function, clicking the "like" button helps the individual to maintain his/her own face and present him/herself as a well-mannered person.

CONCLUSIONS

The subject of the study was 'face' created by participants of a social network. Having analyzed face-management patterns used by Facebook participants and strategies they employ in self-presentation, we came to the following conclusions:

- Social network interactions constitute a fascinating area of investigation. Facebook communication strongly resembles face-to-face communication, in both its pleasant and awkward aspects. However, on the one hand, its online character entails certain limitations, while on the other hand, its virtual digital nature makes it more difficult to control.
- Although the main aim of social networking sites is to provide a platform for meeting friends and communicating with them, the activities their users mainly engage in are self-presentation and self-promotion.
- Encounters in virtual reality differ from face-to-face conversations in that people can enjoy greater freedom in self-presentation and in exerting influence on others' perceptions.
- On Facebook, people display their face both in a literal sense—a representation of their physiognomy, and in a metaphorical sense—their desired self-image, created in the interaction with "friends".
- The face (self-image) that the individuals show to others is not their real face, but a complex of positive attributes they want to be associated with and characterized by ("desired identity" (Schlenker, 2003)).
- As in real life situations, social interaction is not free from acts which can be described as inappropriate, violating norms of ethics. In the Facebook context, unethical behaviour includes boasting, lying, and cheating, which have been discussed here; and harmful, hateful, and offensive speech, which merits further investigation.
- Interaction on Facebook is not devoid of positive aspects: participants' behaviour, apart from being focused on self-face, is aimed at the well-being and face of the other, e.g., other-face-flattering posts and "likes".

REFERENCES

Althen, G. (1988). *American ways: A guide for foreigners in the United States.* Yarmouth, ME: Intercultural Press.

Austin, W. J. (2008). Relational ethics. In L. M. Given (Ed.), *The SAGE encyclopedia of qualitative research methods* (pp. 748–749). Los Angeles, CA: SAGE.

Bauman, Z. (2008). *Does ethics have a chance in a world of consumers?* Cambridge, MA: Harvard University Press.

Bogdanowska, M. (2003). *Komentarz i komentowanie: Zagadnienia konstrukcji tekstu.* Katowice, Poland: Wydawnictwo Uniwersytetu Śląskiego.

Bogdanowska-Jakubowska, E. (2013a, April). *Multiple contexts of face.* Paper presented at the 1st Sosnowiec Symposium, *Communication Across Cultures: Face and Interaction*, University of Silesia, Sosnowiec, Poland.

Bogdanowska-Jakubowska, E. (2013b, May). *Ethics and (im)politeness*. Paper presented at the International Conference, *Impoliteness and Interaction* (Impolin), Bydgoszcz, Poland.

Brown, P., & Levinson, S. C. (1987). *Politeness: Some universals in language usage*. Cambridge, UK: Cambridge University Press.

Ciechowicz, J. (2000). Twarz aktora. In *Twarz: Punt po Punkcie*. Rok pierwszy, Zeszyt pierwszy (pp. 121–130). Gdańsk, Poland: Wydawnictwo Słowo/Obraz Terytoria.

Coleman, L., & Kay, P. (1981). Prototype semantics: The English word lie. *Language*, *57*(1), 26–44.

Durkheim, E. (1915/2001). *The elementary forms of religious life* (C. Cosman, Trans.). Oxford, UK: Oxford University Press.

Flew, A. (1979). *A dictionary of philosophy*. London, UK: Pan Books.

Goffman, E. (1955). On face-work: An analysis of ritual elements in social interaction. *Psychiatry: Journal for the Study of Interpersonal Processes*, *18*, 213–231.

Goffman, E. (1967). *Interaction ritual: Essays in face-to-face behavior*. Chicago, IL: Aldine.

Goffman, E. (1971). *Relations in public: Microstudies of the public order*. New York, NY: Harper Torchbooks.

Ho, D. Y.-F. (1994). Face dynamics: From conceptualization to measurement. In S. Ting-Toomey (Ed.), *The challenge of facework: Cross-cultural and interpersonal issues* (pp. 269–286). Albany, NY: State University of New York Press.

Hornby, A. S., Cowie, A. P., & Gimson, A. C. (1980). *Oxford advanced learner's dictionary of current English* (OALD). Oxford, UK: Oxford University Press.

Hu, H. C. (1944). The Chinese concepts of face. *American Anthropologist*, *46*(1),45–64.

Kant, I. (1991). *Practical philosophy* (M. Gregor, Trans.). Cambridge, UK: Cambridge University Press.

Kemp, S. (2004). *Future face*. With contributions from V. Bruce and A. Linney. London, UK: Profile Books.

Kępiński, A. (1998a). *Autoportret Człowieka (Myśli i Aforyzmy)*. Kraków, Poland: Wydawnictwo Literackie.

Kępiński, A. (1998b). Twarz, ręka: A fragment of *Poznanie Chorego*. 1978. In A. Mencwel (Ed.), *Antropologia kultury* (pp. 196–207). Warszawa, Poland: Wydawnictwa Uniwersytetu Warszawskiego.

Kerbrat-Orecchioni, C. (2005). Politeness in France: How to buy bread politely. In L. Hickley & M. Steward (Eds.), *Politeness in Europe* (pp. 29–44). Clevedon, UK: Multilingual Matters.

Leary, M. R., & Price Tangney, J. (2003). The self as an organizing construct in the behavioral and social sciences. In M. R. Leary & J. Price Tangney (Eds.), *Handbook of self and identity* (pp. 3–14). New York, NY: Guilford Press.

Levinas, E. (1969). *Totality and infinity. An essay on exteriority* (A. Lingis, Trans.). Pittsburgh, PA: Duquesne University Press.

Levinas, E. (1985). *Ethics and infinity: Conversations with Philippe Nemo* (R. A. Cohen, Trans.). Pittsburgh, PA: Duquesne University Press.

Liu, R. (1986). *The politeness principle and 'A Dream of Red Mansions'* (Unpublished master's thesis). Lancaster University, Lancaster, UK.

Locher, M. A. (2006). Polite behavior within relational work: The discursive approach to politeness. *Multilingua*, *25*, 249–267.

Longman Dictionary of Contemporary English (LDCE). (1987). Harlow, UK: Longman.

Maslow, A. H. (1970). *Motivation and personality* (2nd ed.). New York, NY: Harper & Row.

Naylor, L. L. (1998). *American culture: Myth and reality of a culture of diversity*. Westport, CT: Bergin & Garvey.

New Oxford American Dictionary (NOAD). (2010). A. Stevenson & C. A. Lindberg (Eds.). Oxford, UK: Oxford University Press.

Owens, D. (2006). Lying, honesty, and promising. In K. Brown, A. Barber, & R. J. Stainton (Eds.), *The encyclopedia of philosophy of language and linguistics* (pp. 413–415). Oxford, UK: Elsevier.

Ricoeur, P. (1992). *Oneself as another* (K. Blamey, Trans.). Chicago, IL: University of Chicago Press.

Schlenker, B. R. (2003). Self-presentation. In M. R. Leary & J. Price Tangney (Eds.), *Handbook of self and identity* (pp. 492–518). New York, NY: Guilford Press.

Spencer-Oatey, H. (2009). Face, identity and interactional goals. In F. Bargiela-Chiappini & M. Haugh (Eds.), *Face, communication and social interaction* (pp. 137–154). London, UK: Equinox.

Ting-Toomey, S., & Kurogi, A. (1998). Facework competence in intercultural conflict: An updated face-negotiation theory. *International Journal of Intercultural Relations*, *22*(2), 187–225.

Watts, R. (2003). *Politeness*. Cambridge, UK: Cambridge University Press.

Internet sources

https://www.facebook.com/notes/
https://www.facebook.com/principles.php
http://www.theage.com.au

CHAPTER TWO

Mom 2.0: Mothering IN THE Blogosphere

JENNIFER M. RAYMOND AND JODI H. COHEN

INTRODUCTION

For many, the Internet offers the promise of creating space for new and different dialogues. The Internet has opened up the public square, where previously the control over published information resided with the wealthy and influential. Despite the fact that women remain underrepresented in the public sphere of politics in the United States, in the blogosphere, women appear to be staking their claim on the public discourse. The Pew Internet & American Life Project found that half of all bloggers are women (Lenhart & Fox, 2006). Many women blog about their experiences as mothers. These so-called "mommy bloggers" are more likely to write journal-type blogs characterized by their regular posts about family and community-related issues (Stavrositu & Sundar, 2012). "The personal is political", a phrase coined in 1969 during the height of the women's movement, came out of an essay written by Carol Hanisch in 1969 (later published in 1970) in response to criticism of consciousness-raising as being apolitical and too much like therapy. Hanisch contends that we should work to develop a better link between personal experience, theory and action. This chapter examines the ways in which blogs written by "mommy bloggers" can be considered political along three dimensions: direct political commentary, reconstructing the social narrative of motherhood, and the development of agency through a public voice.

THE INTERNET, POLITICAL DISCOURSE AND THE PUBLIC SPHERE

The concept of the public sphere conjures up images of groups of individuals gathered in dialogue, deliberating ideas and working together to garner solutions for public problems (Dahlgren, 2005; Habermas, 2001). In the digital age, much attention has been given to the potential of the Internet for expanding citizen participation and transforming democratic politics (Bennett & Entman, 2001; Chadwick, 2006; Chadwick & Howard, 2010). In discussing the political properties of the Internet, Chadwick (2006), building upon the work of Phillip Agre (2002), offers several conceptual themes including decentralization, participation, community and post-industrialization, that are relevant for understanding the role of mothers who blog. Decentralization refers to the ease of access for publishing, as control is not centralized among one or a few powerful sources. Unlike traditional politics, the barriers for entry are lower. Mommy bloggers embody the shift away from the traditional media value chain. New developments in information technologies have reduced barriers to entry, decentralizing control over media and allowing independent authors to self-publish through platforms such as blogs. These independent authors have control over their content and distribution to consumers, a stark contrast to the previous model in which these things were controlled by corporations.

Given that women in the United States continue to earn less on the dollar than men (Hegewisch, Liepmann, Hayes, & Hartmann, 2010), and lag behind men in asset and wealth accumulation (Deere & Doss, 2006), economic costs for entry are an important consideration. In terms of political involvement, we might also consider that while women are increasingly seeking political roles at the local and state level, the percentage of female elected officials at the national level in the US remains low (Lawless & Fox, 2005). As Lawless and Fox (2008) point out, in the realm of traditional, electoral U.S. politics:

> Women are less likely than men to be willing to endure the rigors of a political campaign. They are less likely than men to be recruited to run for office. They are less likely than men to have the freedom to reconcile work and family obligations with a political career. They are less likely than men to think they are "qualified" to run for office. And they are less likely than men to perceive a fair political environment. (pp. 1–2)

While blogging and running for, or serving in office, are not the same, Lawless and Fox's findings have several implications for understanding how women participate in politics beyond our traditional measure of what constitutes participation, and what we mean by political. Here, a reduction in barriers to participation may take on a different meaning.

Another important concept is that of community or networked individualism (Wellman et al., 2003). It is important to consider how the rise of individualism predates Internet technologies (Wellman et al., 2003). In this case previous technological and social changes, such as industrialization, displaced many mothers from the local tight-knit communities of women who shared information including tips about parenting and relationships. Today's mothers often live farther geographical distances from family members, and may find themselves feeling more isolated and emotionally disconnected. Yet, through the use of new information technologies, such as social media and blogging, many are using the Internet to connect across geographic distances. As Wellman et al. (2003) point out, "This shift facilitates *personal communities* that supply the essentials of community separately to each individual: support, sociability, information, social identities, and a sense of belonging. The person, rather than the household or group, is the primary unit of connectivity" (n.p.). Individuals go online not only to find information but also to find community. This is especially true for health-related issues, where the Internet serves as a site of information sharing and peer support for pregnant women (Cohen & Raymond, 2011), women with breast cancer (Fogel, Albert, Schnabel, Ditkoff, & Neugut, 2002), people living with HIV/AIDS (Mo & Coulson, 2010), and parents of children with diabetes (Merkel & Wright, 2012).

Another useful lens for considering mothers who blog is that of post-industrialization and the Internet. Chadwick (2006) explains Lance Bennett's (1998, 2003) viewpoint that "individual political identity derives not from relatively fixed, collective institutional sources but is increasingly a matter of self-expression and lifestyle choice" (p. 29). Yet, Bennett and Entman (2001) challenge the idea of the personal being political by distinguishing between the public sphere and the policy sphere. While they acknowledge that personal matters may have political dimensions, they define the policy sphere as "that subset of public sphere where ideas and feelings explicitly connect with—are communicated to, from or about—government officials, parties or candidates for office who may decide the outcomes of issues and conflicts facing society" (p. 4). While this is a useful distinction, it becomes problematic when we add a gender dimension. As previously noted, women are less likely to express political ambitions, and therefore we need to be open to different ways of conceptualizing political participation. Second, within the realm of blogging, although women are more likely to write to a blog than men (Garber, 2012), men are consistently listed on the "A-list", or ranked as top bloggers (Lopez, 2009). It is important to consider how reliance on an understanding of the political that is rooted in electoral politics, and a rational approach to policy making that values the objective over the subjective, reinforces the divide between the personal and political that relegates women to the domestic sphere. In other words, by imposing traditional views of what it means to be political on new forms of communication, there is a risk that we will "re-inscribe a public valuing of behaviors associated with educated adult (white) males, and render less visible behaviors associated with members of other demographic groups" (Herring et al., 2004, as cited in Lopez, 2009, p. 735).

"MOMMY BLOGGERS"

It is through the exploration of personal experiences that these women often challenge societal expectations of motherhood and engage in discourse that reflects larger cultural and political debates. In discussing mommy bloggers, Morrison (2011) writes:

> They describe the transmutation of personal feeling and experience into a sense of communal identity and practice, and the possibilities for collective social action that can arise from this identification. This is the structural power of personal mommy blogging. These texts and the communities they support are also, however, intimate enough to allow the expression of a full range of emotional and pragmatic experience, often breaking social taboos constraining who can speak and what can be said about the condition, experience, and role of motherhood. (p. 40)

Yet, Morrison (2011) explains that the private, intimate nature of blogs, combined with the practice of posting anonymously and user pseudonyms, "blocks women's culture's capacity to mobilize political action" (p. 49) due to the separation between their online identities and roles in the non-virtual world.

Lopez (2009) points out that mommy bloggers have been marginalized at times within the community of women who blog. Writing about the 2005 BlogHer conference, Lopez states that "At the end of the conference, a participant announced that if women 'stopped blogging about themselves they could change the world'. The mommy bloggers felt attacked, as if their personal style of writing was somehow less valuable than their colleagues' entries on current events or politics" (2009, p. 730). In response, Alice Bradley challenged this dismissive attitude as failing to recognize the power of the personal. "We're redefining the roles with our blogs.... The unexciting, everyday, in between stuff. But, in doing that, we're also delving into new territory. Into radical territory, I think" (Bradley, as cited in Lopez, 2009).

It is important to situate "mommy blogs" within the larger cultural context of an idealized motherhood that is unattainable for most mothers. Douglas and Michaels (2004b) termed this dynamic the "new momism" and argued that today's mothers are under more pressure than ever before to be perfect. They also point out that this dialogue of the new momism is being played out on the web, from individual mothers who post "family photos, recipes and tips about toddlers"

(Douglas and Michaels, 2004a, p. 313) to websites that offer a never-ending supply of advice and tips about all things motherhood. Douglas and Michaels (2004a) also find that there is a discourse challenging the new momism:

> On-line, mothers get to talk to each other, not just listen to some supposed expert, and the outpouring of support you see women giving each other, about everything from diaper rash to homework assignments (including links to relevant web sites), truly embodies what we used to call sisterhood. (p. 313)

It is here, in that challenge, that the personal is again political. Rather than being passive consumers of experts' advice, mothers are online questioning the advice, and creating their own spaces and their own narratives.

Stavrositu and Sundar (2012) distinguish between two types of blogs: personal journaling and filter blogs. Filter blogs are often focused on social and political issues, include links to other sites that the author(s) have deemed useful and relevant, and take more of an open discussion format. Personal blogs are more internally focused, similar to diaries or personal journals. However, the authors point out that unlike traditional written journals, blogs are public spaces that offer visibility and the ability to attract a following. The authors define women's empowerment as the perception of "connectedness, mastery of control over aspects of one's life and the ability to effect change" (p. 370). The authors propose that blogging offers an opportunity for women to develop a sense of agency, which they define as "the feeling of having a competent, confident and assertive voice" (p. 371). Their findings suggest that blogging is both "agency enhancing" and acts as a vehicle for "community building" (Stavrositu & Sundar, 2012, p. 382). The authors suggest that "those who feel disempowered due to lack of a social network may undertake blogging as a means for meeting and connecting with similar others. Those who feel like making a contribution in the socio-political arena may consider blogging as a vehicle for expressing and honing their political voice" (p. 382). The authors recognize the implication of this for marginalized groups but do not address it directly in their study.

SOCIAL CONSTRUCTION, POLITICAL DISCOURSE AND PUBLIC POLICY

Challenging the social construction of motherhood, and of mothers from marginalized groups has political implications. Schneider and Ingram (1997) posit that the social construction of target groups shapes policy design, including decisions regarding the distribution of rewards and punishments. Schneider and Ingram offer a matrix that illustrates how social construction in public policy takes place along two dimensions: power and deservedness. And, where the target group falls on that matrix will shape the types of policies that are implemented. For example, a less powerful, less deserving group will be seen as deviant and will be subject to policy interventions that seek to punish. Schram (2000) offers a critical analysis of the discourse surrounding welfare mothers to reveal how the discourse of personal responsibility contributes to the negative social construction of poor mothers as undeserving and responsible for their own poverty. And yet, social constructions can change over time, as evidenced by the shifting construction of Japanese Americans from negative, as threats, to positive, as the "model minority" (DiAlto, 2005). In our current culture, one strategy for gaining support for a political measure is to engage in a battle for "hearts and minds", in which politicians or advocates for a cause make emotional appeals rather than logical ones (Brader, 2006). This tactic has been used to build support for causes in the US, from the Iraq war to marriage equality for same-sex couples. One aspect of this often involves changing the social construction from one that is negative to one that is positive. For mothers who are members of marginalized groups, or otherwise outside of the mainstream image of motherhood, blogging may serve as a vehicle for social and political change through offering a counter-narrative designed to change hearts and minds.

METHODS

This research seeks to explore the ways in which mothers who blog use those spaces to challenge and redefine motherhood, and how their participation in the public discourse constitutes the development of a political voice. This research is exploratory and employs qualitative content analysis to examine the writings of mothers who blog. How do mothers who blog use blogging as a vehicle for reconstructing conceptions of motherhood? To what extent do mothers from marginalized groups, including single mothers, women of color, lesbians and young parents, explore issues of identity and inequality in their blogs? In what ways do mothers who blog engage in political discourse through their examinations of the personal? Purposive sampling was used to select eleven blogs written by women representing various identities such as race, ethnicity, sexual orientation, age, and marital status. For this chapter the researchers selected blogs written by women who are members of marginalized groups, or who differ from the mainstream image of the ideal mom (white, heterosexual, middle-class, married, with children without disabilities). The selected blogs include those written by women who are lesbian mothers, women of color, single parents, mothers of multiracial children, adoptive parents, parents of one or more children with disabilities, and a parent of a gender non-conforming child. Blogs were identified by searching through several repositories including BlogHer, the "largest community of women who blog" (About

BlogHer), and The Push Back, which includes the perspectives of teen moms. The selected blogs include several that have been chosen for BlogHer's annual "Voices of the Year" designation.

The data included the "about" section or other entries describing the blog and/or the motivations for blogging as well as over 400 blog entries that appeared in March, June, and September 2013 (see Table 2.1).

Table 2.1. Characteristics of Bloggers and Frequency of Posts.

LP	LGBT parent	30	30	30	90
RM	Mother through birth and adoption	27	23	30	80
DM	Latina mom to biracial and bicultural children	20	17	11	48
YM	African American, became a young mother at age 20	15	10	9	34
LL	Single mother	13	14	13	40
LD	Lesbian Parent	10	6	3	19
TM	Black, Latina, former teen mom	9	11	5	25
IA	Indian American mother	7	11	9	27
RR	Mother of two children, one of whom is gender non-conforming	7	8	9	24
DD	Single mom	6	16	22	44
SL	Mother of two children, one with a disability	3	3	4	10
				Total	441

Data were reviewed and analyzed using a consistent coding-scheme to identify common themes and differences within and across entries. Only blogs that are publicly accessible and do not require the researcher to join or subscribe have been included in this study. Authors of the blogs are not identified by proper name or URL. This study is limited in its small sample size and reliance on popular blogging sites, which may contribute to sampling bias.

RESULTS AND DISCUSSION

The frequency of postings varied from a few (3) per month to writings posted every day. The content of the postings varied as well, and included everything from recipes, reflections on a child's behavior or developmental process, to a commentary on a social or political issue or links to other blogs of interest. It would be easy to read the majority of the postings as being domestically related, and therefore to dismiss them as apolitical, focusing only on those posts that were directly concerned with a policy action or issue; however, in this analysis, consideration is given to how even seemingly banal posts may be understood as a means of discursive politics.

RECONSTRUCTING MOTHERHOOD

Each of the bloggers included in this study made reference to their experience of being a member of a marginalized group, either in their description of their blog, or in one or more blog entries. These women explored issues of identity and inequality in their blogs, sometimes in response to political or cultural events, and other times in response to daily interactions with others. Single mothers have also used their blogs as a place to challenge negative stereotypes, and instead present the reality of single parenting.

LL reflects on what it is like to be a single mom and her list includes:

- Table for two
- Cutting yourself some slack
- Staying open to new experiences.

While these are reflections that many moms can relate to, LL goes on to explain that in doing this exercise she realizes that, "A common theme here, is painting my role as a single mom in the most positive light possible. It's me showing the world that this stereotype doesn't have to be negative."

DD discusses her struggles affording summer care for her children while she works, and links her struggle to the broader issue of childcare: "There needs to be a better system that isn't so broken that $3.38 too much income means you can handle these extremely high child care costs." Here DD links her personal struggles to afford childcare to a broader critique of political policies to support families and children in the US.

One lesbian writer, LD, challenges the normative gender terms for parents and creates a name for herself that is neither "mom" nor "dad". In discussing the reasons for creating the blog, this author cites the following:

- "Need to create a space for myself"
- Realization there were few or no role models of butch lesbian parenting
- Being confronted by the gender binary: "not just mothers and fathers but *feminine* mothers and *masculine* fathers"

Another lesbian mother, LP, sees blogging as serving numerous functions, personal and political: to become a better parent, to connect to others and self, and to make the world safer for her own children by promoting visibility and understanding. Again, in recognizing the issue of lack of visibility and challenging the status quo, LD and LP use their blogs for both personal and political goals.

CHALLENGING OFFLINE OTHERING ONLINE

Several of the authors describe incidents that have occurred offline where they experience the effects of cultural stigma. In these interactions, it is often not just that their families are seen as different, but it is implied that they hold a different, and lower, status in society. These interactions can be viewed as microaggressions, daily indignities that serve as subtle, intentional, or unintentional insults (Sue et al., 2007).

Both LP, a lesbian mother, and RM, a mother via birth and adoption, point out that strangers will often ask personal and intrusive questions about their families, such as:

> When did you get her? Who is the real mom? Are you the aunt? Does she have a dad?

LP explains, "At our daughter's first pediatrician appointment, her doctor asked, 'Who is the real mom?' At a grocery store, the cashier wouldn't let it go, 'Are you the aunt?'"

Here, in her blog, LP responds:

> We didn't get her. She doesn't have a dad. She has two moms: Mommy and Mama. We are both her real moms. We planned for her. We spent a year trying to conceive her. A year dreaming of her, hoping for her. Through first words, first steps, tantrums, bad dreams, parent teacher conferences, and the agonizing public school lottery, we are her parents.

RM describes her experience fielding questions about being a transracial, adoptive family. She explains what is and what is not appropriate to say to adoptive families. "Do not ask me if my kids are adopted in front of them…[I] especially don't appreciate questions like, "Where are they from?" in front of my children". RM issues a reminder for adults to "be sensitive to adopted children, and to understand that fielding questions from strangers (or hearing their mother field questions from strangers) may make them feel self-conscious and "othered". Rather than insulting or dismissing the question askers, both mothers use this as an opportunity to make personal struggles public, and in doing so, educate the reader about ways in which they can create change by being sensitive to different kinds of families.

In the same post discussed above, LP points out that public attitudes about same-sex marriage are growing more positive, linking her personal experience with a political debate about equal rights. Further, she pushes against cultural attitudes that position her family and her children into an "othered" space. She uses her blog to voice a public message and to elicit a public response.

One of the bloggers, DM, who describes her family as biracial and bicultural, sees blogging as a way to both create awareness of their experiences, and also to offer an alternative narrative for her own family. In her mission statement, DM states that:

> Being of mixed race and bicultural parents, the journey of personal identity for (children) will be unlike mine or that of their father's. I wish I could say that I am completely confident in our world to accept my children with open arms, free of racism and ignorance. But sometimes I'm not…I wish for my efforts to, one day, be a source of identity for my children. That they hear my voice in reading their letters. That, no matter where my soul may be, my children feel the comfort and strength in the knowledge of who I am, who they are.

DM challenges the social divisions of race and identity here with a plea for a changing public perspective. Issues of racial identity become public discourse in these personal blogs.

BLOGGING, AGENCY AND COMMUNITY

Through blogging, these women find and help build community. One former teen mom, YM, says it makes her more introspective, and more connected in looking for community:

> While most of us no longer have "the village," an extended network of aunts and cousins who can guide us through motherhood, we can create it ourselves online. As one of the women stated: "remember: you are never, ever, the only one. If you blog it, they will come."

Bloggers often post links to other blogs and comment on each other's blogs, creating a community, and perhaps more importantly, a network where they promote and recognize each other's contributions. Several of the writers have a regularly occurring section where they recognize the work of other bloggers, and offer snippets of other blogs, and links. In some cases, they invite a guest blogger to post on their site, or include a link to another site where their own writing is being featured. In opening personal blogs to other voices and commentary, a discussion critical to social issues is often built, moving these blogs into a space of community.

Through these writings, we also learn about who they are, their professional and personal goals, relationships and financial challenges. They identify themselves as mothers, but they are also writers, thinkers, professionals, educators and leaders in a new, very public conversation about the lives of women. Sometimes their posts are merely reflections on their experiences, while other times they link those experiences to larger social and political forces.

Although the Internet may put mothers under a microscope, the fact that they are living their lives in full view may mean that we get to appreciate the complexities of their lives. In a culture where women's voices are often absent from policy making, they have created an alternative dialogue. YM states that she began blogging "to fill what I thought was a void in the parenting world". As LD, says "I am growing the food I want to eat."

FINDING A POLITICAL VOICE

Nearly all of the women had written entries addressing or commenting on a social issue or political controversy, including the overturning of the Defense of Marriage Act and a New York City (NYC) public awareness campaign targeting teen pregnancy rates. Both of the teen parent (or former teen parent) bloggers wrote about a NYC advertising campaign aimed at preventing teen pregnancy. YM, on her blog, described the ads, one of which shows a baby, eyes red from crying, with the byline, "I am twice as likely not to graduate high school because you had me as a teen." This young mother points out that she could not have seen her future successes when she herself was young and pregnant. She warns of sending a message that young mothers will internalize, thereby contributing to their sense of failure. She directs the reader to statistics on the number of teen parents who suffered from alcoholic parents and physical abuse.

> We miss out on the bigger picture when we paint teen parents as failures before they've had a chance to prove themselves. If you're a teen parent reading this, please know that *I* believe in you.

TM agrees: She sees the campaign as evidence that "NYC and the country is once again failing to meet the needs of its youth". She points out that while New York City is investing in these ads, they have failed to implement a comprehensive sex education program, despite evidence that such programs lead to lower incidences of teen pregnancy.

In this example, both of the blog authors, YM and TM, are using their blogs as a forum for a larger discussion about policy issues. The writers seamlessly move from a personal reflection to a critical analysis of a political culture that demonizes teen sexuality, and maintains inequality through its policy decisions. But they also use their blogs to offer encouragement to other young and teen mothers and to talk honestly about the realities of teen parenting. Unlike the NYC ads, these realities are not all bad. YM mentions some pros of being a young mom:

- Young enough for sleepless nights
- Energy to run around
- More able to relate to what it is like to be a kid

At the top of the cons list is the judgmental stares one receives if perceived to be a teen mother. Here, she uses her public blog to push at the cultural attitudes that cause the judgmental stares, in the hope of fostering a shift in those attitudes, and to offer support to those experiencing similar circumstances, both through advice and humor.

RR, who writes about raising a gender non-conforming son, describes her reaction to receiving a text with the news that the Defense of Marriage Act (DOMA) was overturned:

> I looked at my phone. In our state, my brother can get married when and if he wants to. I looked at my gender nonconforming son. If he grows up to be gay he will be able to get married. All of my LGBTQ friends are finally being treated as human beings deserving of all of the rights, privileges and freedoms that I was granted simply for being straight. I started to cry.

Prior to receiving the news, she was making waffles and taking out the syrup and whipped cream. She put the syrup away, and they celebrated with lots of whipped cream. In this example, the juxtaposition of the domestic activity of making breakfast for children who are unaware of the political battles in the outside world, along with the internal emotional and intellectual response to a major policy change, illustrates the false dichotomy of the personal and the public. The narrative that places women, and especially mothers, as being in a domestic sphere insulated from all things political fails to recognize that one does not leave their public self on the doorstep. As RR's story reveals, concerns about policy issues are entangled with concerns about children's well-being. RR's story challenges us to reject the Western rational approach to politics which devalues subjectivity, and to acknowledge the ways in which policy decisions are deeply connected to our personal lives.

After Guido Barilla, the chairman of a popular pasta company was quoted in the news as making a negative comment about gay families, LP wrote an open letter on her blog. In it she explains that she will be boycotting the company, and points out that words are powerful and harmful:

> In a world where LGBT youth kill themselves too often, in a world where my community is still tortured and murdered for something we can't control, in this world where public opinion has shifted away from your ideas and a lot closer to mine, in this world where nothing is perfect and people are hurting, in this world where you are in a position of power and authority as the chairperson of a major corporation, you need to keep your ideas to yourself. Please. For my family. For my community. For all of us.

A mother caring for her children does not cease to be a public citizen based on her physical location (in the home) or the activity in which she is partaking (cooking, parenting, etc.). In contrast, in both of these examples, it is easy to see how the personal is political. The daily struggles of marginalization, perceived and blatant discrimination, and the desire to have one's family recognized as deserving and protected by the law, are at once intensely personal and deeply linked to policy decisions. Adhering to a rational, objective definition of public discourse would obscure their voices and dismiss their writing as too subjective, personal or irrelevant. And yet, these writers use their blogs to critique and celebrate policy changes, to discuss laws and rights, and to engage in political actions such as boycotts. And the public nature of blogs allows them to engage in discussions and debate with others, across geographic space, and to spread awareness or encourage others to take action through boycotts and campaigns on social and policy issues.

CONCLUSIONS

Examining blogging as a vehicle for women to engage in a discourse from which they have been historically excluded makes it possible to begin to recognize that in blogging the personal is political. Personal voice in public space, in this case, in the blogosphere, has value in its presence. These women are writing about their lives and using their experiences to challenge cultural norms and push for political change. This then links to narratives of good versus bad mothering. The good mother is socially expected and normalized to have one set pattern—that of mainstream media perpetuated through parenting and women's magazines, television shows and advertisements. This narrative does not reflect the experiences of real families, or does it? In considering the blogs in this study we can examine interaction with children, home, and spouses, recognizing the patterning of "good" motherhood, that of maternal sacrifice and the constant assumed joyful experience of Douglas and Michaels's (2004b) New Momism. The highly romanticized view of motherhood in an age where women lack the village of peers has the potential to lead to increased isolation and self-doubt. Yet, the blogosphere and mommy blogs offer a space to encounter and interact with the public and private experiences of other mothers, those presenting a narrative that breaks with these restrictive social conventions. Most who read are seeking representations of their own experiences to normalize what they feel in the face of the daily drama and/or trauma of mothering. While corporations may exploit these anxieties and seek to build a consumer base for products that demonstrate "good" motherhood, these blogs reject that narrative and in doing so, circumnavigate the traditional media value chain.

The American expectations of a happy childhood place untold pressure on mothers to provide just that. This is coupled with social expectations of joy in all experiences of motherhood, all while coiffed, well dressed and in heels, leaving little fluctuation from the 1950s housewife. Yet, it simultaneously adds to the newer pressures of whether or not to work outside of the home, or in a job other than that of housewifery, and the economic needs of families today for dual incomes, along with the continued expectation of "wife" and "mother". The media's constant monitoring of mothering throws self-experience into relief, challenging whether a mother is raising her children the "right" way, providing the relaxed fun-filled day to promote a scripted happy childhood, yet constantly scared by media reports of child death, abduction and other hazards—all while trying to do a better job than the previous generation of mothers. These blogs, instead of working to promulgate standards of social perfection, challenge the ways in which perfection is written. It is not enough to say that the standards of perfection are too high, instead it becomes essential to question the very nature of that assumed perfection, challenging and breaking the media value chain.

Although the majority of the blog entries did not include explicitly political content such as commentary on political races or partisan politics, several of the women did use their blogs as a platform to express their concerns about or reactions to public policies. Perhaps more importantly, the women used their blogs to challenge current conceptions of motherhood and to create alternate public models of families like their own to fill a gap or to challenge the negative constructions they had encountered. Given the link between social construction and policy design, taking steps to own their narrative can be seen as engaging in a politics of changing hearts and minds. Finally, given the research on women's lack of desire to seek out electoral office, more research is needed into how blogging and other forms of digital engagement may contribute to fostering a sense of agency, and to what extent this sense of agency translates into political participation, the development of a political voice and a willingness to take on a leadership role.

REFERENCES

Agre, P. E. (2002). Real-time politics: The Internet and the political process. *The Information Society, 18*(5), 311–331.

Bennett, W. L., & Entman, R. M. (Eds.). (2001). *Mediated politics: Communication in the future of democracy*. Cambridge, UK: Cambridge University Press.

BlogHer. (n.d.). About. Retrieved from http://www.blogher.com/about-this-network

Brader, T. (2006). *Campaigning for hearts and minds: How emotional appeals in political ads work*. Chicago, IL: University of Chicago Press.

Chadwick, A. (2006). *Internet politics: States, citizens, and new communication technologies*. New York, NY: Oxford University Press.

Chadwick, A., & Howard, P. N. (Eds.). (2010). *Routledge handbook of Internet politics*. London, UK: Routledge.

Cohen, J. H., & Raymond, J. M. (2011). How the Internet is giving birth (to) a new social order. *Information, Communication & Society*, *14*(6), 937–957.

Dahlgren, P. (2005). The Internet, public spheres, and political communication: Dispersion and deliberation. *Political Communication*, *22*(2), 147–162.

Deere, C. D., & Doss, C. R. (2006). The gender asset gap: What do we know and why does it matter? *Feminist Economics*, *12*(1–2), 1–50.

DiAlto, S. J. (2005). From "problem minority" to "model minority": The changing social construction of Japanese Americans. In A. L. Schneider & H. M. Ingram (Eds.), *Deserving and entitled: Social constructions and public policy* (pp. 81–103). Albany, NY: State University of New York Press.

Douglas, S., & Michaels, M. (2004a). Dr. Laura's neighborhood: Baby wearing, nanny cams, and the triumph of the new momism. In S. Douglas & M. Michaels, *The mommy myth: The idealization of motherhood and how it has undermined all women* (pp. 298–330). Toronto, Canada: Free Press.

Douglas, S., & Michaels, M. (2004b). Introduction: The new momism. In S. Douglas & M. Michaels, *The mommy myth: The idealization of motherhood and how it has undermined all women* (pp. 1–27). Toronto, Canada: Free Press.

Fogel, J., Albert, S., Schnabel, F., Ditkoff, B. A., & Neugut, A. (2002). Use of the Internet by women with breast cancer. *Journal of Medical Internet Research*, *4*(2), e9.

Garber, M. (2012, April 27). The digital (gender) divide: Women are more likely than men to have a blog (and a Facebook profile). *The Atlantic*. Retrieved from http://www.theatlantic.com/technology/archive/2012/04/the-digital-gender-divide-women-are-more-likely-than-men-to-have-a-blog-and-a-facebook-profile/256466/

Habermas, J. (2001). *The structural transformation of the public sphere: An inquiry into a category of bourgeois society*. Cambridge, MA: MIT Press.

Hanisch, C. (1970). The personal is political. In S. Firestone & A. Koedt (Eds.), *Notes from the second year: Women's liberation* (pp. 76–78). New York, NY: Radical Feminism.

Hegewisch, A., Liepmann, H., Hayes, J., & Hartmann, H. (2010). Separate and not equal? Gender segregation in the labor market and the gender wage gap. IWPR Briefing Paper, 377. Retrieved from http://www.iwpr.org/publications/pubs/separate-and-not-equal-gender-segregation-in-the-labor-market-and-the-gender-wage-gap

Lawless, J. L., & Fox, R. L. (2005). *It takes a candidate: Why women don't run for office*. New York, NY: Cambridge University Press.

Lawless, J. L., & Fox, R. L. (2008). *Why are women still not running for public office?* Washington, DC: Brookings Institution.

Lenhart, A., & Fox, S. (2006, July 19). Bloggers. Pew Internet & American Life Project. Retrieved from http://www.pewinternet.org/2006/07/19/bloggers/

Lopez, L. K. (2009). The radical act of 'mommy blogging': Redefining motherhood through the blogosphere. *New Media & Society*, *11*(5), 729–747.

Merkel, R. M., & Wright, T. (2012). Parental self-efficacy and online support among parents of children diagnosed with type 1 diabetes mellitus. *Pediatric Nursing*, *38*(6), 303–308.

Mo, P. K., & Coulson, N. S. (2010). Living with HIV/AIDS and use of online support groups. *Journal of Health Psychology*, *15*(3), 339–350.

Morrison, A. (2011). "Suffused by feeling and affect": The intimate public of personal mommy blogging. *Biography*, *34*(1), 37–55.

Schneider, A. L., & Ingram, H. M. (1997). *Policy design for democracy*. Lawrence, KS: University Press of Kansas.

Schram, S. (2000). *After welfare: The culture of postindustrial social policy*. New York, NY: New York University Press.

Stavrositu, C., & Sundar, S. S. (2012). Does blogging empower women? Exploring the role of agency and community. *Journal of Computer-Mediated Communication*, *17*(4), 369–386.

Sue, D. W., Capodilupo, C. M., Torino, G. C., Bucceri, J. M., Holder, A., Nadal, K. L., & Esquilin, M. (2007). Racial microaggressions in everyday life: Implications for clinical practice. *American Psychologist*, *62*(4), 271–286.

Wellman, B., Quan-Haase, A., Boase, J., Chen, W., Hampton, K., Díaz, I., & Miyata, K. (2003). The social affordances of the Internet for networked individualism. *Journal of Computer-Mediated Communication*, *8*(3), 0–0. Advance online publication. doi: 10.1111/j.1083-6101.2003.tb00216.x

CHAPTER THREE

Virtual Local Public Sphere: The Role of New Media in Creating a Contemporary Local Democracy

ILONA BIERNACKA-LIGIEZA

INTRODUCTION

This chapter explores how the quality of the democratic process can be augmented by new communication technologies used on the local level. Firstly, the chapter presents some solutions which are being introduced to improve local administration and information systems in Poland. The chapter examines the contemporary structure of local e-government in selected regions in Poland (the top-down process). Secondly, the chapter focuses on the development of local community e-participation (the bottom-up process), by carrying out an analysis of the impact of ICT on contemporary communication between local politicians and their voters. Using both quantitative and qualitative methods of research, I endeavour to analyze how the power of ICT is used by local communities in regions with diverse economic capacities.

Participation is one of the most important elements of democracy and is closely associated with a number of processes that link up with communication and social decision-making processes. These processes, to a greater or lesser extent, use ICT technologies and the Internet as an aid, even though they themselves are not dependent on the Internet. This chapter looks at the ways the affordances of the Internet and Web 2.0 services apply (or not) on the level of local democracy.

Globalization does not render locality irrelevant, but challenges it, as was emphasized, for instance, by the concepts of glocalization (Featherstone, Lash, & Robertson, 1995, pp. 25–44) or translocality (Appadurai, 1996). In general, these concepts suggest that encounters of the local and the global can be productive in terms of modifying locality by placing it in the wider context of the global and vice versa. In the case of using digital technologies in a local context, we are not interested in the width but in the depth. Looking at the implementation of the digital technologies in local communities, we are not concerned with the question of how the local gets modified by the global, but if it can become intensified. Some scholars provide sceptical accounts of the decaying sense of participation in the life of local communities and argue that in the late modern period real (off-line) local communities dissolve into isolated individuals (Putnam, 2001). Potential intensification of the local participatory energy on and through the Internet is therefore more important in that it is missing even in the real life of local communities.

THEORETICAL FRAMEWORK

Concept of locality in the globalized world

The impact of globalization on local media and society within specific cultural and national contexts could, thus, be multi-faceted. Many scholars (Hafez, 2007; Hegde, 2005; Thussu, 1998, 2007a, 2007b) analyzing today's media trends notice that global media companies are aware of local needs and they adjust their programs to the local context. Moreover, year after year, it is becoming more apparent that locality is perceived as one of the most important factors of the media economy. The process of mutual cooperation could be seen on the local, national and global level. The process of strengthening both the local and global media is becoming increasingly noticeable in more countries each year. This tendency allows media scholars to assume that globalization, characterized by a multiplying audience, does not necessarily lead to cultural homogenization but, rather, reinvigorates cultural diversity in new ways.

On the one hand, current trends such as technological convergence, free movement of goods, services and capital, as well as market mergers and acquisitions, often jeopardize the potential growth of local cultures, particularly in developing countries and in transition countries. Cultural industries are increasingly concentrated in the hands of a few players who have advanced technical capacities for producing and distributing creative products.

On the other hand, in order to flourish, what local cultures need is not to be preserved unchanged, like insects in amber, but to live and develop in their own ways as they themselves choose. And in this, they can benefit from the use of new tools of information, knowledge and communication, which they can obtain only by increasing their connections to the world at large. Cultural exchange is also a key factor in breaking down the barriers that prevent good relations among people and it can serve as a powerful instrument of "preventive diplomacy".

Bauman, in his deliberations on globalization, has devoted a lot of attention to locality and its retardation in the contemporary world. We no longer need a material carrier to transmit information, so Bauman decided that 'a town and local people have little to do with the local community' (Bauman, 1998, p. 37). Quoting Lazarfeld, he concluded that in the globalized world there exists no "local agora", no place for the opinions of local authority; a place in which 'plans of actions are developed, private matters become public, opinions are created, courts are organized and punishments given' (Bauman, 1998, p. 37). It seems, however, that these local debate forums still exist, and, what is more, they create new spaces for public debate.

The process by which, in the globalized world, individual cultures tend to decrease in importance or to be overwhelmed by giving room to a single global culture, is often a source of concern. The resulting bewilderment materializes in one of two ways: exaggerated devotion to the past, often a reinvented past, in the name of tradition and the opposite tendency, namely the non-critical adoption of any cultural input coming from the outside.

Arjun Appadurai describes the production of locality as the object of ethnography. For him, "locality is an inherently fragile social achievement" that must be maintained carefully against various kinds of odds, especially through ritual ones. Not only boundary maintenance, or a foundational ritual, but also rites of passage produce locality as both a spatial construction and as a way of embodiment—through the production of local subjects. The glocal approach suggests that local cultures may be valorized and revitalized through the means and opportunities offered by globalization in order to make them a source of enrichment for all the individuals involved. Instead of a superficial interest for local habits and folklore, glocalization involves the belief in an active multiculturalism based on the acknowledgement and valorization of differences between cultures, and on the promotion of cultural exchanges whereby people from diverse societies can express and communicate their visions, values and traditions to one another. Robertson ultimately hopes to dispel the 'notion of homogenization of all cultures' by the forces of transnational capital (Robertson, 1995, p. 25). Glocalization is not what Thussu (1998) refers to as 'desi globalization—when foreign business interests and media emphasize their native credentials to present a more acceptable face of globalization' (p. 46). Instead, Luke argues, 'glocalization attests that every global, virtualizing force is met by a stubborn alterity, a dialectical intensification of both globalism and localism' (Luke, 1997, p. 89). Concerning the implementation of a new communication technologies structure into the local public sphere, we must take into consideration not only challenges but also doubts and threats connected with global technology development, and it is one of the main issues of this chapter.

Affordances of the new media and democracy

Nowadays, the one-way media, which are characteristic of mass society and include the press, radio and television, are losing to the interactive, digital means of communication. New information and communication technology (ICT) may serve not only for work or entertainment, but also for building up the society. We associate with ICT such hopes as, for example, to expand the opportunities for public information about the intentions of the government or to increase participation of citizens in co-decision making about the shape of the state, which is particularly important in the face of declining interest in participation in public life. The impact of ICTs on political processes and state-citizen relations is determined by means of such concepts as tele-democracy, digital democracy, cyber-democracy and e-democracy. Regardless of the name and scope of the concept, common to these ideas is the belief that various features of new technologies—interactivity, faster mode of information, communication feedback—may, in a positive way, have an influence on democratic mechanisms (Białobłocki, Moroz, & Nowina-Konopka, 2004; Chadwick, 2006; Cindio & Schuler, 2012; Nowina-Konopka, 2009; Zissis & Papadopoulou, 2009).

New communication technologies are being used by local communities mainly in two forms, as e-government (top-down process) and e-participation (bottom-up process). There is no doubt that ICT is a strong support for local administration. A proper and smoothly functioning e-government system seems to be standard for each democratic country. Moreover, due to the spread of Web 2.0 media,[1] the perception of representation is being reconstructed. Web 2.0 itself may not strongly affect citizens' attitudes towards community involvement and participation, but can be used to create conditions for a more involving, inclusive and transparent democratic culture.

The two processes mentioned above (top-down and bottom-up) are two halves of e-democracy. As we can see, new communication technologies cause many changes in the contemporary local public sphere. These may be changes in how the internal organization of the public sector works—i.e., the technology can be used to improve collaboration and integration between different levels of government and between offices. The second type is aimed at increasing the availability of online information about the work of public institutions and the fact that the public sector will try to arrange its activities for the benefit of the people so that the centre of activity is shifted towards self-service (Grönlund & Andersson, 2007; Nam, 2010; Yates, Gulati, & Tawileh, 2010). According to Trechsel and Mendez:

> e-democracy consists of all electronic means of communication that enable/empower citizens in their efforts to hold rulers/politicians accountable for their actions in the public realm. Depending on the aspect of democracy being promoted, e-democracy can employ different techniques for: 1. increasing the transparency of the political process; 2. enhancing

the direct involvement and participation of citizens; 3. improving the quality of opinion formation by opening new spaces of information and deliberation. (2005, p. 5)

E-democracy relates to those uses of ICTs which provide either novel or more efficient, practicable means for citizens to exercise influence in the governing process. In other words, this term applies when ICTs are used to revolutionize the relationship between the citizen and the representative. E-government, however, is a term that can be invoked to describe those uses of ICTs which do one of two things. First, under the paradigm of organizational theory, they may make the interaction between different agencies and different bureaucrats more efficient, as they do for private firms. Second, they may make the relationship between the government bureaucracy and the citizen, in the sense of a political consumer, more comfortable and efficient by reducing transaction costs. To put it another way, when a citizen can pay a fine or fill out a property tax form online, this is an example of e-government. In many cases, e-government and e-democracy initiatives may emerge at the same time as various levels of government that increase their reliance upon and familiarity with ICTs. Regardless of who takes the initiative, these actions may result in unidirectional or bidirectional processes. For several years, governments throughout the world have been seeking to provide electronic access to government services. Key reasons for this public sector reform have been to increase the efficiency of government operations, strengthen democracy, enhance transparency, and provide better and more versatile services to citizens and businesses (Coe, Paquet, & Roy, 2001; Giritli, 2009; Ho, 2002 Ifinedo & Singh, 2011).

According to Macintosh and Whyte, e-participation means the use of ICTs to broaden and deepen political participation by enabling citizens to connect with one another and with their elected representatives. The emphasis of this definition is the involvement of all stakeholders in democratic participatory decision making, instead of just the top-down initiatives of the governments (Macintosh & Whyte, 2008). Romsdahl understands e-participation as one of the many methods of public deliberation. Public deliberation is not a new concept in itself, but e-participation holds potential to revitalize it (Romsdahl, 2005, p. 44). On the other hand, some scholars approach the concept of e-participation from a critical point of view (Fountain, 2001; Wallsten, 2007).

Specificities of the new media use in the local context

The Internet is well known for its suggestive spatial dimension and strong, though replicated, geography consisting of areas that are experienced as local. The capacity to motivate people's concentration on specific shared "places" was one of the earliest noticed phenomena described as creation of virtual communities (Rheingold, 1993). Geographical proximity is not required. It is an 'imagined community' or a 'community without proximity', consisting of people who have never met but enter into more intimate relations in the virtual world than they do in reality with the people living in the same town or house (Barney, 2004).

It is worth noting that along with the only virtual communities, there are still local communities that exist both online and off-line, despite having the required tools and possibilities to create a virtual community. There are also communities which do not have access to digital tools because they either do not feel the need to use them, or they are "digitally excluded" and have no access to the technology, and thus only exist in the physical world. It is worth noting that, in a way, traditional local media also integrate real-life communities because most people living in a given region or town perceive themselves as a part of the community only in their minds and rarely enter into direct interaction with each other (Anderson, 2006). Urry (2000), deliberating on the community mobility in a 'network society', noticed that Bell and Newby (1976) have identified three useful categories concerning the meaning of the community: proximity, locality and community. These categories are also useful in the discussion of the local media, because one can identify different kinds of media used for communication by a given community. The Internet and its Web 2.0 services are used by many as a space for debate, intervention and grassroots journalism, which are activities that may also have local-specific functions.

The first opportunity which the Internet presents is the chance to create a local debate forum. It is a community of people who live in the same place, go to the same institutions to take care of official matters, are subject to the same rules set by the authorities, etc. Another potential of the Internet is the possibility to fill the gap in the traditional media market. Where there is a lack of "official" information, and there are too few journalists in remote places, it is possible to generate a communicative platform on the Internet, which would be based on a bottom-up initiative coming from the citizens.

The capacity of new media to increase the quality of democracy has been a source of conflict between the sceptics and the utopians ever since the debate over digital democracy commenced. The same goes for the Internet in the local context. Studies exploring the involvement of local communities in political debates and decision making via ICT at the beginning of the twenty-first century showed diversified interest from the citizens' side, and researchers had different opinions about the digital public sphere at the local level (Hoff, Horrocks, & Tops, 2000; Norris, 2001; Wilhelm, 2000, 2004). The first experiences of a virtual commune or city were initiated from those countries which were familiar with highly advanced communication technologies (e.g., the USA [California], the Netherlands [Amsterdam], Germany [Berlin], Denmark [Jutland], Sweden [Gothenburg]). Nowadays, we can see dozens of e-democracy initiatives, both in countries with highly developed ICTs and a long democratic tradition (e.g., Norway [Modalen, Agder, Larvik, Molde];

Finland [Tampere]) and those marked by a rebirth of democracy and average ICT development (e.g., Poland [Małopolska, Lower Silesia]; the Czech Republic [Prague, Brno]). Regarding this rapidly growing transformation of the local governance structure, researchers are much less sceptical of ICTs being used as one of the main tools of that transformation than they had been at the beginning of that process (Jeitziner, 2009; Meier, 2009; Orihuela & Obi, 2007). Upon analyzing the influence of the ICTs on democracy, we are able to see that new communication technologies may increase access to political decision makers and, in a broader sense, contribute to public opinion formation both on global and local issues. The key element is that the Internet has a low threshold: ICT makes it much easier for "ordinary people" to get through with their messages than any other medium.

Local government has a critical role to play in this e-democracy process as the branch of formal democracy that is closest to real people and real communities, that deals with people's local concerns, and that helps people shape the places in which they live. Most local governments in western democratic societies prioritize the implementation of the Web 2.0 agenda, but they are also conscious that in the end the real import of Web 2.0 is not about the use of online tools, but rather in the extension of the Web's collaborative, participative logic to all of the council's activities. And yet, when we look at the state of affairs in eastern democracies (e.g., Poland), we see local government scarcely using Web 2.0 technologies. Despite the fact that discussion forums give local people the opportunity to talk to each other about the issues that they identify as important, councillors very rarely use blogs, though increasingly they do use Twitter to share their thinking or to update the community on their activities. Councils in Poland very rarely use Facebook Fan pages to communicate with the public. When it comes to local dialogue and debate on the net, the experiences are different in countries with a stable democracy and high technological development (e.g., Scandinavia) as compared to regions of developing democracy and lower technological impact (e.g., Poland). Analyzing the case of Poland, it can be seen that communication within a delimited group, for instance a political party organization, renders the best communication results. In contrast, large, open debate forums are more troublesome. If the participants are not committed, the quality of the discussion suffers, and therefore the debates die out quickly. Some debates have had a more uncivilized tone than we are used to in public debates, often instigated by anonymous contributions or contributions under a false name. Finally, on the negative side, right-wing extremist groups have used some discussion forums to spread racist messages. The Internet's low free-speech threshold that should be a clear democratic advantage, can, unfortunately, also be a problem.

Of course, there are also many positive examples from the net-based debate. In particular, both the scope and quality are affected when citizens have a chance to become involved in specific issues, which the politicians are then forced to deal with. In these cases, the net functions as an extra channel in addition to meetings, petitions, etc. The net debate very rarely reaches 100 percent participation. We can treat a result just over 50 percent as a success. In comparison, only a small minority writes letters to the editor or takes the floor at public meetings. Moreover, some of the participants in the net debate would never write a letter to the editor, or speak out—for the simple reason that they do not subscribe to a newspaper or attend public meetings. Finally, success or failure cannot be "measured" only by the number of active participants, but must also be measured by how many people visit the websites in question and keep informed on the debate (Millard, 2006; Porwol, O'Donoghue, & Breslin, 2012).

So, can ICT further local democracy by creating the new setting of the local public sphere? This question is pertinent in light of the current problems in democratic organization, which are highlighted by two factors. The first one is that the processes of political governance are fragmented and complex and therefore difficult for ordinary citizens to grasp. The second one is that the traditional channels, which formed the basis of democratic organization for more than a hundred years, have weakened, and the gap between ordinary people and the political elite seems wider than before. It is therefore natural to search for reforms in democracy, and among these, to consider the potentials of ICT.

METHODOLOGICAL CONSIDERATIONS

Aims of the research

When we look more closely at the local governance across Europe, we can clearly see that different ways of strengthening citizens' trust in local authorities and the creation of platforms of public dialogue are important factors that shape contemporary democracy. Local communities search for solutions that will help in the realization of the essential principles of community communication, which are public trust and social dialogue. Both of these elements strengthen the sense of responsibility for the region, which positively influences the quality of the local governance and all other institutions that create the local public sphere. The above needs must be met by creating sufficient digital communication platforms. Keeping all these aspects in mind, the main aim of the chapter was to analyze democratic challenges and problems associated with new information and communications technology (ICT) being implemented by a local communication system in Poland. Based on the results of the research, the author was able to:

- gather new knowledge about the potentials and limitations of ICTs in terms of democratic participation and governance;
- learn about strategies (adjusted/not adjusted to community expectations) for information society creation and making local politics more intelligible for the citizen;
- influence the communication policy of different regions.

Research questions

Can ICTs further democracy by creating the public sphere as a new communication environment? This question is pertinent in light of the current problems in democratic organization, which are evidenced by two factors:

1. first, that the processes of political governance are fragmented and complex, and therefore difficult for ordinary citizens to grasp;
2. second, that the traditional channels, which formed the basis of democratic organization for more than a hundred years, have weakened and the gap between ordinary people and the political elite seems wider than before. It is therefore natural to search for reforms in democracy, and among these, to consider the potentials of ICT. Those factors also raise more specific questions for Polish researchers such as: How have ICTs changed the functioning of local government in Poland? Do ICTs support political communication? Are ICTs used as platforms for local debate? Are ICTs used mainly as tools for transmitting information from the dominant, one-sided communication? Do ICTs support local democracy?

Technical aspects of the research

This analysis is based on both qualitative and quantitative research as well as website content analysis. A comparative survey has been carried out in different regions of Poland. The key aspects for choosing communes were as follows:

1. economy (rural, semi-urbanized, urbanized);
2. location (east/west/central part of Poland);
3. population (demographic structure).

The data gathered in this analysis were obtained through:

1. documents, reports, statistics data analysis;
2. interviews with: politicians, clerks, journalists, entrepreneurs—the purpose of interviews was to determine how the increased use of ICT changes work

procedures, routines and involvement in associations internally in the organizations and interaction between citizens and politicians/administration;

3. interviews with citizens—a representative sample of the citizens in selected municipalities were asked questions about their knowledge of local politics, participation in associations/ institutions/ local politics, perception of influence on local politics, attitudes towards local democracy, use of ICTs, etc. In order to gauge general changes in the citizens' participation and their relationship with the local government, questions were repeated to a random sample of citizens (62) in each municipality;
4. the content analysis of chosen municipalities' websites was based on parameters that focus on the character of the net communication. The data gathering entailed the collection and registration of material that focuses on political and community communication—'whole site approach' of both official documents (e.g., administrative documents, official e-mail contact, e-news, e-petitions, etc.) and unofficial texts and links (e.g., chat rooms, blogs, social media, etc.).

Reasoning behind the methodology

Because the digitization process has a diverse course in different cultures, it is worth conducting some deeper studies based on sociological methods. Using both quantitative and qualitative aspects of research, it is being analyzed how the power of ICTs is used by local communities in regions with diverse economic capacities. Is there a big difference between them at the local level? Moreover, consistent with the following methodology, we may also check the implementation of ICT tools for building up contemporary democracy in Poland. Over the past decade, local public spheres all over the world were exposed to similar external driving forces, such as technological change, internationalization, and concentration of media ownership as well as developments in public administration. So thus it seems interesting to look at each single case and try to determine how each country is trying to cope with all those challenges.

RESEARCH RESULTS

Main actors of local community life online: Municipalities, local political parties, NGOs

At the beginning of the empirical studies presentation it is crucial to explain the two main terms being used interchangeably to discuss Polish local administration structure. Both terms—*'commune'* and *'municipality'*—are used to name Polish 'gmina' (one of the levels of the Polish local government system). The term 'commune' has more geographic and organization connotations, and 'municipality' is rather interpreted as a more administrative term, more often like 'commune administration sector'. 'Municipality' is dedicated to city/town commune.

The most prevalent form of local communities' online presence is the websites prepared by the municipalities, local political parties, and NGOs. Research conducted in Polish communes over the last decade proved that they have become more transparent due to their visibility and activity on the Internet (Biernacka-Ligięza, 2010; Guzik, 2004; Nowak, 2011; Nowina-Konopka, 2009; Żygulski, 2004). A vast majority of them can be contacted via e-mail, and most have their own websites. What is more, the content and level of information provided on the municipal website varies significantly. On the pages of some municipalities, vast amounts of information are provided, while others limit themselves to publishing only an address or telephone number. At the beginning, many municipalities treated their websites as a hobby or fringe activity, much less important than the ordinary work of the commune. Currently, the communication network is becoming one of the most important instruments for many communities and, increasingly, it is becoming more professional as more municipalities actively use the Internet, and newly arrived residents are eager to turn to electronic solutions.[2]

It is necessary to look closer at smaller communes in different regions of the country; 12 communes from 3 (three) different regions of the country were chosen:

- Lower Silesia (Western Poland): Wałbrzych, Świdnica, Dzierżoniów, Jaworzyna Śląska;
- Podkarpacie (Eastern Poland): Krosno, Sanok, Jasło, Rymanów;
- Łódzkie Voivodship (Central Poland): Sieradz, Zduńska Wola, Łask, Zelów (see Table 3.1).

We should refer not only to the presentation of the municipality as a political and administrative unit, but also to the institution and organization operating within its area.

Table 3.1. Communes' Websites Content.

	Contact information	Council meetings	Online debates	Online forms
Wałbrzych	x	x	–	x
Świdnica	x	x	–	x
Dzierżoniów	x	x	–	x
Jaworzyna Śląska	x	x	–	x
Krosno	x	x	–	x
Sanok	x	x	–	x
Jasło	x	x	–	x

	Contact information	Council meetings	Online debates	Online forms
Rymanów	x	–	–	x
Sieradz	x	x	–	x
Zduńska Wola	x	x	–	x
Łask	x	–	–	x
Zelów	x	–	–	x

Source: Own description, 2013.

All municipalities covered by the survey have their own websites, most of which are extensive and comprehensive in their provision of detailed information. The most complete websites (e.g., Sieradz, Wałbrzych) are replete with diverse, well-structured information. One can access extensive services, such as, for example: opening hours of the various public institutions such as the library, information on the operation of kindergartens, the school common room, tax information, the superintendent, planning-town office, or the latest community news. Moreover there are announced cultural or sports events together with information about opening hours and training schedules at the local sports club. As we can see, municipalities' websites provide a variety of information, ranging from directions for driving to school, through the announcement of entertainment shows, up to submitting an application for a place in kindergarten. Still, not many citizens in Poland are able to apply for a position in kindergarten through the Internet because they have not yet met both the safety and the technical requirements, including the protection of personal data. Security of web-based communication is still a challenge for Polish municipalities, but administrations are making steady improvement. Thus, in the near future, it is expected that—according to the plan of information society development—submitting applications electronically should be possible soon in most Polish municipalities.[3]

Many municipalities also publish the results of public opinion surveys carried out by the public service sector (e.g., Dzierżoniów commune regularly posts results of each year's customer satisfaction survey). Information is updated quite regularly (especially in developed communes) and the residents who frequently visit websites of municipalities can keep up with information about public services. They can also easily figure out where to look for more detailed information. Municipal websites also contain links to other sites including institutions and public office sites where you can ask questions about public services.

Websites of local governments do not engage in party politics, but the content is not fully devoid of political questions because quite often it provides various forms of access to the agendas of their meetings. Infrequent for Polish services is the provision of information about what occurs at the meetings of the council, the municipal executive board and committees, although not in all municipalities is information given in the same degree of detail. There is information about the meetings and agendas of different kinds and about decisions taken that can also be quickly learnt and accessed from the network. In this respect, small municipalities do not differ at all from the big ones: website users are informed in the same way about the resolutions of the municipality by the small communes of Jasło or Jaworzyna Śląska and the bigger communes such as Sieradz or Wałbrzych. The difference is, however, in the amount of information. In addition, large communes seem to have more professional websites. Some sites include links to a source of information about the provincial council and local elections.

The list of issues raised at council meetings and the municipal executive board and other committees is presented in electronic services, in order to make it easy to find out those issues in which local governments are currently engaged. But only some municipalities give detailed information about current political issues. However, municipalities are present on the Internet primarily as providers of public services. The political aspect is not omitted, but it is not readily available in many communes, as the information is not posted on the main sites; therefore, to find information about the activities of municipalities, as political organizations, or information about municipal policies, one would need to go either to the microsite, or directly to these sites by browser, or via commercial information services. The information services of some communes provide a list of politicians, including their phone numbers and e-mail addresses, but in many cases one cannot always find the information represented by the political parties. However, for the most part, politicians are only mentioned as members of the municipal executive board; getting a mention on this list is sometimes difficult. The websites of municipalities very rarely have links to local political parties. None of the Polish municipalities analyzed in this paper posted links to the local political parties' websites.

When we look at local parties' websites, we can find information about people to contact and opportunities to establish closer relations with representatives of the parties. However, we cannot say that this information is open space for dialogue. One can make contact—by phone or via e-mail—with the President or other members of the party. Whether this will be a two-way contact—between a voter and a member of the party or between the citizen and the politician—or whether it contributes to public debate on the Internet, depends on how parties treat such notifications. In Poland, sadly very few local parties create opportunities for active participation in political dialogue at the local level through the network for the residents. Only within a former voivodship centre (Wałbrzych, Sieradz, Krosno) is a local political debate on the network more visible, yet it still does not constitute predominant dialogue space for the local public sphere. It also seems that these forums are not used too extensively. Neither do the larger nor smaller political parties offer discussion groups or other opportunities that expand the debate on the network. In some municipalities it is the smallest local party or municipal association which offers such a function (e.g., OBS).

In varying degrees, information about offers of different NGOs can be found. Some of these associations have complex websites, while others do not have websites at all and are only mentioned in the municipal service. Lists like these are written according to the same pattern as the traditional presentation of organizations in the written information issued by local governments, such as brochures describing what is happening in the district. This includes offers from both the municipality and NGOs.

It follows that all analyzed actors of local public life (municipalities, political parties, NGOs) are able to inform residents fairly well of democratic processes, but they are doing worse with allowing residents to have an active democratic influence. Websites of the main actors of the local public sphere have the potential to serve as a quality information source. Attempts to enrich the websites with interactive engines that would enable citizens to use their own voice are rare. When they use the Internet, the most important thing for them is probably not political participation of citizens but the services that the municipality offers. The actors are focused here on high quality gained by the new technologies—the role of citizens is not as accentuated as "the role of co-owners" (Winsvold, 2007).

Attempts to increase civic engagement—through discussions or direct decision making—are rare and do not function very well. Among the chief reasons for this are probably the facts that the forums are in no way related to the political decision-making process in communities, and that local politicians do not engage in debate.

Where the network is a communication space, it is not the municipalities that initiate it but local or regional newspapers with their online versions, or commercially owned local information services (e.g., www.doba.pl; www.wałbrzyszek.pl); sometimes political parties are an exception. Also, local portals with discussion forums (e.g., www.walbszyszek.com; www.krosno24.pl; www.doba.pl; www.sieradzanie.pl) can be indicated as the sphere of political debate, and Internet users take up important matters. This offer is, however, still limited. With regard to the news website, the common use of the Internet is something different from using the Internet as a channel of communication between the municipality and residents.

Websites of local public actors as a news source and an arena of participation

At the beginning of this century, small municipalities in Poland were subjected to criticism. The municipalities were criticized for lack of professionalism and the municipalities' websites did not even deserve to be referred to as Web pages. This criticism even then was not justified. The smallest municipalities did not and still do not differ from the largest ones in terms of informing the public about services or about the meetings of the municipal council. Differences are primarily based on the amount of information, rather than on its quality, or type, or the manner of communication. Large municipalities have more information to share, such as the Krosno municipality website, which is seen to have more content than the Rymanów municipality site. Moreover, the shape, form and quality of the website design are determined by the commune budget, which, unfortunately, in the case of small municipalities, is sometimes quite limited. It must be admitted that the quality of Web pages in Polish municipalities in 2002 left much to be desired (especially when it came to small municipalities). The passing decade definitely changed the image of the Polish e-community and the difference between large and small municipalities in the network primarily refers to the quantity rather than quality of the information published on the website of the municipality.

For residents of the communities analyzed in this chapter, the Internet at the beginning of this century was not a very important source of information about local issues. Only a few people read the mayor's and other politicians' statements that appeared on the network (less than 1% of Poles). Only 1% of the population of Poland was actively involved in Internet political debates.[4] Today the situation is slightly different, especially when it comes to the Internet as a source of information, which for many residents of Polish communities is precisely the most important place where they seek information relevant to them about the region (approx. 39%). However, they do not seek such information at the municipal sites, but rather use the commercial information services such as www.krosno24.pl; www.swidniczka.pl; www.doba.pl; www.walbrzyszek.pl, etc. The local newspaper also continues to serve as an important source of information about the municipality (approx. 31%).[5] Of course, paper publications are more often accompanied by electronic editions. Today, almost every local title has its own page on the Internet.

Considering the opportunity to participate in political discussions on the Internet, it may not be surprising, since there are few possibilities to discuss politics on the network, that such engagement is limited and also very often linked to specific political parties. Since few residents are members of political parties, we cannot expect that participation in the existing newsgroups will be high.

However, it might have been expected that the number of people who have seen or read posted statements of mayors or other local politicians on the Web would be much greater. Such statements can be found not only on the municipal website and on the websites of parties, but also in newspapers, which remain much more popular than the electronic versions (only 3% of inhabitants of Poland have become familiarized with these statements through the Internet).

It is worth indicating that in Poland the Internet is a very important source of information about the region, its culture, tourist attractions and the economy, but most respondents (76% of Poles)[6] stated that the Internet is still not an important source of information about local politics. Taking into account that over 34% of Poles found that the local newspaper is an important source of information, it can be concluded that the Internet, as a source of information about local politics and as an arena to exchange views on political issues, is still in its early stages of development.

If the use of the Internet as a source of information in the local context is not very extensive, then the use of the Internet as an opportunity for participation in local public life is almost negligible. The possibilities for inviting residents to the political debate in the municipality, such as in newsgroups or via feedback and reactions to the proposals of politicians are not often used in Poland. It appears to be improving, and in the last two years we have found more municipalities where we can encounter some positive examples of public dialogue being followed on the Internet. (For example, in the Dzierżoniów commune twice a year, an open dialogue is being followed with citizens about service quality at the local administration offices. Taking part in the debate were the mayor, high management of the council, politicians, and clerks. Participants of the discussion evaluate the administration and suggest some changes that can improve the quality of local administration service).

CONCLUSION

We can see, though, that local government is leading the way in the use of new technologies and is trying to connect online and off-line activity. One thing should be underlined: central government support for good practice in the use of new technologies in local government. Local governments need to use the Internet more proactively but this commitment must be backed by online transparency. The Internet proved to be, for the majority of analyzed communes, mainly a tool for conveying information and providing services on the appropriate level, very rarely used as a platform for debate. It can be noticed that the local newspaper still plays an important role in building a local democracy and a local identity (in a printed and electronic version), where readers can find both sources of information and also have the opportunity to participate in the debate, although local news sites are becoming even more popular (often a commercial initiative, or an additional activity of local publishers/broadcasters) and usually defeat the press.

Regrettably, Polish local politicians are scarcely "visible" on the Internet, as it is rather difficult to find information about local political parties that do not provide up-to-date information to their constituencies. Poles generally do not search for information about local politicians/politics on the Internet because they show little interest in this area of local activity and are more active in the fields of sport, education, or culture. So the analysis presented above brings about one very important observation about the lack of Web 2.0 activity in Polish local politics. Local politicians need to adjust their communication attitudes and they should become more open to social networking technologies to engage citizens in public debate. They need to allow access to social networking sites from council IT systems. It is necessary to bear in mind that there are few hard and fast rules about the use of Web 2.0 technologies. Different tools should be applied in different ways to different problems at different times. For the 21st-century politician, it is important to be open-minded, experimental, willing to engage in dialogue and to question (or allow others to question) existing hierarchies and ways of working. Achieving successful outcomes will involve uncertainty and productive chaos along the way, and it is essential to adopt a mindset that is comfortable with this way of working with people. Collaboration is becoming a more vital currency than control. In time it will become redundant to talk about 'using the Web' as these techniques and tools become fully integrated into the way in which councils work.

To sum up, one has to conclude that the Internet can contribute to the reconstruction of the local public sphere because it is a convenient method of communication. Any content can be put online and it does not require special skills. In a situation in which the local media lose their meaning, the Internet could fill the gap. It also provides an opportunity for citizens to participate in a bigger debate in which more people are engaged than would be the case with the TV or newspapers. The Internet also creates a possibility to have a debate on socio-political issues and to organize political marketing online. However, it is rarely used, especially in small towns and villages. The analysis shows that despite rapid development of technology and growing social participation opportunities, local communities rather slowly adjust to these changes, as they do not organize initiatives, and they do not fully realize the potential of the Internet.

FUTURE RESEARCH DIRECTIONS

As demonstrated above, e-government cannot sensibly be separated from society and public sector developments. These include both societal and technological trends, as well as an understanding of the different cultural and social realms that tend to characterize e-government developments and which are likely to remain important in the future. Some or all of these societal, technological and public sector trends will need to be taken into account by any (regional) e-government initiatives. Due to those reasons, it is worth monitoring changes and the social impact of ICT over the local communities. It seems also important to investigate how the new strategy for developing ICT in Poland will be adjusted into the social expectations, and if all European, national and local solutions connected with establishing and developing an electronic democracy system increase participation.

BIBLIOGRAPHY

Anderson, B. (2006). *Imagined communities: Reflections on the origin and spread of nationalism.* London, UK: Verso.

Appadurai, A. (1996). *Modernity at large: Cultural dimensions of globalization.* Minneapolis, MN: University of Minnesota Press.

Barney, D. (2004). *Network society.* Cambridge, UK: Polity Press.

Bauman, Z. (1998). On glocalization: Or globalization for some, localization for some others. *Thesis Eleven, 54*, 37–49.

Bell, C., & Newby, H. (1976). Communion, communialism, class and community action: The sources of new urban politics. In D. Herbert & R. Johnston (Eds.), *Social areas in cities* (Vol. 2). Chichester, UK: Wiley.

Białobłocki, T., Moroz, J., & Nowina-Konopka, M. (2004). *Społeczeństwo informacyjne: Istota, rozwój wyzwania.* Warszawa, Poland.

Biernacka-Ligięza, I. (2010, July). *Local communication matters?: Local information services in the creation of the civic society—The case of Poland.* Paper presented at the IAMCR Conference, Communication and Citizenship: Rethinking Crisis and Change, Braga, Portugal.

Chadwick, A. (2006). *Internet politics: States, citizens and new communication technologies.* New York, NY: Oxford University Press.

Cindio, F., & Schuler, D. (2012). Beyond community networks: From local to global, from participation to deliberation. *Journal of Community Informatics, 8*(3). Retrieved from http://www.ci-journal.net/index.php/ciej/article/view/908/933

Coe, A., Paquet, G., & Roy, J. (2001). E-governance and smart communities—A social learning challenge. *Social Science Computer Review, 19*(1), 80–93.

Cooper, P., & Kulawczuk, P. (Eds.). (2008). *Electronic self-government communication: Innovative tools of public interest advocacy.* Warsaw, Poland: Institute for Private Enterprise and Democracy.

Cullen, R., & Sommer, L. (2010, January). *Participatory democracy and the value of online community networks: An exploration of online and offline communities engaged in civil society and political activity.* Paper given at the 43rd Hawaii International Conference on System Sciences, Honolulu, Hawaii.

Dahlgren, P. (2009). *Media and political engagement: Citizens, communication, and democracy.* New York, NY: Cambridge University Press.

Featherstone M., Lash S., & Robertson R. (1995). *Global modernities.* London, UK: Sage.

Fountain, J. E. (2001). *Building the virtual state: Information technology and institutional change.* Washington, DC: Brookings Institution Press.

Giritli, N. K. (2009). E-governmentality: On electronic administration in local government. *Electronic Journal of e-Government, 7*(1), 55–64.

Grönlund, Å., & Andersson, A. (2007). E-government research 2003–2006: Improvements and issues. In D. Norris (Ed.), *Current issues and trends in e-government research* (pp. 247–288). Hershey, PA: Idea Group.

Guzik, R. (2004). Polskie miasta i gminy wiejskie w Internecie—Geografia społeczeństwa informacyjnego. In J. Słodczyk (Ed.), *Rozwój miast i zarządzanie gospodarka miejską*. Opole, Poland: Miasta w okresie przemian.

Habermas, J. (1989). *The structural transformation of the public sphere: An inquiry into a category of bourgeois society*. Cambridge, UK: Polity Press.

Hafez, K. (2007). *The myth of media globalization*. Cambridge, UK: Polity Press.

Hargittai, E., & Walejko, G. (2008). The participation divide: Content creation and sharing in the digital age. *Information, Communication and Society, 11*(2), 239–256.

Haug, A. V. (2007). Local democracy online: Driven by crisis, legitimacy, resources, or communication gaps? *Journal of Information Technology and Politics, 4*(2), 79–99.

Hegde, R. S. (2005). Disciplinary spaces and globalization: A postcolonial unsettling. *Global Media and Communication, 1*(1), 59–62.

Held, D. (2006). *Models of democracy*. Cambridge, UK: Polity Press.

Hoff, J., Horrocks, I., & Tops, P. (Eds.). (2000). *Democratic governance and new technology: Technologically mediated innovations in political practices*. London, UK: Routledge.

Ifinedo, P., & Singh, M. (2011). Determinants of eGovernment maturity in the transition economies of Central and Eastern Europe. *Electronic Journal of e-Government, 9*(2), 166–182.

Jeitziner, B. (2009). Zielsetzung und Umsetzung eines webbasierten Wahlhilfesystems für Parlamentswahlen. In A. Meier (Ed.), *eDemocracy & eGovernment: Stages of a democratic knowledge society* (pp.178–183). Berlin, Germany: Springer.

Kies, R., Mendez, F., Schmitter, P., & Trechsel, A. (2004). *Evaluation of the use of new technologies in order to facilitate democracy in Europe*. STOA 116. European Parliament Report. Retrieved from www.europarl.europa.eu/stoa/publications/studies/stoa116_en.pdf

Klotz, R. J. (2004). *The politics of Internet communication*. Lanham, MD: Rowman & Littlefield.

Kluszczyński, R. (2001). *Społeczeństwo informacyjne—Cyberkultura—Sztuka multimediów*. Kraków, Poland: Rabid.

Layne, K., & Lee, J. W. (2001). Developing fully functional e-government: A four stage model. *Government Information Quarterly, 18*(2), 122–136.

Lee, J., & Kim, S. (2012, September). *Active e-participation in local governance: Citizen participation values and social networks*. Paper presented at the EGPA Conference, Bergen, Norway.

Lilleker, D., & Jackson, N. (2010). Towards a more participatory style of election campaigning: The impact of Web 2.0 on the UK 2010 general election. *Policy & Internet, 2*(3), 69–98.

Luke, T. W. (1997). New world order or neo-world orders: Power, politics, and ideology in informationalizing glocalities. In M. Featherstone, S. Lash, & R. Roberston (Eds.), *Global modernities* (pp. 91–107). London, UK: Sage.

Macintosh, A., & Whyte, A. (2008). Towards an evaluation framework for eParticipation. *Transforming Government: People, Process & Policy, 2*(1), 16–30.

Meier, A. (Ed.). (2009). *E-democracy and e-government: Stages of a democratic knowledge society*. Berlin, Germany: Springer.

Millard, J. (2006). E-governance and e-participation: Lessons from Europe in promoting inclusion and empowerment. Budapest, Hungary: UDESA Workshop.

Ministry of Interior and Administration (MSWiA). (2008). *The strategy for the development of the information society in Poland until 2013*. Retrieved from https://www.itu.int/net/wsis/review/inc/docs/rcreports/POL/StrategyForTheDevelopmentOfTheInformationSociety.pdf

Morrison, J., & Newman, D. (2001). Consultation and participation in New Labour's Britain and beyond. *International Review of Law, 15*(2), 171–194.

Nam, T. (2010, January). *Whither digital equality? An empirical study of the democratic divide.* Paper presented at the 43rd International Conference on System Sciences, Honolulu, Hawaii.

Norris, P. (2001). *Digital divide: Civic engagement, information poverty and the Internet worldwide.* New York, NY: Cambridge University Press.

Nowak, J. (2011). *Aktywność obywateli online: Teorie a praktyka.* Lublin, Poland: UMCS.

Nowina-Konopka, M. (2009). Politycy lokalni a nowe typy komunikacji politycznej w Internecie. In M. Jeziński (Ed.), *Nowe media i polityka: Internet, demokracja, kampanie wyborcze.* Toruń, Poland: Wydawnictwo Adam Marszałek.

Orihuela, L., & Obi, T. (2007). E-government and e-governance: Towards a clarification in the usage of both concepts. In T. Obi (Ed.), *E-governance: A global perspective on a new paradigm* (pp. 26–32). Amsterdam, The Netherlands: IOS Press.

Papadopoulou, P., Nikolaidou, M., & Martakos, D. (2010, January). *What is trust in e-government? A proposed typology.* Paper presented at the 43rd International Conference on System Sciences, Honolulu, Hawaii.

Porwol L., O'Donoghue, P., & Breslin, J. G. (2012, October). *Social inclusion and digital divide: eParticipation dilemmas in municipalities.* Paper presented at the 6th International Conference on Theory and Practice of Electronic Governance, Albany, NY.

Pratchett, L., Wingfield, M., & Polat, R. K. (2006). Local democracy online: An analysis of local government Web sites in England and Wales. *International Journal of Electronic Government Research, 2*(3), 75–92.

Putnam, R. D. (2001). *Bowling alone: The collapse and revival of American community.* New York, NY: Simon & Schuster.

Robertson, R. (1995). Glocalization: Time-space and homogeneity-heterogeneity. In M. Featherstone, S. Lash, & R. Roberston (Eds.), *Global modernities* (pp. 25–44). London, UK: Sage.

Romsdahl, R. J. (2005). Political deliberation and e-participation in policy-making. *Comparative Literature and Culture, 7*(2). Retrieved from http://dx.doi.org/10.7771/1481-4374.1264

Rose, L. E. (2002). Municipal size and local nonelectoral participation: Findings from Denmark, the Netherlands, and Norway. *Government and Policy, 20*(6), 829–851.

Rose, L. E. (2004). Local government and politics. In K. Heidar (Ed.), *Nordic politics: Comparative perspectives* (pp. 164–182). Oslo, Norway: Universitets forlaget.

Snellen, I. (2003). E-knowledge management in public administration: The agenda for the future. *Knowledge Management in Electronic Government, Lecture Notes in Computer Science, 2645*, 70–75.

Thornton, W. (2000). Mapping the 'glocal' village: The political limits of 'glocalization'. *Continuum: Journal of Media & Cultural Studies, 14*(1), 79–89.

Thussu, D. K. (1998). *Electronic empires—Global media and local resistance.* New York, NY: Oxford University Press.

Thussu, D. K. (2007a). *Media on the move: Global flow and contra-flow.* London, UK: Routledge.

Thussu, D. K. (2007b). *News as entertainment: The rise of global infotainment.* Thousand Oaks, CA: Sage.

Torpe, L., & Nielsen, J. (2004). Digital communication between local authorities and citizen in Denmark. *Local Government Studies, 30*(2), 230–244.

Trechsel, A. H., & Mendez, F. (2005). *The European Union and e-voting.* London, UK: Routledge.

Urry, J. (2000). *Sociology beyond societies: Motilities for the twenty-first century.* London, UK: Routledge.

Wallsten, K. (2007). Agenda setting and the blogosphere: An analysis of the relationship between mainstream media and political blogs. *Review of Policy Research, 24*(6), 567–587.

Wilhelm, A. (2000). *Democracy in the digital age*. London, UK: Routledge.

Wilhelm, A. (2004). *Digital nation: Toward an inclusive information society*. Cambridge, UK: Cambridge University Press.

Winsvold, M. (2007). Municipal websites in the local public debate: Supplying facts or setting agenda? *Nordicom Review, 28*(2), 7–23.

Yates, D. J., Gulati, G. J., & Tawileh, A. (2010, January). *Explaining the global digital divide: The impact of public policy initiatives on digital opportunity and ICT development*. Paper presented at the 43rd International Conference on System Sciences, Honolulu, Hawaii.

Zissis, D., & Papadopoulou, A. (2009). Competent electronic participation channels in electronic democracy. *Electronic Journal of E-Government, 7*(2), 195–208.

Żygulski, W. (2004). E-govrnment-rozwiązanie przyszłości. *Marketing, 10*(3), 2–12.

Sources

Author's survey: Conducted between 2002–2010. Place of survey: former walbrzyskie voivodship (counties: dzierzoniowski; swidnicki; walbrzyski). Quantitative questionnaires among inhabitants: 2000 (based on telephone survey). Qualitative interviews with local politicians, officials, local journalists, representatives of NGOs: 34.

Reports

Administracja publiczna w sieci 2002 – czy rzeczywiście bliżej obywatela (2002) Internet Obywatelski, Warszawa.

eEuropa – Społeczeństwo informacyjne dla wszystkich (2000) Monitor Integracji Europejskiej nr 35, Urzędu Komitetu Integracji Europejskiej, Warszawa.

Strategia rozwoju społeczeństwa informacyjnego (2008) Ministerstwo Spraw Wewnętrznych i Administracji, Warszawa.

Rozwój regionalny w Polsce – raport (2009). Ministerstwo Rozwoju Regionalnego, Warszawa.

United Nations (2003) World Public Sector Report 2003: *E-government at the Crossroads*, ST/ESA/PAD/SER.E/49, New York.

Statistics

2002–2011 reports of: Central Statistics Office (GUS); Eurostat; Internet World Statistics; Millward Brown SMG/KRC; PBI; Gemius; municipalities presented in the paper.

NOTES

1. Web 2.0 is a term coined by O'Reilly Media in 2004. The term Web 2.0 has many definitions, and includes the use of tools such as social networking sites, videosharing sites, blogs and wikis. However, what makes Web 2.0 new and important is its capacity to change the relationship between the Internet and its users. According to Lilleker and Jackson, Web 2.0 is about interacting with web-based content, adding comments, or uploading files. Each visitor is able to have shared ownership over a site. This implies a change in power structures and a shift in organizational thinking towards models based on equal partnership rather than elite dominance (Lilleker & Jackson, 2010).
2. Source: Customer service assessment—survey which is followed by the Dzierżoniów commune as part of the ISO directives evaluation process.
3. Source: Ministry of Interior and Administration (MSWiA), 2008, *The Strategy for the Development of the Information Society in Poland until 2013.*
4. Source: Author's own research, 2007.
5. Source: Author's own research, 2009.
6. Source: Author's own research, 2009.

Part Two:
Momentous Challenges in Uncharted Territory: Advertising and Public Relations

CHAPTER FOUR

Effects of Communication in Public and Media Rationale: Result Measures of Public Relations

GUILLEM MARCA, KATHY MATILLA, AND ANDRÉA OLIVEIRA

INTRODUCTION

Use of traditional media has been challenged by communication directors as a result of the emergence of new media and e-communities. Social media offers insightful analytical resources, and studies show that it greatly influences audiences' decision making. As a result, the disconnection between organizations and the media needs to be thoroughly analyzed.

The effects achieved by professional interventions can be found in the final evaluation of communication plans, brought about by initial research and goal setting. There are several effects (knowledge, attitude promotion, behavioral changes, etc.), and each of them is useful to evaluate a certain type of goal or process stage. It is important for professionals to distinguish what type of results they are measuring, and what information can be gained.

There is extensive and varied terminology for the concise classification of the different categories of "result" in English literature. In communication evaluation literature, the most recurrent terms are *output*, *outtake* and *outcome*. However, there are many more (*outlet*, *input*, *outgrowth or outflow*), even if there is no consensus on their specific meanings among different authors. It is not the access to information that constitutes the main challenge for the communication professional maintaining the value chain vs. paradigm shift that affects the breaking point of the public sphere. Instead, it is the discrimination of the type of information needed according to the goals set. The credibility that traditional media still enjoys, even in its digital format, can be a starting point for public relations professionals when thinking about strategy.

THE GRIM REALITY OF THE RESULTS

From a simplified (and grim) perspective, Pestana and Daniels (2011) present a vision of public relations functioning in three stages, thus establishing the basis for the most complex matrix of results evaluation that the industry and academia have had at their disposal in the past half century:

- In a first phase, public relations activity is developed; a story is created and told.
- Then, in the second phase, the story is distributed through third parties who act as intermediaries.
- In the third phase, the intermediaries communicate the story to the public and to the target audience.

All of this happens to accomplish specific business results.

Although the vision is very much simplified, the authors distinguish three phases between monitoring establishment, public relations activity and intermediaries and audiences, which are the rationale of the discipline.

The strategic planning models of communication and public relations are structured in stages that can range from four (Cutlip, Center, & Broom, 2005; Marston, 1963), to ten (Broom & Dozier, 1990; Gregory, 2006). All of them have at least two stages in common that aim to obtain data from different sources, types and formats: the investigation stage and the evaluation stage. In practice, communication and public relations professionals work with information that comes from research from the aforementioned two stages, which are preliminary or posterior to the implementation of its planning and action.

Beyond the classic socio-demographic and psychographic data used in the disciplines of advertising and marketing for each audience, data about notoriety, perception, opinions and behaviors, among others, become blocks of knowledge that practitioners should be able to handle easily to allow for proper decision making. These blocks of information come from two types of data: results from investigations prior to interventions and results of final evaluations. When performed during implementation (formative evaluation), there is allowance for modification and correction, which seeks to avoid or mitigate failure (Oxley, 1989).

RESULT MEASURES IN PUBLIC RELATIONS EVALUATION

The essential requirements to accomplish subsequent investigation (evaluative) include management commitment, correct goal setting, selection of the most appropriate result measurements, determining the best way to gather and organize this data and informing the board of directors (Seitel, 2002). Therefore, we observed that the importance of managing the gathered knowledge is vital in evaluations.

There are many different types of result measurements, and each one is useful to evaluate a goal type or process phase, and it is important for the practitioner to distinguish what type of result measurement they are using along with what information can be extracted from it. Thus, if goals that involve change (relational, attitudinal, behavioral) are set, the collected data should adhere directly to this element of change. It is wrong to manage media coverage data thinking that it will directly influence the element of change. Media evaluation data explains the media, not the stakeholders, although media can play an important role in public opinion (L'Étang, 2009).

English-speaking culture has an extensive terminology to concisely classify the different result categories, while in the Spanish language there is only one term: "result". This subdivision of the concept allows for a standardized data classification that facilitates knowledge management acquired through investigation and evaluation. Oft-repeated options in literature about communication evaluation are output, outtake and outcome (Likely, 2003; Lindenmann, 2002; Paine, 2007; Robina, Amisha, & Gregory, 2006; Stacks, 2002, 2006); however, and as we shall see, there are many more and not all authors agree on their specific meanings.

Fraser Likely (2003) provides the widest variety in terms of result measurement categorizing, relating it to a scale that includes five levels of monitoring. The higher the level, the more complex the management of data is. Occupying the first level is the outlet, which is the result measurement that evaluates the exhaustiveness of the communication system and channel selection.

Likely defines the second level as the result of evaluating the communication products generated. For that, he establishes four types of result measurements: input, throughput, output and outtake. In this case, the data collected are related to the creation and development of the communicative product, product distribution through the channel and the result-reactions that messages embedded in each product have generated in each audience.

Input refers to the time and resources used by the professional in order to produce tactic material (Robina et al., 2006).

Outputs are the immediate data of a public relations campaign —those issues that are visible at first sight. In actions focused on press or media, the output measurement consists of counting the number of appearances in the media (Lindenmann, 2002; Robina et al., 2006; Stacks, 2006). This is considered to be the final stage of a communication product, resulting from production and distribution. Conversely, Paine (2007) adheres them to the production, asserting that outputs are the physical elements of a public relations program, which is anything published or produced directly by the public relations team.

Outtake measurement gathers information that determines if groups of key audiences have received the targeted messages, if they had paid attention, understood the messages, and if they would be able to reproduce them somehow (Lindenmann, 2002; Robina et al., 2006; Stacks, 2006). Paine adds that outtakes are the perception data generated by the outputs.

Outcome measurements are the only typology that Likely (2003) includes in the third level of his classification. This step uses new data and manages data produced in lower levels, focusing on the communication program as a collection of products with the same message directed at the same interest groups in a similar time interval. Outcomes are data related to the effect generated by communication actions. They evaluate if disseminated communications have become an opinion, attitude or create change in all or part of the key target audiences (Lindenman, 2002; Paine, 2006; Robina et al., 2006). In this category, Stacks (2006) also includes comprehension and knowledge transformations.

The penultimate level is the outgrowth. Outgrowth gathers primary and secondary data to assess the relationship of the organization with different audiences and the consequences around the concept of reputation (Likely, 2003). Stacks (2006, pp. 19–20) refers to outgrowth as "the culminating effect of all programs and communication products on the stance of an organization perceived by stakeholders or the public; a statistical result used as a dependent variable in some investigation". In this sense we might also consider the term outflow, coined by Robina et al. (2006), which collects data about long-term effects resulting from public relations work.

Finally, Likely (2003) aligns the role of communication and public relations with the organization. He uses "outlook" to denominate those results where the data of actuation and communication management face a multi-category list of organization strategy.

The different result measurements determined, based on the perspective of different authors, refer to data about level of knowledge, opinions, perceptions, etc. Table 4.1 shows the different categories defined by expert authors in this field.

Table 4.1. English-Language Terms for Result Measurement Categories.

Authors	System	Resources/ Production	Distri-bution	Knowl-edge	Percep-tions	Attitude	Opinion	Conduct	Reputa-tion	Relation-ships	Long term effects
Lindenmann (2002)			*output*	*outtake*		*outcome*	*outcome*				
Likely (2003)	*outlet*	*input*	*output*	*outtake*		*outcome*	*outcome*		*outgrowth*	*outgrowth*	
Stacks (2006)			*output*	*outtake*	*outcome*	*outcome*	*outcome*	*outcome*	*outgrowth*		
Paine (2006)		*output*			*outtake*	*outcome*	*outcome*	*outcome*			
Robina et al. (2006)		*input*	*output*	*outtake*		*outcome*	*outcome*				*outflow*

Beyond the theoretical provisions formulated by Likely (2003) and other authors, the most frequently used data by practitioners for evaluation includes budget compliance, knowledge levels and attitude changes, media response, stance, the price of actions or sales changes (Haywood, 1984). However, in 2010 practitioners agreed that measuring the outcome was preferable to measuring the output effect (AMEC, 2010).

From this literature review, we can establish a clear parallel between the terms output, outtake and outcome, as presented by different authors, and the three phases that simplify public relations operations: activity, intermediaries and audiences (Pestana & Daniels, 2011).

THE PARADIGM SHIFT

In "The Shift Towards Outcomes", Pestana and Daniels (2011), distinguish three overlapping phases in the shift towards outcomes. These phases establish the effects of public relations with strategic value:

- From the eighties to the present there has been an interest in measuring outputs of traditional media (one to many), highlighting visibility and feeling axes.
- From the nineties to the present, this concern extends to outputs connected to external data for traditional and digital media, which has involved a decade-long technological evolution (one to many). Thus, the measurements of visibility and feeling exposed in phase one remain. Additionally, external factors from media are linked to them, including sales results or market shares as well as the first attempts at awareness and perception studies.
- In the final phase, started in 2005 and continuing to the present moment, the measurements range from outputs to outcomes in traditional, digital and social media (many to many). This phase combines measurement and market monitoring models with engagement measurement, which, in the words of Watson (2012), is the "measurement of the participation of the public and the interested parts with the organization that is trying to communicate with these groups and others who chose to enter into some dialogue or response".

Paine (1995) was one of the first public relations consultants who focused on Internet coverage monitoring, highlighting information flow speed, which is also "splendidly dynamic and unfortunately malleable", given that it undergoes constant change. The approach of pre-social Internet monitoring was similar to the press coverage measurements: counting the number of names of organizations or product mentions.

Only fifteen years later, social media technologies have unleashed an implementation of systemic theories of public relations, first illuminated by Grunig and Hunt (1984), and further developed by Murphy (1989) and Dozier, Grunig and Grunig (1995).

Based on a systemic perspective, which stemmed from the symmetrical bidirectional model (Grunig & Hunt, 1984), audiences are considered to be social actors who are able to make changes in the organization's environment and influence its operation. Grunig and Hunt also emphasize the need to manage the conflicts between audiences and organizations through dialogue and negotiation.

Audiences are social actors who are able to make use of communication strategies to defend their interests; they can negotiate with the organization in order to benefit from this relationship (Murphy, 1989, 1991). Audiences are collectives that are willing to find, through dialogue, a solution to the conflicts that emerge from their relationship with the organization, without relinquishing their own interests and goals. This solution benefits both parties (Dozier, Grunig, & Grunig, 1995). The active role of the audience, theorized since 1984 (Grunig & Hunt) and revived by the emergence of social media, means that public relations professionals must reorganize and standardize their methods to perform well and demonstrate their value. However, with the appearance of social technologies, the emergence of technologies capable of monitoring them soon followed, resulting in an unprecedented amount of data.

The International Association for the Measurement and Evaluation of Communication (AMEC) and the Institute for Public Relations (IPR) use the Barcelona Declaration of Measurement Principles. It consists of seven principles that are the result of a decade of progress in the evaluation profession. These include (AMEC, 2010):

1. The importance of goal setting and measurement.
2. Effect measurement (outcome) is preferable to the measurement of the actions (outputs).
3. The effect on business results can and should be measured whenever possible.
4. Media measurement requires quantity and quality.
5. Advertising Value Equivalents (AVE) are not a value of public relations.
6. Social media can and should be measured.
7. Transparency and Reliability are paramount to sound measurement.

Directly or indirectly, all of these principles attempt to establish the effects of evaluations rather than the effect that communication has on the public. These principles are the first step in reorganization and standardization. We highlight three examples that enhance the measurement of effects:

- Measurements should have an integral approach that includes elements of traditional and social media, changes in the mindset of the interested parties, comprehension, attitude and behavior, according to each case, and the effect had in business results (Principle 1).
- Results should include changes in perception, comprehension, attitude and behavior, relating them to sales, donation, brand value, corporative reputation, employee commitment, public policies, investment decisions and other changes in the interested parties (audiences), linked to an organization, non-profit, government or entity, as well as the beliefs and behaviors of interested parties (Principle 2).
- Research surveys should be used to either isolate a change in sales, sale preferences or an attitude change resulting from a public relations initiative (Principle 4).

Apart from appealing to the assessment of detrimental effects on the measurement of outputs, principle 5 rejects the use of AVEs (Advertising Value Equivalents), the most common form of measurement that calculates the cost of space in the media that journalists create as a consequence of the intervention of public relations professionals. AVEs are not an outcome measurement of a public relations campaign; they reduce public relations to media appearances. As Pestana and Daniels (2011) assert, this is "a crude measurement of potential cost savings, not an earned value".

Finally, as for the sixth principle, the implementation of the symmetrical bidirectional model mentioned above has been standardized due to the emergence of social media. For the authors of the Barcelona Declaration, social media measurement is a discipline itself, since an "exclusive metric" does not exist. It requires specific goals and indicators clearly defined by the organizations, and the analysis of the content should be complemented with search data and web navigation, as well as organization sales data, CRM data, surveys and other methodologies. As for social media, and conventional media, the quantity and quality of assessments are critical and must focus on "conversations" and "communities", and not just coverage. We will observe the effects of communication with the former.

CONCRETION AND STANDARDIZATION

Reviewing the literature published on evaluation in public relations, we are able to find elements to quantify each result measurement. Below, we focus on the most common: output, outtake and outcome.

Output is formed by data analysis of media content (number of pieces, number of contacts, number of people exposed, etc.), exhibitions and events measurement (number of participants, participant typology, interviews, etc.) and surveys, which determine message exposure, issues, concepts, etc. (Grunig & Hunt, 2003, Lindenmann, 2002). Cutlip, Center and Broom (2005), Wilcox and Cameron (2006), Stacks (2002, 2006) and Paine (2006) also include elements of self-elaboration or production, such as the number of press releases, articles produced, photographs, brochures and other elements.

The outtake gathers data from surveys (all kinds), focus groups and ethnographic studies (based on observation, participation and role techniques). Outtakes also use other more specific techniques, including the legibility test (Cutlip et al., 2005) or the signaled stopping technique (Grunig & Hunt, 2003).

The outcome can be obtained from information gathered through surveys, focus groups, before/after opinion surveys and ethnographic studies, projects specifically designated to determine changes in opinion, attitude or conduct patterns. Normally, these are based on experimental studies and require a multivariable analysis and model construction (Lindenmann, 2002).

It could be argued that the challenge in recent years has not been the access to information, but rather the discrimination of what information is necessary according to the goals. We observed that there is previous literature regarding the definition and classification of results information. However, beyond the academic world, the use of different categories in results measurements is uncommon. To choose amongst a great deal of data is always complex, but depending on the issue, the degree of sensitivity is higher. After the Barcelona Declaration, Pestana and Daniels (2011) note that there are seven principles that create a matrix known as "The Valid Metrics Framework".

The creation of a matrix needs content designation for the two axes, one vertical and the other horizontal. The vertical axis is "Communication Phases", which uses the three stages of a simplified vision of public relations operation, also described at the beginning of this chapter: public relations activity, the effects on the intermediaries and, lastly, the effects on a target audience.

For the horizontal axis, a simplified version of the communication effects is aligned, focusing on five effects. Jeffrey (2013) presents them while associating each with a question-cum-definition:

- Awareness — are intermediary and target audiences aware of one's efforts?
- Knowledge — are these audiences becoming clearer about the facts?
- Interest — are they giving consideration to one's offer?
- Support — have they moved toward supporting the offer?
- Action — are they taking action in measurable business outcomes?

Progress in achieving measurements for each matrix helps in demonstrating the campaign's success: vertically (from production to outcomes) and horizontally (through the five stages of communication), where the objective is to advance diagonally from the upper left corner to the lower right corner.

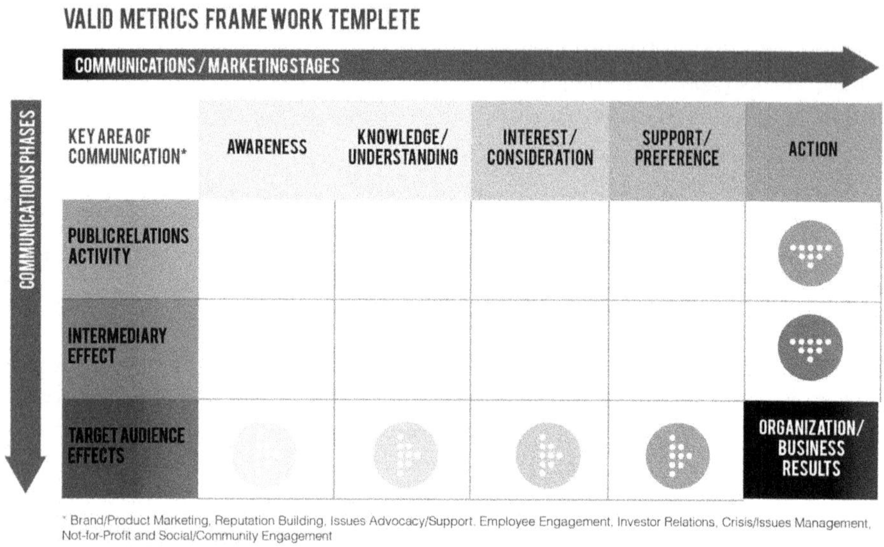

Image 4.1. Valid Metrics Framework Template.
Source: *The Valid Metrics Framework* (Pestana & Daniels, 2011)

As observed in the first module of the matrix, the authors have developed a framework adaptable to eight types of campaigns or key communication areas; it will be possible to extract consequent indicators from them. The designated areas are Brand/Product Marketing, Reputation Building, Issues Advocacy/Support, Employee Engagement, Investor Relations, Crisis/Issues Management, Not-for-Profit and Social/Community Engagement.

The Valid Metrics Framework focuses on the paradigm shift public relations evaluation and displays a succession of standards for specific measurements.

The horizontal Public Relations Activity concentrates the measurement of the efforts on the development of activities. Typically, these measurements are developed between awareness and support. In most communication areas, the most important elements include:

- Content creation (number of activities created, videos/podcasts)
- Traditional media engagement
- Social media engagement (numbers of blog posts, blogger events, blogger briefings, Twitter posts, community site posts and events)
- Influencer engagement (activities undertaken to drive engagement forward, such as the number of Facebook and Twitter posts, community site posts, etc.)
- Stakeholder engagement (same as influencers case)

- Events/speeches (offline community events and traditional media outreach)

With data collected only from public relations activities, it is impossible to know if the activities had any effect; they are just a measure of effort (Jeffrey, 2013).

This data can be compared later with the resulting response and business activity, and can also be attributed to business results.

In the horizontal Intermediary Effect, public relations professionals check if intermediary audiences respond to public relations activities. Nowadays, these intermediary audiences are media, bloggers and key influencers (third parties). The depth obtained in the bottleneck of communication indicates the depth of our success.

If we want to measure Awareness in intermediary audiences we measure:

- Audience reach (traditional and social media)
- Impressions/Target audience impressions
- Number of articles
- Video views
- Frequency
- Prominence
- Share of voice
- Earned media site visitors/day
- % share of a conversation

In the case of Knowledge/Understanding, we consider:

- Key message alignment (traditional and social media)
- Accuracy of facts
- % share of a conversation

In the Interest/Consideration case, we consider:

- Key message alignment
- Frequency of (positive) mentions
- Expressed opinions of consideration or interest
- Social network Followers
- Retweets/Shares/Linkbacks
- % share of a conversation

Lastly, for Support/Preference:

- Endorsement by journalists or influencers
- Rankings on industry lists
- Expressed opinions of preference
- Social network fans
- Likes

According to the AMEC Framework, support/preference is the last expected effect from intermediaries, and is focused on the communication goals of the organization. In the "action" column, we only find effects expected from the target audience.

The sought-after effects by the public relations discipline are in the horizontal "Target Audience effects". In order to achieve them, two previous steps must be aligned: public relations actions and Intermediary Effect. If the previous steps are not successful, it is very difficult to achieve effects in the target audience.

If we want to measure Awareness, we use:

- Unaided awareness
- Aided awareness
- Owned media site visitors per day
- Social network channel visitors

For Knowledge/Understanding:

- Knowledge of company/product attributes, features and Brand association and differentiation for the key area of Brand/Product Marketing
- Knowledge of issue and Knowledge of client POV for the key area Issues Advocacy/Support
- Knowledge of company profile and key area offers for Reputation Building
- Knowledge of company/product attributes and features, and Brand association and differentiation for the key area of Social/Community Engagement

In the case of Interest/Consideration, we consider:

- Relevance of brand (to consumer/customer) for the key area of Brand/Product Marketing
- Relevance of issue (to stakeholder) for the key areas of Issues Advocacy/Support
- Relevance of company (to stakeholder) for the key area of Reputation Building

- Relevance of brand (to consumer/customer) for the key area of Social/Community Engagement
- Visitors to website
- Click-through to site
- Time spent on site
- Downloads from site
- Calls
- Event/meeting attendance

Lastly, for Support/Preference:

- Attitude increase for the key areas of Brand/Product Marketing and Social/Community Engagement
- Attitude change for the key areas of Issues Advocacy/Support
- Attitude change for the key area of Reputation Building
- Stated intention to buy for the key areas of Brand/Product Marketing and Social/Community Engagement
- Brand preference/Loyalty/Trust for the key areas of Brand/Product Marketing and Social/Community Engagement
- Quote requests for the key areas of Brand/Product Marketing and Social/Community Engagement
- Trials for the key areas of Brand/Product Marketing and Social/Community Engagement
- Increase in reputation drivers, e.g., Trust, Admiration, for the key area of Reputation Building
- Belief in corporate branding for the key area of Reputation Building
- Enhanced relationships with key stakeholders for the key area of Reputation Building
- Endorsement for all areas
- Links to site for all areas

The most significant difference in the Target Audience Effects is the existence of the "action" effect, the supreme rationale in most communication actions, and consequence of all of the effects of the communication bottleneck. In this module's target audience/action, the effects for each key area are significantly different, which is clearly not the case for most of the previous models:

- For the Brand/Product Marketing area, the expected actions by the public are sales, market share, cost savings, generation of leads and customer loyalty.
- For the key areas of Issues Advocacy/Support, the following actions are expected: active advocates, letters of support (to parliament members,

congress, etc.), registrations (to join support groups), donations, passed or blocked legislation/regulation, cost savings.

- As for the Reputation Building area, actions expected are market share, share price, talent retention and recruitment, cost savings, customer loyalty, passed or blocked legislation/regulation.
- Finally, in the area of Social/Community Engagement, the effects to measure are active advocates, brand engagement, leads/sales, revenue, market share and cost savings.

All of these effects, on intermediaries and on target audiences, are nowadays accompanied by monitoring and measuring tools that allow for the evaluation of public relations activities, in terms of outcomes and outgrowth.

INTERMEDIARY EFFECT

Not only has the emergence of social media changed the information industry and traditional media, but it has also transformed the public relations industry. For this industry, social media goes hand-in-hand with management demand for accountability. Managers conclude that evaluation standardization and a search for new parameters of effects measurement are necessary.

Both elements have modified the relationship established between public relations and journalists, and between organizations and media. AMEC's proposal (2010) and its concretion by Pestana and Daniels (2011) proves the opposite. For many years, traditional media had been the "intermediaries" of public relations: they transmitted the message and brought about effects to the public. However, these effects were measured incorrectly and without a standardized pattern. With the new framework of evaluation, focused on outcomes, the efficiency of the intermediary becomes objective, which relocates the influence of the press. In this sense, some of the forgotten values of the eighties have reappeared, when newspapers and magazines were the main tools for publicity and later for promotions, and public relations were evaluated with AVEs (until the present moment). Now it is possible to recognize the value of those who are the real storytellers: the journalists.

At present, the traditional press has a competitor in its role as intermediary between organizations and audiences: social media. One competitor who acts concurrently as many competitors. These days, many of the audiences that have been the only target in public relations have the capacity of influencing their peers through technological democratization of message emission and the capacity to give feedback. Now, any member of a group can be the influencer, but he or she must earn this role, building an image according to this new role. This situation has always existed because, in terms of opinion leaders, experts or stakeholders had been part of the audience map of public relations professionals. Therefore, the difference lies in the ease of new members becoming influencers, displacing those who had previously played that role.

Furthermore, social technology allows for measuring the effects of new influences. Its efficacy as well as its capacity for consolidating communication models was already asserted by public relations gurus of the twentieth century (Dozier et al., 1995; Grunig & Hunt, 1984; Murphy, 1989, 1991), and can now be demonstrated with objective data.

From the public relations perspective, a chain has been broken, but much has been gained. The ability to demonstrate the effectiveness of actions allows for discrimination between valid and non-valid intermediaries. This, in turn, contributes to the creation of communication strategies based on solid research (Cuenca, 2012) and evaluation (Matilla & Marca, 2012) that enhance the creation and accomplishment of goals in communication plans.

From the traditional media point of view, gaining value should also be a key factor. As Ramonet (2011) suggests, mass media "had never experienced a trauma as they are now experiencing with the impact of the Internet, which is just 20 years old". Journalists are the ones who can enforce their know-how to regain an actual shared space with bloggers and other intermediaries that are building their image from zero. To do this, media should go back to what they were and be the first ones to highlight the profiles of the press professionals, who are often displaced by the share of reader's comments, who, consequently, act as providers of free content, turning each headline into a micro social network.

Today, press, like other intermediaries, is the ultimate goal for many public relations intermediation activities. Within this new context, they must defend their space and occupy new spaces from which they can influence their audiences, improving their image capital and capitalizing their experience and education with the creation of opinions, contents and stories, along with capturing new talent. By making use of these resources, journalists will be as influential as other intermediaries, but with a higher status to differentiate them.

REFERENCES

AMEC-International Association for the Measurement and Evaluation of Communications. (2010). *Barcelona declaration of measurement principles*. London, UK: AMEC. Retrieved from http://amecorg.com/wp-content/uploads/2011/08/Barcelona Principles for PR Measurement.pdf

Broom, G. M., & Dozier, D. M. (1990). *Using research in public relations*. Englewood Cliff, NJ: Prentice Hall.

Cuenca, J. (2012). *Auditorías de relaciones públicas*. Barcelona, Spain: UOC.

Cutlip, S. M., Center, A., & Broom, G. M. (2005). *Effective public relations* (9th ed.). Englewood Cliffs, NJ: Prentice Hall.

Dozier, D. M., Grunig, L. A., & Grunig, J. E. (1995). *Manager's guide to excellence in public relations and communication management*. Mahwah, NJ: Lawrence Erlbaum.

Gregory, A. (2006). Public relations and planned communication. In R. Tench & L. Yeomans (Eds.), *Exploring public relations* (174–197). Harlow, UK: Prentice Hall.

Grunig, J. E., & Hunt, T. (1984). *Managing public relations*. Forth Worth, TX: Harcourt Brace Jovanovich College.

Grunig, J. E., & Hunt, T. (2003). *Public relations management*. Barcelona, Spain: Gestión 2000.

Haywood, R. (1984). *All about public relations: How to build business success on good communications*. Berkshire, UK: McGraw-Hill.

Jeffrey, A. (2013, March). *Social media measurement: A step by step approach: Using the AMEC valid metrics framework*. Paper presented at the International Public Relations Research Conference, Miami, FL. Retrieved from http://www.instituteforpr.org/topics/social-media-measurement-a-step-by-step-approach/

L'Étang, J. (2009). *Public relations: Concepts, practice and criticism*. Barcelona, Spain: UOC.

Likely, F. (2003, June). *Considerations when building a performance scorecard for your communication function*. Paper presented at the IABC International Conference, Toronto, Canada.

Lindenmann, W. (2002). *Guidelines for measuring the effectiveness of PR programs and activities* (Rev. ed.). Gainesville, FL: IPR-Institute for Public Relations.

Marston, J. E. (1963). *The nature of public relations*. New York, NY: McGraw-Hill.

Matilla, K., & Marca, G. (2012). The accountability gap: The use of preliminary and evaluative research in Spain. *Public Relations Review*, *38*(5), 825–830.

Murphy, P. (1989). Game theory as a paradigm for the public relations process. In C. H. Botan & V. Hazelton (Eds.), *Public relations theory* (pp. 173–192). Mahwah, NJ: Lawrence Erlbaum.

Murphy, P. (1991). The limits of symmetry: A game theory approach to symmetric and asymmetric public relations. *Public Relations Research Annual*, *3*(1–4), 115–131.

Oxley, H. (1989). *The principles of public relations*. London, UK: Kogan Page.

Paine, K. (1995). Monitoring publicity on the Internet. *Public Relations Tactics*, *2*(8), 8–9.

Paine, K. (2006). Designing and implementing your communication's dashboard: Lessons Learned Institute for PR. Retrieved from http://www.instituteforpr.org/wp-content/uploads /Commu nication_ Dashboard.pdf

Paine, K. (2007). *Measuring success: The communicator's guide data-driven to measuring public relationships*. Durham, NH: KDPaine & Partners.

Pestana, R., & Daniels, M. (2011, June). *Lisbon summit valid metrics workshop 3*. Paper presented at the 3rd European Summit on Measurement, Lisbon, Portugal. Retrieved from http://amecorg.com/wp-content/uploads/2011/12/Lisbon-Summit-Vaild-Metrics-Workshop-3-June-2011.pdf

Ramonet, I. (2011). *The explosion of journalism*. Madrid, Spain: Clave Intellectual.

Robina, X. J., Amisha, M. M., & Gregory, A., (2006). Evaluation in use: The practitioner view of effective evaluation. *PRism Online PR Journal*, *4*(2), 1–11.

Seitel, F. P. (2002). *Public relations theory and practice*. Madrid, Spain: Pearson Education.

Stacks, D. W. (2002). *Primer of public relations research*. New York, NY: Guilford.

Stacks, D. W. (2006). *Dictionary of public relations measurement and research*. Miami, FL: Institute for Public Relations.

Watson, T. (2012). The evolution of public relations measurement and evaluation. *Public Relations Review*, *38*(3), 390–398.

Wilcox, D. L., & Cameron, G. T. (2006). *Public relations: Strategies and tactics* (8th ed.). Boston, MA: Pearson / Allyn and Bacon.

CHAPTER FIVE

Hot Brands ARE Cool: The Temperature Scale AS A Tool FOR Branding IN A Digital Society

PATRÍCIA DIAS

INTRODUCTION

The contemporary society has been described as 'Information Age' (e.g., Drucker, 2001), 'Digital Age' (e.g., Levinson, 1999) and 'Network Society' (Castells, 1996/2005), among other expressions that refer to the pervasiveness of digital technologies in contemporary daily activities and to the increase of information and communication fluxes and access to technological tools.

Branding experts have pointed out the importance of brands in contemporary society, as they have become reference points in a message-cluttered and over-stimulating context (e.g., Cooke, 2012; Davis, 2009; Olins, 2003). In a market of abundance, where the offers exceed demand, brands are crucial in order to get the attention of customers and potential customers (Davenport & Beck, 2002) and to help consumers in their decision-making, as brands can be the decisive difference between offers which are similar in price and quality (Davis, 2009). Following Kapferer's (1991/2000) argument that a brand can become, over time, independent from particular products, services and organizations, Kornberger (2010) offers a sociological approach to brands, observing that brands are nowadays appropriated by customers to express their own identity, thus resulting in emotional attachments to brands.

Brands are, nowadays, a crucial strategy asset for organizations striving to survive in highly competitive, turbulent and ephemeral markets and struggling to be the prevailing stimulus in stimuli-saturated environments.

Following previous approaches to the notion of digital brand (e.g., Adamson, 2008; Cocoran, 2011), this chapter discusses how brands should be in order to be successful in the contemporary digital context. In addition, it approaches branding from the perspective of communication sciences, understanding the notion of a brand being successful as its ability to communicate the messages intended by the organization and to generate the desired images and reputation.

THEORETICAL FRAMEWORK

The theoretical framework can be summarized in the argument that the concept of communication process is applicable to branding and relevant for the understanding of this phenomenon. This argument is grounded on two assumptions: a) branding can be thought of as a communication process where an organization communicates a brand and its stakeholders (mainly clients and potential consumers) form corresponding images, which cumulatively result in reputation; and b) the contemporary society is the context of branding as a communication process, and the particular features of this context are shaped by the widespread, frequent and intense use of digital technologies. Within the communication sciences, Media Ecology stands out as the most relevant school of thought that sustains the assumptions presented above.

BRANDING AS A COMMUNICATIONAL PROCESS

Branding is the process of managing and communicating a brand. It has traditionally been approached from a marketing perspective, focused on brand management, but it can also be thought of as a communicational process between the organization and its stakeholders. This communicational perspective on branding is relevant to discuss the effectiveness of a brand concerning awareness, brand image and reputation.

Following one of the most traditional approaches to communication, Shannon and Weaver's (1949/1998) model, organizations assume the role of 'sender', the communicated brand is the 'message', the different stakeholders are the 'receivers', and their perception and interpretation of the brand results in the brand image (Kapferer, 1991/2000). Reputation is the outcome of the cumulative exposure to the brand, thus being a synthesis of several brand images formed (Dowling, 2001). Concerning the notion of feedback, several authors within organizational communication argue for a paradigmatic shift in the communication models and practices between organizations and their stakeholders from a unidirectional relationship to a dialogical one (e.g., Cornelissen, 2004/2009; Davis, 2009; Kunsh, 2003). Several traditions within communication sciences also highlight the importance of the context to effective communication, as semiotics and symbolic interactionism, for instance. The sharing of cultural meanings, values, mental categories and frames of reference facilitates similar perceptions and understandings of signs (e.g., Barthes, 1957/2007b, 1967/1990, 1985/2007a; Fauconnier & Turner, 2002/2003). Thus, the contemporary society can be thought of as the context of contemporary branding.

Concerning the effectiveness of branding, effective communication occurs when the understanding of the receiver corresponds to the intention of the sender. In this sense, several authors argue that effective communication is highly improbable or even impossible (e.g., Berger, 1982; Luhmann, 2000, 2002/2012; Watzlawick, Bavelas, & Jackson, 1967). Thus, branding is effective when the stakeholder's brand image corresponds to the strategic goals set by the organization for the brand it communicates.

CONTEMPORARY SOCIETY AS THE CONTEXT FOR BRANDING

Identifying the main features of the contemporary society becomes relevant for branding under the assumption that brands can result more effectively in the intended brand images when they allude to meanings, values and frames of reference shared on a social and cultural level.

Not only in communication sciences, but in social sciences as a whole, digital technologies are often pointed out as one of the most distinctive and characteristic features of contemporary society. Digital technologies are associated to a new economic cycle (e.g., Bell, 1973; Castells, 1996/2005; Drucker, 2001; Machlup, 1962/1972; Perez, 2002; Porat, 1977; Tapscott & Williams, 2010; Toffler, 1980), to a change from modernity to postmodernity (e.g., Baudrillard, 1986/1989; Lipovetsky & Charles, 2004/2005; Poster, 1995/2000) or at least for a different stage of modernity (e.g., Bauman, 2000; Beck, 2008; Giddens, 1990/2002, 1999), and to significant social changes (e.g., Castells, 1996/2005; Rainie & Wellman, 2012). Some authors argue that the effects of digital technologies are deeper, operating at a cognitive level (e.g., Levinson, 1999; McLuhan, 1964/1994), and thus identify changes in the human contemporary cognitive structures resulting from the widespread, frequent and intense use of digital technologies (e.g., Carr, 2010; Jenkins, 2006; Manovich, 2002; Pink, 2005; Prensky, 2001, 2006; Shirky, 2010; Tapscott, 2008). Cognition includes both stimuli perception and understanding (Fauconnier & Turner, 2002/2003; Maturana & Varela, 1980). Therefore, this chapter explores the hypothesis that branding will be more effective if it takes into account both culturally shared symbolic meanings and shared cognitive structures that enframe the perception and understanding of a message, i.e., the cognitive-semiotic context.

CONTEMPORARY COGNITION

Notions such as Marshall McLuhan's (1964/1994) conception of media as extensions of men, Martin Heidegger's (1949/1977) enframing as the essence of technology or Jean Baudrillard's (1986/1989) hyperreality as the ultimate stage of simulation emphasize the strong effects of technology at a cognitive level. Recent research has reinforced these insights by providing findings on concrete cognitive effects of digital immersion, i.e., the generalized, frequent and intense use of digital technologies (Jenkins, 2006). Within Media Ecology, Paul Levinson (1999) argued that McLuhan's electronic age has already given place to a new age, whose beginning was brought about by the internet. In the contemporary digital age, the convergence between the internet and mobile devices is enabling the full concretization of the global village and retribalization. Thus, in the same way that the print age enhanced the preponderance of the vision that began with the literacy age, digital media are even cooler than electronic media, therefore emphasizing their cognitive effects such as the acoustic space, mosaic thinking, or holistic perception.

The cognitive effects of digital immersion were first studied in relation to videogames (Gee, 2005, 2007; Johnson, 2006; Prensky, 2001). Empirical research and experiments revealed, for instance, that frequent videogamers develop a better perception of tridimensional space (Green & Bavelier, 2006), have better eye-hand coordination (Gee, 2005, 2007; Johnson, 2006; Kutcher & Kutcher, 2007; Tapscott, 2008), perceive a greater amount of visual information and faster (Green & Bavelier, 2006), react quicker to stimuli (Gee, 2005, 2007; Johnson, 2006; Tapscott, 2008), have greater ability to multitask (Gee, 2005, 2007; Prensky, 2006; Tapscott, 2008), learn better through trial-and-error situations and easily improvise (Gee, 2005, 2007; Johnson, 2006; Prensky, 2006; Tapscott, 2008) and have better abilities of connecting, networking and collaborating (Castells, 1996/2005, 2009; Shirky, 2010; Tapscott & Williams, 2006, 2010). Both Marc Prensky (2001) and Lev Manovich (2002) observe a change from linear reasoning to parallel thinking, and observe that this new cognitive structure is best suited to the network structure of digital media. Research has shown that newspaper readers tend to go through the pages sequentially, as readers of the same contents in the online edition follow more unstructured and random reading patterns (Michael, Keller, Carpenter, & Just, 2001). Less enthusiastic approaches also observe negative cognitive effects of digital immersion such as the reduction of attention spans (Davenport & Beck, 2002; Scott, 2006/2013) and difficulties in dealing with information overloads (Carr, 2010).

There are also more general approaches that consider digital immersion the main distinction between generations, such as Mark Prensky's (2001) concept of digital natives, Don Tapscott's (1998, 2008) idea of net generation or Marc McCrindle's (2006) proposal of generation Y. On the other hand, Mark Baurelein (2008) considers this generation the dumbest ever, highlighting its lack of reading habits, for instance. Nicholas Carr (2010) observes how the cognitive effects of digital technologies have changed reading itself, which is currently more superficial and quick (skimming). Tapscott (2008) interposes by pointing out the good academic and professional performance of net geners. Shirky (2010) also argues that digital media stimulate the cognitive surplus that resulted from the passive interaction of receivers with mass media, i.e., a combination of attention, energy and time that is currently stimulated and engaged by digital media, resulting in greater collaboration, innovation and productivity. Concepts such as hypertextual brain (Prensky, 2001), participatory culture and distributed cognition (Jenkins, 2006) and collective intelligence (Federman & de Kerckhove, 2003; Flew, 2002/2008) reinforce this argument. Daniel Pink (2005) also agrees that technologies have released men from concrete, specific and repetitive tasks, thus freeing their cognitive resources, time and effort for more creative activities. Thus he observes the establishment of a new balance in the human cognitive structures, as both the hemispheres of the brain (the left, more linear and sequential, and the right, more emotional and creative) are equally stimulated by digital media.

Attempting to describe contemporary cognition, assuming that it is shaped by digital immersion, Table 5.1 presents a comparison between McLuhan's description of the cognitive features shaped by electronic media and more recent findings on the cognitive effects of digital media.

Table 5.1. Features of Contemporary Cognition Which Is Shaped by Digital Immersion, in Comparison to Marshall McLuhan's Description of the Cognitive Effects of Electronic Media.

		Cognitive effects of digital media Other authors								
		Carr	Gee	Jenkins	Johnson	Levinson	Pink	Prensky	Shirky	Tapscott
Cognitive effects of electronic media Marshall McLuhan	From unisensorial to multisensorial stimulation	✓	✓	✓	✓	✓	✓	✓	✓	✓
	From intense to engaging stimulation	✓	✓	✓	✓	✓	✓	✓	✓	✓
	From the left to the right hemisphere of the brain				✓		✓	✓		✓
	From linear to mosaic thinking	✓	✓	✓	✓	✓	✓	✓	✓	✓
	From linear to acoustic space					✓	✓			✓
	From reason to emotion and intuition			✓	✓	✓	✓	✓	✓	✓
	From cause-and-effect to holistic understanding	✓	✓	✓	✓	✓	✓	✓	✓	✓

EMPIRICAL STUDY

The empirical stage of this research intends to test whether a brand can communicate more effectively if it takes into account, both in its format and content, its cognitive-semiotic context characterized in the theoretical framework. In order to test this hypothesis, a longitudinal and comparative case study was explored, including 15 rebranding cases of big Portuguese corporations. The criteria for selection of these corporations was being generally known to the Portuguese population, so that we could consider that the receivers of their communication (or the targets of their branding) shared the same cognitive-semiotic context. McLuhan's (1964/1994) categories of hot and cool were adopted in order to develop a temperature scale that allowed the comparison of previous and current brands according to the previously identified cognitive and semiotic features of contemporary society.

THE TEMPERATURE SCALE

McLuhan (1964/1994) categorized media according to their type of shaping of cognitive effects. This categorization was binomial, as media could be classified as hot or cool according to three interrelated criteria: a) the amount of senses they stimulated; b) the intensity or quality of their content; and c) the degree of engagement or participation they caused in the receivers. McLuhan added that hot media tend to exclude the receiver and are usually light-on, while cool media tend to include the receiver and are usually light-through. The author also highlighted that when a medium's classification was not coherent in all criteria, the degree of engagement or participation caused should prevail over the others.

Levinson (1999), applying McLuhan's concepts to digital technologies, pointed out that media change and evolve, and therefore their classification as hot or cool may also change over time. The author gives the example of how cinema has become cooler and how writing reverses from hot to cool on SMS messages. Thus, the classification of media should be, according to Levinson (1999), not absolute but relative, i.e., media are not classified by themselves but in comparison to other media. In addition, the author claims that this classification stems more from use practices than from technological features.

Federman and de Kerckhove (2003), who have applied McLuhan's thinking to management, suggest that hot and cool should be considered as the two extremes of a continuum rather than two binomial categories. This approach to the concept of media temperature emphasizes the fact that this classification is relative and also considers the possibility of different degrees of temperature, thus reflecting in a more rigorous manner different classifications obtained in each of the three criteria considered.

Grounded on these developments suggested by McLuhan's followers, this research proposes a temperature scale with six degrees—freezing, cool, fresh, warm, hot and burning—as theoretical framework for understanding the adjustment between features of the brand, both in format and in content, and its cognitive-semiotic context. Thus, the temperature scale is theoretically grounded on McLuhan's (1964/1994) concepts of hot and cool and also on more recent contributions from Media Ecology (Federman & de Kerckhove, 2003; Levinson, 1999; Postman, 1993; Watson & Blondheim, 2007), and it was adopted as an empirical tool that enabled the relative positioning of brands — previous and new — according to the results of the methods applied, i.e., a visual content analysis and a visual semiotic analysis (Rose, 2001/2007; van Leeuwen & Jewitt, 2001/2004). This relative positioning enabled the comparison not only of brands among themselves but also between brands and the contemporary cognitive-semiotic context, which is assumed to be supercool (Baudrillard, 1986/1989).

METHOD

The empirical research design considers the cases of rebranding of big Portuguese enterprises occurring between 2004 and 2011—a total of 15—as a case study, presenting a longitudinal and comparative perspective on the issue (Bouma & Atkinson, 1987/1995). This case study was explored in two stages using mixed methods in order to triangulate results (Berg, 1989).

In the first stage, two types of visual analysis were applied to the logotypes representing each brand, taking into account that the logotype is considered the main form of expression, identification and representation of the brand by several authors in the field (e.g., Kapferer, 1991/2000; Olins, 2003; Schultz, Hatch, & Larsen, 2000; Seruya, 2009). A content analysis was applied in order to evaluate the relationship between the rebranding processes and the cognitive features of the contemporary context, and a semiotic analysis was applied in order to evaluate the relationship between the rebranding processes and the semiotic features of the contemporary context, both as reported above.

In addition, in the second stage, documental analysis and in-depth interviews were used to determine how each organization evaluated the communicational effectiveness of their rebranding. The interviewees were a total of 15, one member of each organization that was or had been involved in the respective rebranding process.

SPSS was used to process the data resulting from the visual content analysis and the visual semiotic analysis. The interviews were face-to-face and the audio was recorded and later processed in NVivo. The documental analysis focused on news dating from the week after the launch of each rebranding process in the main Portuguese mainstream media, traditional and online, and also on documentation provided by most organizations studied. This information was organized in analysis grids and later integrated with the results from the interviews.

DESCRIPTION OF THE CASE STUDIES

The 15 cases of rebranding studied were the following, presented chronologically and with the indication of the sector of each organization:

a) RTP; media group; rebranding in January 2004
b) CTT; mail distribution; rebranding in October 2004
c) EDP; energy provider; rebranding in 2004 and July 2011
d) TAP; airplane company; rebranding in February 2005
e) TMN; telecommunications; rebranding in September 2005
f) BES; bank; rebranding in January 2006

g) Crédito Agrícola (CA); bank; rebranding in September 2006
h) Montepio; bank; rebranding in October 2006
i) Optimus; telecommunications; rebranding in January 2008
j) BANIF; bank; rebranding in January 2008
k) PT; telecommunications; rebranding in May 2009
l) Porto Editora; publishing; rebranding in January 2010
m) SONAE; retail and distribution; rebranding in February 2010
n) Novabase; IT; rebranding in December 2010
o) SIC Radical; TV channel; rebranding in May 2011

DISCUSSION

The visual content analysis

The visual content analysis was theoretically framed within the thought of McLuhan (1964/1994) and the above presented characterization of the contemporary cognitive structures, and also methodological guidelines from Rose (2001/2007) and van Leeuwen and Jewitt (2001/2004). The previous and new logotypes were analyzed according to 5 categories with a variable number of variables each that could assume a value varying from 0 to 4. This coding was later converted to a scale from 0 to 100, which allowed the positioning of each brand along the temperature scale adopted as reference. Table 5.2 lists the categories, and variables considered.

Table 5.2. Categories and Variables Considered for Coding in the Visual Content Analysis.

Categories	Variables
Graphics	Shapes Filling Definition Complexity Positioning Relationships Perspective
Font	Shapes Filling Complexity Case Positioning Relationships Perspective

Categories	Variables
Color	Definition Hue Tonality Saturation Relationships
Composition	Positioning Relationships Graphics/name dichotomy Intertextuality
Variability	Variation Animation

Table 5.3 lists the score obtained by each logotype and Figure 5.1 presents their positioning on the adopted temperature scale.

Table 5.3. Score Obtained by the Previous and New Brands in the Visual Content Analysis.

Brands	Previous	New	Temperature variation
RTP	26 [*Hot*]	36 [*Warm*]	10
CTT	34 [*Warm*]	42 [*Warm*]	8
EDP	36 [*Warm*]	37 [*Warm*]	1
TAP	28 [*Hot*]	41 [*Warm*]	13
TMN	47 [*Warm*]	59 [*Fresh*]	12
BES	28 [*Hot*]	39 [*Warm*]	11
CA	31 [*Hot*]	48 [*Warm*]	17
Montepio	31 [*Hot*]	41 [*Warm*]	10
Optimus	25 [*Hot*]	74 [*Cool*]	49
BANIF	34 [*Warm*]	50 [*Fresh*]	16
PT	30 [*Hot*]	35 [*Warm*]	5
Porto Editora	31 [*Hot*]	44 [*Warm*]	13
SONAE	51 [*Fresh*]	67 [*Cool*]	16
Novabase	25 [*Hot*]	46 [*Warm*]	21
SIC Radical	49 [*Warm*]	53 [*Fresh*]	4
EDP	37 [*Warm*]	66 [*Fresh*]	29

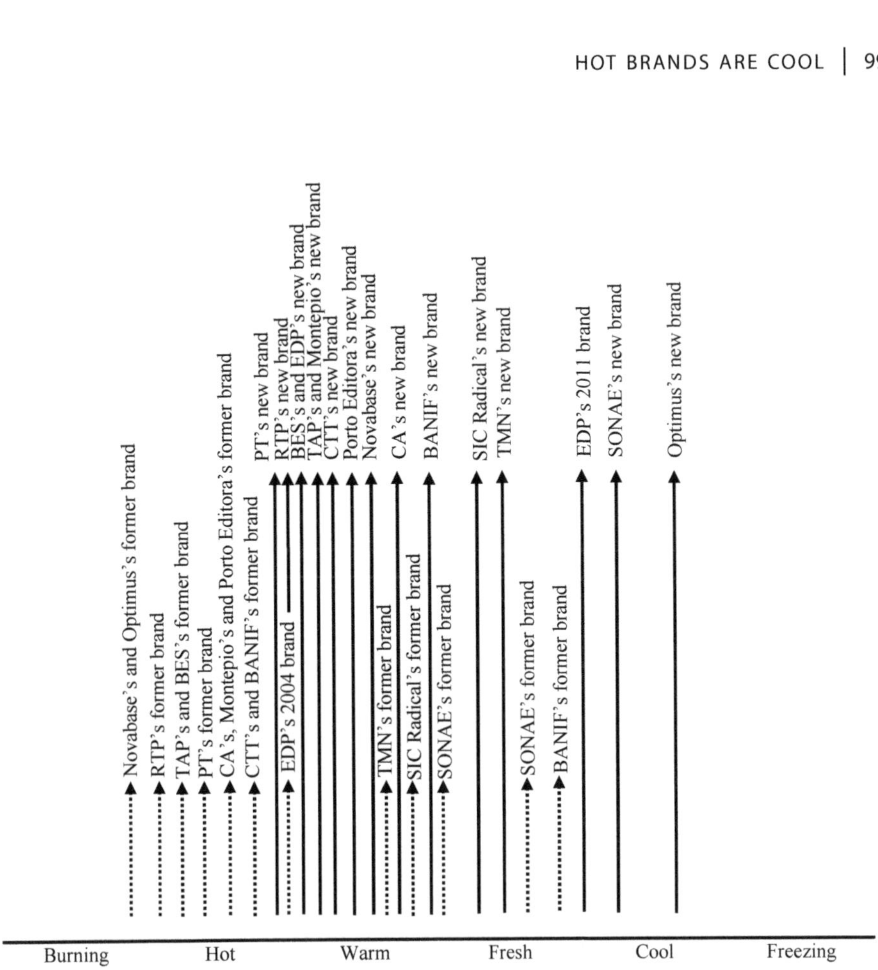

Figure 5.1. Positioning of the Brands Along the Temperature Scale, Following the Score Obtained in the Visual Content Analysis.

THE VISUAL SEMIOTIC ANALYSIS

The semiotic analysis of the logotypes followed closely the work of Barthes (1957/2007b, 1967/1990, 1985/2007a), and also methodological guidelines from Rose (2001/2007) and van Leeuwen and Jewitt (2001/2004). Thus, three main steps were followed: a) identification and description of the signs present in the logotype; b) identification and description of denotative and connotative significations; and c) identification of anchors and meaning transferences. The data resulting from this analysis were later codified into five elements, whose presence and/

or repetition was counted and later converted to a scale varying from 0 to 100, in order to enable the longitudinal comparison between former and new brands and comparison in relation to the visual content analysis.

For the visual semiotic analysis, the presence and/or repetition of five different elements was counted and added, and the logotypes were positioned on the temperature scale according to the total score obtained. The five main elements considered were: a) number of denotative meanings; b) number of connotative meanings; c) number of metaphors and other style figures; d) number of references and appellation (Williamson, 1978); and e) number of *studium* and *punctum* (Barthes, 1980/2010). Table 5.4 lists the score obtained by each logotype. Figure 5.2 presents the positioning of all the brands along the temperature scale.

Table 5.4. Score Obtained by the Previous and New Brands in the Visual Semiotic Analysis.

Brands	Previous	New	Temperature variation
RTP	55	74	19
CTT	90	85	-5
EDP	36	81	45
TAP	80	137	57
TMN	67	112	45
BES	54	73	19
CA	57	65	8
Montepio	79	119	40
Optimus	105	83	-22
BANIF	124	104	-20
PT	91	93	2
Porto Editora	45	85	40
SONAE	120	147	27
Novabase	39	100	61
SIC Radical	49	65	16
EDP	81	83	2

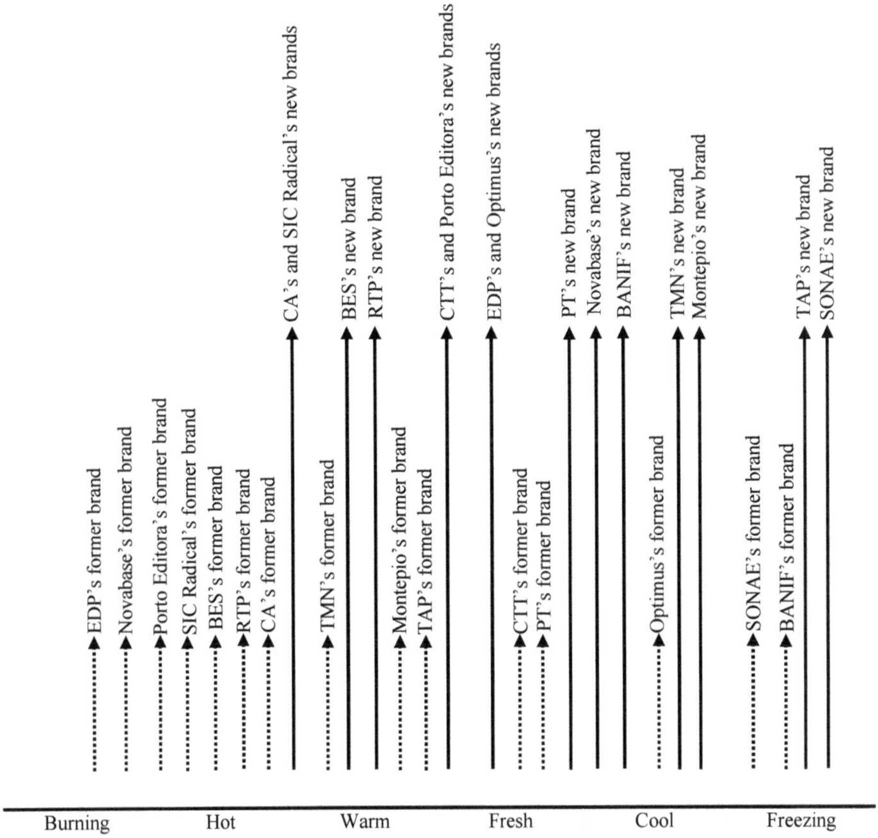

Figure 5.2. Positioning of the Brands Along the Temperature Scale, Following the Score Obtained in the Visual Semiotic Analysis.

THE DOCUMENTAL ANALYSIS AND INTERVIEWS

The interviews took place in October and November 2011. The audio was recorded and later organized in analysis grids resorting to the software NVivo. The interviewees were one member of each organization that had been involved in the rebranding process. This criterion resulted in the participants being mainly from the executive level in the communication or marketing departments.

The interviews were semi-guided and addressed the following main issues: a) Which were the motivations for the rebranding?; b) Which were the goals set for the new brand?; c) Which are the main advantages and disadvantages of the former and the new brands identified by the interviewee?; and d) How does the organization evaluate the rebranding process (from a communicational standpoint)? The information collected in the interviews was complemented with documents provided by some of the organizations and with the analysis of news in the main mass media in Portugal (press and television) during the week following the launch of the new brands.

Concerning the motivations for rebranding, 12 out of the 15 interviewees referred to the need to stay up-to-date, to modernize the brand, or to in some way keep up with societal trends, consumer behavior trends and competitors, thus showing the close relationship between the brand and its cognitive-semiotic context.

When comparing the former and the new brands, most organizations struggled to update their brand and to appeal to new targets while maintaining the elements that were more closely related to the organizational identity. Organizations found diversified solutions to answer this issue that varied from conducting merely a light restyling (e.g., CTT) to radically changing every aspect of the brand (e.g., BANIF).

The evaluation of the communicational effectiveness of each new brand was a sensitive issue, and the studied organizations had different postures in making information available and being transparent. The research design tried to mitigate this limitation by determining success according to the goals previously set by each organization for their new brand. However, it was not possible to gather all the necessary information from all the organizations. Even so, all organizations consider their new brands more successful than the former in communicating their brand and in generating the intended brand images. Some of the organizations (e.g., TMN, BANIF) described adjustments that were made to the new brand following the initial feedback from collaborators, clients and other stakeholders, thus enhancing its communicational effectiveness.

FINDINGS

Although the former and new brands are more or less evenly distributed along the temperature scale, there is a concentration of the previous brands in the hotter half of the scale and of the new brands in the cooler half of the scale. This trend is more evident in the results of the content analysis of the formal elements of the logotypes. However, the results are not solid enough to support the claim that the brands adjust their semiotic features to those of the cognitive-semiotic context by becoming cooler in the undergone rebranding processes.

Relating these results with the findings from the documental analysis and the interviews, the communicational effectiveness of each brand was perceived, by each organization, in relation to the goals defined for the rebranding process.

Thus, organizations that defined unspecific and/or unrealistic goals faced disappointing results that might not be so bad necessarily. Besides, a few enterprises were reluctant to provide all the information required by the researcher, particularly financial data.

However, although each rebranding process had specific goals and the organizations studied as well as their stakeholders are diversified, it was possible to draw some conclusions. The new brands which have formal features best suited to the contemporary cognitive structures, that allude to more meanings and to more ambiguous meanings and which have more levels of meaning are more engaging and involving, and generally considered more successful by their own organizations. Pedro Boucherie Mendes, CEO of the TV channel SIC Radical, whose brand became cooler in the rebranding process, states that "When choosing what to watch, people first exclude and then choose. That's why it is important to have an ambiguous brand, so that people won't exclude that option right away." Rebranding into a cooler brand helped this cable channel whose main viewers were male teenagers to conquer other segments such as young adults (25 to 35) and females.

Cooler brands are also considered more effective in generating identification and emotional relationships, which is coherent with the fact that the criteria that varied the most between previous and new brands were appellation and *punctum*. Color was the most important feature associated with appellation and *punctum*. For instance, there were several brands maintaining or adopting variations of the national flag's colors, red and green, and also blue, as the sea is one of the Portuguese's main cultural references.

On the other hand, the brands with less meanings and/or less levels of meaning are more effective in communication when the goal was to discard unwanted meanings. For instance, Crédito Agrícola wanted to lose the association with rural areas and farmers as its main clients and this goal was achieved by rebranding to a hotter brand. By removing the ground from its logotype, the bank lost its association with the growth of plants and with agriculture, thus becoming appealing to a wider set of targets. The same happened to BANIF, a bank which was founded in Funchal, on Madeira Island. The former logotype was green and blue, inspired by the sea and the forest, and included signs related to sailing, such as chains and knots. By changing completely to an indigo logotype featuring a centaur, the organization was able to keep its brand polysemic while dissociating from its insularity and becoming closer to all Portuguese.

Thus, the adjustment between the cognitive and semiotic features of the brand to those of the contemporary environment is not related to better communicational effectiveness only when this adjustment occurs by attunement. A contrast at the semiotic level can be more effective in communicating the intended message and in achieving the goals set by each organization. Besides, the contemporary media landscape and organizational environment, particularly as it pertains to marketing and advertising, are cluttered with messages, saturated with stimuli (Davis, 2009). Although social media marketing experts highlight the importance of having engaging brands and building active communities (Kerpen, 2011; Qualman, 2009; Tuten & Solomon, 2012), simply becoming aware of the brand is an indispensable step to being engaged with a brand's digital presence. Thus, the brands which are best suited to the contemporary cognitive-semiotic context are those which are mostly cool but have some hot features. These brands are more effective in gaining attention in an overcrowded context due to their hot features, but are also more effective in retaining that attention, as their cool features are particularly suited to generating involvement, engagement and participation.

CONCLUDING REMARKS AND FUTURE RESEARCH

In conclusion, this paper shows that applying this cognitive and semiotic analysis, along with the temperature scale, to brands can be a useful methodology for helping organizations communicate their brands more effectively. In addition, it can contribute to enhancing creativity and communication effectiveness in brand design and in branding.

In the future, this research line aims to develop, test and validate a more intuitive and user-friendly temperature scale that combines both the cognitive and the semiotic features and that enables the adjustment, by attunement or contrast, between the organization's goals, its communication tools and the societal context that can be regularly used as a working-tool in organizations.

REFERENCES

Adamson, A. (2008). *Brand digital: Simple ways top brands succeed in the digital world*. Basingstoke, UK: Palgrave Macmillan.

Barthes, R. (1990/1967). *The fashion system*. Berkeley, CA: University of California Press.

Barthes, R. (2007a [1985]). *Elementos de semiologia*. Lisboa, Portugal: Edições 70.

Barthes, R. (2007b [1957]). *Mitologias*. Lisboa, Portugal: Edições 70.

Barthes, R. (2010 [1980]). *Camera lucida*. New York, NY: Hill and Wang.

Baudrillard, J. (1989 [1986]). *America*. New York, NY: Verso.

Bauman, Z. (2000). *Liquid modernity*. London, UK: Polity Press.

Baurelein, M. (2008). *The dumbest generation: How the digital age stupefies young Americans and jeopardizes our future (or, don't trust anyone under 30)*. New York, NY: Tarcher/Penguin.

Beck, Ü. (2008). *World at risk*. Hoboken, NJ: Wiley.

Bell, D. (1973). *The coming of the post-industrial society: A venture in social forecasting*. New York, NY: Basic Books.

Berg, B. (1989). *Qualitative research methods for the social sciences*. Boston, MA: Allyn and Bacon.
Berger, C. (1982). *Language and social knowledge: Uncertainty in interpersonal relations*. New York, NY: Hodder Arnold.
Bouma, G., & Atkinson, G. B. J. (1995 [1987]). *Social science research: A comprehensive and practical guide for students*. Oxford, UK: Oxford University Press.
Carr, N. (2010). *The shallows: What the Internet is doing to our brains*. New York, NY: W. W. Norton.
Castells, M. (2005 [1996]). *A sociedade em rede*. Lisboa, Portugal: Fundação Calouste Gulbenkian.
Cocoran, I. (2011). *The art of digital branding*. New York, NY: Alworth Press.
Cooke, P. (2012). *Unique: Telling your story in the age of brands and social media*. Ventura, CA: Regal.
Cornelissen, J. (2009 [2004]). *Corporate communication: A guide to theory and practice* (2nd ed.). London, UK: Sage.
Davenport, T., & Beck, J. (2002). *The attention economy: Understanding the new currency of business*. Boston, MA: Harvard Business School Press.
Davis, M. (2009). *The fundamentals of branding*. Lausanne, Switzerland: AVA Academia.
Dowling, G. (2001). *Creating corporate reputations: Identity, image and performance*. New York, NY: Oxford University Press.
Drucker, P. (2001). *The essential Drucker*. Oxford, UK: Butterworth-Heinemann.
Fauconnier, G., & Turner, M. (2003 [2002]). *The way we think: Conceptual blending and the mind's hidden complexities*. New York, NY: Basic Books.
Federman, M., & de Kerckhove, D. (2003). *McLuhan for managers*. Toronto, Canada: Viking Canada.
Flew, T. (2008 [2002]). *New media: An introduction*. Oxford, UK: Oxford University Press.
Gee, J. P. (2005). *Why video games are good for your soul*. New York, NY: Common Ground.
Gee, J. P. (2007). *What video games have to teach us about learning and literacy*. New York, NY: Palgrave Macmillan.
Giddens, A. (1999). *Runaway world: How globalization is reshaping our lives*. London, UK: Profile.
Giddens, A. (2002 [1990]). *As consequências da modernidade*. Oeiras, Portugal: Celta Editora.
Green, C. S., & Bavelier, D. (2006). Effect of action video games on the spatial resolution of visuo-spatial attention. *Journal of Experimental Psychology: Human Perception and Performance, 32*(6), 1465–1478.
Heidegger, M. (1977 [1949]). The question concerning technology. In D. Krell (Ed.), *Martin Heidegger: Basic writings* (pp. 287–317). New York, NY: Harper & Row.
Jenkins, H. (2006). *The convergence culture*. New York, NY: New York University Press.
Johnson, S. (2006). *Tudo o que é mau faz bem: Como os jogos de vídeo nos estão a tornar mais inteligentes*. Lisboa, Portugal: Lua de Papel.
Kapferer, J. N. (2000 [1991]). *A gestão de marcas: Capital da empresa*. Mem Martins, Portugal: Edições CETOP.
Kerpen, D. (2011). *Likeable social media: How to delight your customers, create an irresistible brand, and be generally amazing on Facebook (& other social networks)*. New York, NY: McGraw-Hill.
Kornberger, M. (2010). *Brand society: How brands transform management and lifestyle*. Cambridge, UK: Cambridge University Press.
Kunsh, M. (2003). *Planejamento de relações públicas na comunicação integrada*. São Paulo, Brazil: Summus Editorial.
Kutcher, S., & Kutcher, M. (2007). Understanding differences of a cognitive and neurological kind: Digital technology and human brain development. *Syndicated Research Project*. Canada: nGenera.
Levinson, P. (1999). *Digital McLuhan: A guide to the information millennium*. New York, NY: Routledge.
Lipovetsky, G., & Charles, S. (2005 [2004]). *Hypermodern times*. London, UK: Polity Press.

Luhmann, N. (2000). *The reality of mass media*. Stanford, CA: Stanford University Press.
Luhmann, N. (2012 [2002]). *Introduction to systems theory*. London, UK: Polity Press.
Machlup, F. (1972 [1962]). *The production and distribution of knowledge in the United States*. Princeton, NJ: Princeton University Press.
Manovich, L. (2002). *The language of new media*. Cambridge, MA: MIT Press.
Maturana, H., & Varela, F. (1980). *Autopoiesis and cognition: The realization of the living*. Dordrecht, The Netherlands: Kluwer.
McCrindle, M. (2006). New generations at work: Attracting, recruiting, retraining and training generation Y. Sydney, Australia: McCrindle Research.
McLuhan, M. (1994 [1964]). *Understanding media*. Cambridge, MA: MIT Press.
Michael, E. B., Keller, T. A., Carpenter, P. E., & Just, M. A. (2001). fMRI investigation of sentence comprehension by eye and by ear: Modality fingerprints on cognitive processes. *Human Brain Mapping*, *13*(4), 239–252.
Olins, W. (2003). *A ma®ca*. Lisboa, Portugal: Verbo.
Perez, C. (2002). *Technological revolutions and financial capital*. Cheltenham, UK: Edward Elgar.
Pink, D. (2005). *A whole new mind: Why right-brainers will rule the future*. New York, NY: Penguin.
Porat, M. (1977). *The information economy: Definition and measurement*. Washington, DC: U.S. Department of Commerce.
Poster, M. (2000 [1995]). *A segunda era dos media*. Lisboa, Portugal: Celta Editora.
Postman, N. (1993). *Technopoly*. New York, NY: Vintage Books.
Prensky, M. (2001). Digital natives, digital immigrants. *On the Horizon*, *5*(9), 1–6.
Prensky, M. (2006). *"Don't bother me Mom, I'm learning": How computer and video games are preparing your kids for twenty-first century success and how you can help!* St. Paul, MN: Paragon House.
Qualman, E. (2009). *Socialnomics: How social media transforms the way we live and do business*. Hoboken, NJ: Wiley.
Rainie, H., & Wellman, B. (2012). *Networked: The new social operating system*. Cambridge, MA: MIT Press.
Rose, G. (2007 [2001]). *Visual methodologies*. London, UK: Sage.
Schultz, M., Hatch, M. J., & Larsen, M. (2000). *The expressive organization*. New York, NY: Oxford University Press.
Scott, D. M. (2013 [2006]). *The new rules of marketing and PR: How to use social media, online video, mobile applications, blogs, news releases, and viral marketing to reach buyers directly* (4th ed.). Hoboken, NJ: John Wiley and Sons.
Seruya, J. M. (2009). *Gestão da identidade organizacional: É PT!—A marca interna da Portugal Telecom*. Parede, Portugal: Principia.
Shannon, C., & Weaver, W. (1998 [1949]). *The mathematical theory of communication*. Chicago, IL: University of Illinois Press.
Shirky, C. (2010). *The cognitive surplus: Creativity and generosity in a connected age*. New York, NY: Penguin Press.
Tapscott, D. (1998). *Growing up digital: The rise of the net generation*. New York, NY: McGraw-Hill.
Tapscott, D. (2008). *Grown up digital: How the net generation is changing your world*. New York, NY: McGraw-Hill.
Tapscott, D., & Williams, A. D. (2006). *Wikinomics: How mass collaboration changes everything*. New York, NY: Portfolio.
Tapscott, D., & Williams, A. D. (2010). *Macrowikinomics: Rebooting business and the world*. New York, NY: Porfolio.

Toffler, A. (1980). *The third wave.* New York, NY: Bantam Books.

Tuten, T. L., & Solomon, M. R. (2012). *Social media marketing.* Upper Saddle River, NJ: Pearson Prentice Hall.

van Leeuwen, T., & Jewitt, C. (2004 [2001]). *The handbook of visual analysis.* London, UK: Sage.

Watson, R., & Blondheim, M. (2007). *The Toronto School of communication theory: Interpretations, extensions, applications.* Toronto, Canada: University of Toronto Press.

Watzlawick, P., Bavelas, J. B., & Jackson, D. D. (1967). *Pragmatics of human communication: A study of interactional patterns, pathologies, and paradoxes.* New York, NY: Norton.

Williamson, J. (1978). *Decoding advertisements.* London, UK: Marion Boyars.

CHAPTER SIX

The Advertising Offer in the New Media Landscape

ARACELI CASTELLÓ-MARTÍNEZ AND JUAN MONSERRAT-GAUCHI

INTRODUCTION

This chapter offers an analysis of the new trends among advertisers in commercial communication. The current landscape of media, platforms and new advertising forms constitutes a new challenge for the advertising sector. It is necessary to develop new approaches to work processes, audience planning and measurement, and return on investment. It is also necessary for advertising agents to adapt their current role to the new media landscape.

The analysis of the new trends in advertising is illustrated with many examples of advertising campaigns developed in Spain and other countries in new platforms and based on new advertising formulas. This chapter describes the new advertising trends in the use of social television, branded content, social networks, real-time social marketing, augmented reality, digital signage systems, ambient marketing, print media and cinema.

The use of the new forms of communication to reach the target audience represents a drastic change in the relations and work processes that existed between the advertiser, the advertising and media agency, the media and, of course, the audience. The way in which consumers relate to media and brands has changed completely and, therefore, communication professionals are now obliged to constantly adapt their strategies to the changes brought about by the diversification of media and their consumption by users. These changes also require advertisers to constantly carry out research to identify better ways to empathise with the receivers of their messages and to be able to assess the effectiveness of such messages.

The latent question throughout this chapter is, if new forms of advertising have emerged strongly in the new communication landscape as a result of the proliferation of new media and platforms and as a result of the diversification of consumers' preferences, what are the dominant forms of advertising and how can we measure their impact and effectiveness?

An analysis of the new forms of advertising is necessary to answer the research question and to start to understand the ways in which we can measure their effectiveness and impacts. It is necessary to establish other ways of measuring audiences and calculating the return on investment, which are essential to evaluating the impact on the target audience, the worth of the agency that developed the advertising strategy, and the return on investment of such strategy for the advertiser.

The conclusions section of this chapter includes the reflections of various authors on the methods to measure and evaluate the impact, audience and, ultimately, success of an advertising campaign on the new media landscape. Naturally, it is not easy to point to a concrete method that is valid for all new advertising formats. However, based on the description of the different trends and the positions and methods adopted already by some of the protagonists of the advertising sector, this chapter starts to address this question.

THE NEW MEDIA LANDSCAPE

The communication industry is going through a period of profound changes generated not only by the fall of investment in communication and advertising,[1] but also by other factors such as the more proactive and critical role of citizens, their new purchase and consumption attitudes, the digitisation of content, and the philosophy 2.0 of collaborative environments like the social media. These changes and the saturation of conventional forms of advertising have prompted advertisers to come up with new formulas to reach their target audience in a more segmented, effective and profitable way, which also should manage to engage the audience emotionally.

The knowledge society and the transition from the transmission paradigm to the participation paradigm in the "postmodern dialogue with audiences" (Pérez-Latre, 2003, p. 322) are forcing media and advertisers to implement participatory, experiential and empathetic forms of communication to respond to the needs of the multitasking citizen who simultaneously consumes contents from different platforms.

The interactive dimension of digital consumption (Marshall, 2004, p. 51) has changed the conception of audience in collaborative environments and participatory technologies, to such an extent that none of the mass communication theories that became popular during the 20th century seems to be "particularly prepared to explain, predict, or even serve the great changes that are taking place in our media institutions, the message system and audiences" (Bryant & Miron, 2004, p. 697).

Almost two decades ago, Negroponte (1995) had already predicted that "the next evolutionary step in television" would be "the transfer of a part of the intelligence from the sender to the receiver" (p. 34), which, as we will see in the following sections, has become a reality with the emergence of social television. According to Scolari (2008), the one-to-many model of mass communication is in crisis (p. 73) while the interactivity of digital media has rendered useless the founding categories of the cultural process (production-sender and consumption-receiver): "by participating in the control of contents, the user of interactive media ends up becoming part of that content. Paraphrasing McLuhan, it could be said that in the new forms of digital communication the user is the message" (p. 98).

In addition to being audience, public and consumer, the receiver of these new forms of communication is "content co-producer, distributor and consumer" (Bermejo Berros, 2008, p. 49), in the context of a participatory culture in which the unidirectional character that has traditionally characterised the conventional media makes no sense anymore, while effective communication puts the prosumer precisely at the centre of the process, according to the philosophy 2.0.

Scolari (2008) describes these hyper-mediations in the theory of interactive digital communication, which assert the active role of the receiver and consist of "processes of exchange, production and symbolic consumption that take place in an environment characterised by a large number of individuals, media and languages that are technologically interconnected to each other in a grid pattern" (pp. 113–114).

In the current media landscape, characterised by constant change and diversification of platforms, companies are increasingly aware of the need to carry out an "integrated communication strategy" (Victoria Mas, 2005, p. 51) while communication professionals are faced with the challenge of designing fully integrated strategies adapted to the new habits of consumers and developing contents capable of generating conversations with users, in search of a new approach: transmediality.

The concept of transmedia storytelling was originally introduced by Henry Jenkins in an article published in *Technology Review* in 2003, which highlighted the media convergence towards the inevitable flow of content through multiple channels (Scolari, 2013, p. 23). Transmedia narratives are stories told through multiple media, designed and produced in an integrated manner. As Scolari (2013) points out, according to the media expert, Jak Boumans, cross-media is defined by four criteria:

Production involves more than one medium that support each other with their specific strengths.
It is an integrated production.
Content is delivered/accessible on a range of devices such as PCs, mobiles, television sets or set-top boxes, etc.
The use of more than one medium needs to support one theme/story/one purpose/one goal/one message, depending on the type of project (pp. 25–26).

New technologies "affect audiences' lifestyles, interests and use of leisure time" (Pérez-Latre, 2011, pp. 43). In the era of the post-interruption, characterised among other things by audience fragmentation due to the multiplicity of channels, corporate communication and advertising must be based on the distribution of hypermedia and multiplatform contents. Transmediality and participatory culture go hand in hand in the new era of communication, and merge in phenomena such as social television.

Today, companies, products and brands are facing the need to implement emotional communication; to interact with a more committed citizen; to tell stories through a close, coherent, transparent and credible narrative that offers a valuable proposition to customers; to transmit a vocation of service; and to complement users' purchase and consumption experience.

Companies must be capable of generating engagement beyond the mere commercial transaction, and it is here where corporate and advertising transmedia storytelling allows companies to tell stories and friendly experiences through various media and to provide informative content and entertainment (advertainment) of interest to the user.

This new media landscape affects, directly, the advertising offer of the various platforms of each of the advertising media (television, Internet, print press, magazines, supplements, outdoor advertising and cinema), which have been forced to supplement their portfolio of traditional advertising formats with new formulas capable of producing the engagement demanded by advertisers and the transmediality that should characterise advertisements.

If advertising is still the main form of finance for the media and the media audience is the exchange currency that allows the economic quantification and commercialisation of advertising space, it is necessary to review the new advertising solutions that the media have offered to meet advertisers' needs in terms of visibility, efficiency and return on investment in the new communication landscape.

In general, the new advertising campaigns are eager to prioritise the user experience design[2] and to generate added value, by adapting the communication campaign to the usability of each device in order to promote transmediality. The following sections describe some of the innovative communication strategies that advertising and media agencies are developing and that are also being offered by the media platforms as advertising and corporate communication solutions, including many examples of real campaigns carried out by advertisers.

TELEVISION BECOMES SOCIAL

With the dissolution of boundaries between media platforms, which has given rise to transmediality, any offline content generates opinions on social networks in a bidirectional way. Everything revolves around live content, which users manipulate and consume through the medium, platform, device and format of their choice (Tomé, 2011, p. 57). In addition, media exposure habits have changed due to the simultaneous consumption of multimedia content by the user which has been, in turn, motivated by the digitisation process.

In view of the wide penetration of social networks, media platforms such as television stations have become aware that users do not want to be mere receivers and thus put at their disposal tools to review and direct their programming in order to become part of the great social network.

The term "social television" refers to the use of alternative channels, such as the social platforms, as spaces of interaction and conversation around what happens in the programmes broadcast by television.

Social television is increasingly becoming a new way of watching television,[3] to such an extent that the active participation of audiences in real time is understood as the content itself, and is mixed up with the original content into a single message (Tomé, 2011, p. 61) and influences the development of TV programmes. Sometimes, even the interaction between programme and viewer becomes the centre of attention.

These aspects justify the importance that the integration of social networks has acquired in TV programming and marketing strategies and the discourse of the TV networks. TV stations also compete to be leaders in social networks, which become a real-time meter of the popularity of the programmes and the public's feedback. The analysis of social television does not only quantify the amount of people who talk about TV shows, but also allows us to know what is being said about the programmes and brands associated with these broadcasts.

Social television puts new energy into television shows and allows the establishment of closer relations between the thousands of people that are watching the programme at the same time. The second screen enriches the visual experience of the viewer and, at the same time, improves the connection with the consumer. In this context of transmediality, television can no longer be understood without social networks.

From the point of view of advertising, social television opens new horizons to advertisers, which has the ability to amplify the dissemination of its message, provided it is integrated into the discourse of the television programme, and proposes new activities that encourage interaction with the user through the second screen.

An example is Heineken's Star Player app for iPhone,[4] which brings together different apps, mobile marketing, advertising and social television. Heineken, official sponsor of the UEFA Champions League since 2005, offered users a way to make the experience of watching the football matches of this competition on television more fun, more active and more social.

With this free app for iPhone, fans could test their instincts and try to predict the results of the match in order to accumulate points. The user accumulating the highest score in a single game up until the semi-finals would travel with 3 friends and Heineken to the final in Munich on 19 May, 2012.

This strategy complemented Heineken's Legendary Football campaign, based on spectacular ads whose protagonists were famous football players who recalled their greatest moments in the UEFA Champions League.

As we can see, today's brands have the opportunity to participate directly in the television discourse and thus exploit audiences' receptivity towards content that allows them to interact and enrich their multi-screen experience.

WHEN THE BRAND IS BEHIND THE CONTENT: BRANDED CONTENT

There are two reasons why advertisers focus their efforts on new spaces and forms of communication: advertising saturation and the search for new strategies to attract users' attention and create a connection with them. All of this has led an increasing number of advertisers to focus their efforts on spaces in which brand and product are integrated in the content (as it happens with product placement). In addition, companies are now creating their own content to share with users, as in the case of branded content, which aims to interact and share experiences instead of merely advertising a product or service (Del Pino, Castelló, & Ramos-Soler, 2013, p. 20). As Regueira (2011) points out, the main objective of branded content is "to offer experiences, not ads" (p. 218).

Branded content is currently one of the most appealing options of corporate communication and advertising used by advertisers to materialise their content strategies, due to its advantages to tell the story, values and corporate position of the brand through a purpose-created narrative.

In general, branded content is an information and/or entertainment space with audiovisual contents whose production has been fully or partly developed by the brand. In other words, branded content is at the service of the brand from the moment of its conception, although the brand is not always explicitly present in it. One of the characteristics of most branded content is its transmediality, since it allows the generation of multi-channel stories and offers users the possibility of participating in the conversation about content in social media.

In this advertainment formula the limits between information, entertainment and advertising are blurred; advertisers aim to offer users valuable contents; and the potential of content to become viral through the social networks is crucial.

The first edition of the study on branded content carried out in Spain, "ContentScope",[5] published by Grupo Consultores in December 2013, conceives this communication strategy as:

> a new 'di-advertising' discipline that has long term objectives, that does not aim to increase (or at least does not focus on) sales, that is based on emotion, in proximity, in the brand-person link (the term consumer is not valid), and that does not even include the visualisation of the brand.

In the survey carried out for this study, communication professionals highlight engagement, brand image, visibility, and interaction with consumers as the main added values of branded content in comparison to other communication options. In the definition of this form of communication, survey respondents highlighted the content generated by the brand as the differential aspect of branded content:

Table 6.1. Definition of Branded Content.

Content generated by the brand	47.2
Content integration	33.1
Relevant content for consumers	23.2
Differentiation from advertising	22.5
Promotion of the brand's values	21.8
Generation of added value for customers	16.2
Non-intrusive character	12.7
Innovation	11.3
Attractive formula	11.3
Entertainment	9.9
Engagement	4.2
User-brand interaction	2.8
Emotional form	1.4

Source: Grupo Consultores.

The synergy that branded content enables between brands and content is coherent with the current post-advertising age, in which advertisers are eager to create relationships with people and to speak the same language (Solana, 2010). In short, branded content allows advertisers to generate and deliver memorable and relevant content that depicts the brand less aggressively than traditional advertising and by linking the central theme of the content to the brand's differential values in such a way that the content is attractive, practical and non-intrusive from the point of view of the citizen.

Red Bull is a brand that has managed to communicate its values through branded content and, in turn, has reinforced its brand image thanks to its association with certain communication activities and contents. This brand has managed to create an association with risk, adventure, extreme sports and insanity in a perfect symbiosis, to such an extent that it has won the first place, worldwide, in the first "Social Video Equity Report", carried out by Goviral, which ranked the 100 most powerful brands in branded content in 2012.

Extreme competitions, sports challenges and other events, such as Félix Baumgartner's epic free fall, all are sponsored by the Red Bull brand, which has redesigned its advertising discourse to leave aside its characteristic funny and spicy messages in order to reposition the brand, by emphasising the emotional part of these challenges.

To commemorate the 15th anniversary of its Red Bull Music Academy project, in 2014 the brand premiered on the Internet the documentary titled, *What Difference Does It Make? A Film About Making Music.*[6] The documentary, directed by Ralf Schemberg, depicts the challenges faced by people devoted to making music.

There are examples of branded content in Internet, cinema, radio and television. In the Internet, brands have taken advantage of their presence in YouTube to offer content to their audiences. For example, Heineken offered the online reality series *Dropped*;[7] Cornetto offered *Cupidity*;[8] Patagonia offered *Worn Wear: A Film About the Stories We Wear*;[9] Dove offered *Dove Real Beauty Sketches*; and Invisible Children offered the successful documentary, *Kony 2012*, which has been watched more than 99 million times on YouTube.

In cinema one of the most notorious examples is the Bollywood film, *Sólo se Vive una Vez* ("You only live once") (*Zindagi Na Milegi Dobara*), which was shot in Spain and has had a great impact among Indian society and has helped to boost tourism in Spain. The film, which won seven awards at Filmfare (Bollywood's Oscars), narrates the journey of three Indian friends throughout Spain. Pamplona's Festival of San Fermín, Seville, Barcelona and Buñol's Tomatina festival are some of the places and events experienced by these friends. The film has been watched by more than 70 million people in India while the number of Indians visiting Spain has gone from about 70,000 to nearly 200,000. Most Indians visiting Spain were young like the film's protagonists.

Sólo se Vive una Vez is considered as an example of branded content because the Spanish Government, through its tourism institution, *TurEspaña*, reached an agreement with film producer Excel Entertainment to provide financial assistance in exchange for the promotion of Spain. In fact, before the screening of the film, it was accompanied by the commercial spot, "You Need Spain".[10]

In 2014, another outstanding example of branded content came to movie theatres: *The Lego Movie*. In its release in the United States, the film grossed more than 69 billion dollars, becoming the second best release of February. Inspired by the movie, Lego created a video game and new merchandising, such as toys inspired by the characters.

In Spain there are several examples of branded content in radio and television. During 2013 this format became popular on Spanish television, with the broadcast of several fiction series and documentaries sponsored by brands: *Tenemos Chico Nuevo en la Oficina* ("New guy at the office") by Banco Santander; *Coca-Cola Music Experience* by Coca-Cola; *Psicodriving* by Honda; *Viaje al Interior de la Cultura* ("Journey inside culture") by Telefónica; and *Código Emprende* ("Do it code") by BBVA.

On the radio, Vodafone sponsors *Vodafone Yu* in Los40, while the Spanish beer brand San Miguel sponsors *Un Lugar Llamado Mundo* ("A place called earth"), a programme inspired by the song of the brand's ad starring Mika, in Europa FM.

SOCIAL MEDIA

The proliferation of online platforms at the service of marketing and corporate communication, which are derived from the Web 2.0 and are fundamentally based on the integration of content, has led to the use of collaborative environments such as Facebook and Twitter as channels for advertising and corporate communication, sales and customer service. With them, companies seek to achieve conversion, loyalty and recommendation, taking into account the role played by social influence on the purchase and consumption behaviour of users. This is because social networks have become a space for conversation between users, companies and brands.

Integrated communication in social platforms, more than ever before, puts current and potential consumers at the centre of the communication process, following the philosophy 2.0.

The presence of companies and brands in new digital environments is a reality motivated by the great advantages of the social platforms in the field of corporate communication. These platforms offer possibilities for business management based on the establishment of relationships (the "client first" philosophy), the generation of social branding, the segmentation and customisation of messages, the conversion through recommendation and virality, and the experiential marketing aimed at the generation of customer engagement (Castelló Martínez, 2010, pp. 79–98).

However, in order to establish a relationship with brands on social networks users demand tangible benefits and reject such aspects as the misuse of personal data, the excessive presence of advertising or updates, and the use of inadequate communication tones or styles (either too informal, too incredible or too distant and institutional).

To ask for users' interaction (through likes, comments or shares) in exchange for gifts in order to grow rapidly in terms of numbers of followers can be counter-productive for the brand, as it can generate negative perceptions (the brand may be perceived as begging for attention and belittling the user), generate forced traffic, and the dismissal of true fans. Based on this idea, Burger King Spain implemented a strategy that is an example of how social media marketing can be used to, simultaneously, generate virality and notoriety, contribute to the brand's marketing and sales goals, and even to test a product.

Burger King promised the public that if its Spanish Facebook account reached 250,000 followers by 22 April 2013, the company would give free fries to all of its Spanish customers on Friday, 26 April. The campaign was announced on 16 April, when Burger King Spain's Facebook fan page had just over 100,000 fans. This figure was almost tripled in just seven days thanks to a television campaign and sponsored posts in Facebook.

A few weeks earlier Burger King had changed its French fries because it was aware that they were one of its least-valued products, so the challenge aimed to give free samples of the new product and make lots of fuss with a viral social strategy.

Since it opened its Facebook page, Burger King has been one of the most outstanding advertisers in terms of risky campaigns carried out in the social network. An example is the campaign carried out in December 2013 in Norway to identify the true fans. The brand gave users the option to identify themselves as true Burger King fans or to declare themselves as not much of a fan and accept a free Big Mac, the best-known product of its rival: McDonald's.[11]

Those who declared themselves as true fans gained access to a page with exclusive content, while those who preferred the Big Mac were banned from Burger King's Facebook page. The brand lost 30,000 fans, but highlighted the loyalty shown by 8,000 fans with whom it could interact more effectively from that moment on.

In 2009 the brand had already generated controversy with the *Whopper Sacrifice* campaign, which offered a free Whopper to all those willing to eliminate ten Facebook friends who would be notified that their "friend" preferred a free Whopper over their friendship. The campaign was active for 10 days until Facebook intervened and blocked it on the grounds of privacy issues.

In Twitter, beyond the paid-for advertising options offered by the platform (promoted tweets, promoted accounts and promoted trending topics), which are in their testing phase and are not yet available for any account, brands have also seized the opportunity to interact with the user and amplify the dissemination of their advertising campaigns by carrying out communication activities based on hashtags.

Starbucks created the @tweetacoffee account so that users could give a cup of coffee to one of their followers, who would receive on their mobile a $5 ticket to spend on Starbucks.[12]

In Romania, Coca-Cola conducted the campaign *#LetsEatTogether*,[13] which invited Romanians to find a companion to enjoy food and avoid eating alone, based on Coca-Cola's association of the lunch time with happiness. Statistics showed that 6 of every 10 Romanians ate alone so, together with McCann Erickson/MRM Worldwide Romania, Coca-Cola decided to launch a campaign that would help people to meet around a plate of food, and thus contribute to their happiness.

The idea was very successful among the Romanian population, and even among famous people. In addition, the tweets sent with the hashtag *#LetsEatTogether* were processed and broadcast live on television. The brand complemented this campaign with street marketing, in which a famous chef travelled in a caravan to various Romanian cities to surprise some of the people who had used the hashtag.

REAL-TIME SOCIAL MARKETING

We live in the era of real-time marketing. The difficulty in reaching consumers requires brands to be constantly prepared to detect any opportunity to connect emotionally with them. Today, successful marketing is done in real time, and this requires the media agency to have a 24/7 knowledge of the platforms through which the brand transmits its message and of the contents shared by users in these platforms. The immediacy of the conversation in social media has allowed "just-in-time" marketing, which is closely linked to the brand's online reputation management.

Examples of real-time marketing are the activities carried out by some brands with presence in social media during the 2013 Super Bowl, the biggest sports event in the United States, and the interaction between Kit Kat and Oreo with a Twitter user. In the first case, Oreo and other brands such as Tide detergent and Calvin Klein published in their Twitter accounts funny messages and images about the ten-minute Super Bowl blackout that occurred after Beyoncé's half-time performance.

In the case of Oreo, it posted an image of a black background lit by an Oreo Cookie titled, "Power out? No problem". The brand was able to react because it had fifteen community managers connected and prepared to act immediately if something happened. It was real-time marketing which achieved great results: more than 15,000 retweets and 6,000 favourites in just a few hours.

Oreo also starred in another real-time marketing action along with Kit Kat when Kit Kat challenged Oreo to Tic-Tac-Toe to win the affections of Laura Ellen, a female Twitter user who tweeted, "Can tell I like chocolate a bit too much when I'm following @KITKAT and @Oreo hahahahahah". However, Oreo politely declined to engage in the gameplay and instead ate Kit Kat's chocolate cross. To carry out a marketing strategy in real time it is important to listen to the conversations of users, which is not easy to do in the age of big data. The new generation of *Mad Men* requires advertising agents and planners able to process and analyse, with the tools available, the huge volume of information available on the digital platforms about consumers and brands, which can be used in brand communication activities.

DIGITAL SIGNAGE AND AUGMENTED REALITY IN OUTDOOR ADVERTISING

Outdoor spaces offer advertisers a wide variety of ad formats to communicate their messages in a simple but very notorious and powerful way. If advertising pieces are created according to the characteristics of the external environment they can be eye-catching, convey the brand's message and achieve its communication objectives through the use of the right content and format.[14]

Digital signage and augmented reality also follow the trend towards transmediality, multi-screen consumption and the search for interaction with the user like the adverting campaigns developed in social media, real-time marketing, social television and branded content, whose potential increases when applied to the external environment.

Similar to the futuristic reality of legendary science fiction films, dynamic digital signage[15] constitutes an evolution in digital advertising that allows advertisers to offer richer and interactive content.

This concept refers to the evolution of static outdoor and in-store advertising which, jointly, allows advertisers to offer dynamic, personalised and interactive contents. It is known as the "fourth screen", as a perfect complement to television, the computer and mobile devices.

This new medium is based on a set of technologies and computer solutions that enable the creation, distribution and publication of advertising, promotional and/or informational content through the use of electronic devices. These devices allow the display of content in a dynamic way and in real time, in one or multiple locations for a particular audience.

Digital signage is the digital evolution of outdoor advertising and point-of-sale (POS) advertising, through the use of screens, projectors and touch panels. It is a medium that, therefore, emerges from the combination of the Internet and the external environment and is strengthened with the interaction of users through their mobile devices and social networks.

The combination of social networks, mobile marketing and digital signage helps advertisers to get in touch with the online and offline audience, through cross-media advertising campaigns. Digital signage devices can send personalised information related to products to consumers' mobile devices on the point-of-sale, just like in the futuristic film, *Minority Report.*

With these screens, mobile devices can become a tool to improve the shopping experience, to attract new customers and to meet the needs of customers. Digital signage has also been combined with augmented reality to make advertising more memorable thanks to the brand experience that it can generate.

An example of these initiatives is Pull & Bear's *Pull Your Look*[16] campaign, which included screens in stores and fitting rooms to offer consumers the opportunity to interact, choose their look, take a picture of their new look, and share it on social networks.

Nonetheless, the two most internationally renowned digital signage screens are McDonald's in Piccadilly Circus (London)[17] and Forever21's in Times Square (New York).[18] McDonald's invited tourists to have an interactive experience with the brand, through entertaining content that users could photograph and videotape. The campaign managed to convince the public to post their pictures on Flickr, to share their videos on YouTube and to comment about the snapshots on Facebook, thus becoming a cross-media digital campaign, as shown in the campaign video.

With regards to augmented reality, it can be defined as the combination in real time of physical, real-world environments and elements with virtual elements by means of technological devices. Augmented reality is based on a set of technologies that allow the real-time superposition of computer-generated images, sounds and information over real-world elements. In this way, fictional elements can be created digitally and users can interact with them.

Virtually all mobile devices launched by the major technology brands in recent years include among their features a Global Positioning System (GPS) and photo and video cameras. These features and the relative ease in developing specific smartphone apps have enabled the emergence of various utilities that give users additional information about what they are seeing on their smartphone screens.

There are apps specifically designed to create augmented reality experiences, such as Layar, which enables the creation of our own reality layers and the possibility of, for example, playing a video about a restaurant when users point their mobile phone camera to a sign located in a tourist street. There are several interesting examples of the application of augmented reality in the field of marketing.[19] An example of an advertising campaign based on augmented reality is the app developed by Starbucks on the occasion of the celebration of Valentine's Day in 2012: Starbucks Cup Magic, which gave users the opportunity to send very special virtual greetings to their loved ones.[20]

The combination of augmented reality with geo-positioning and other forms of marketing, communication and advertising such as ambient marketing and social media marketing allows media agencies to develop very innovative forms of advertising to achieve the advertiser's media and communication goals.

AMBIENT MARKETING

In order to generate notoriety and attract the public's attention in an ingenious way, ambient marketing uses elements of the environment, beyond the advertising formats of the external environment, to integrate the brand or convey an advertising message in a creative and attractive way.

Ambient marketing actions must be able to communicate the values of the brand and the message it wants to convey in a visually attractive way. An example is Coca-Cola's "healthy lift" message, which was part of the brand's wider *Four Commitments to Fight Overweight and Sedentary Lifestyle* campaign, which encouraged people to take the stairs instead of the lift.

For this purpose, the Coca-Cola team created a structure that looked just like the lifts in a shopping centre in Barcelona: it had the same iconography and light and sound effects of any lift. The difference was that when the doors opened people did not find an elevator cabin, but red stairs with the message "If you climb the stairs you are changing the statistics". Three mini spy cameras were placed in the call button to record the surprise of the protagonists. Ambient marketing goes beyond what is known as street marketing, since it is characterised by integrating the brand in the environment in a creative way, reinventing everyday items for communication and advertising purposes for the benefit of the brand and the product, while street marketing includes any marketing action or technique whose objective is to promote products and services in public places by attracting potential clients' attention and establishing direct contact with them.

In ambient marketing any object from the urban or external environment can become an advertising tool. One example is the statue of Isabel II of Spain located in Madrid's Plaza de Isabel II, customised by Correos, a postal service company, and the Zapping Village agency.

Metro stations have been also customised according to the objectives of a product, service or brand. On the occasion of the premiere of *The Lego Movie*, the advertising team installed in Milan a fake underground entrance with more than 190,000 Lego blocks.

Sometimes it is the advertisers who create the urban artefacts, as in the case of IBM, which placed a peculiar billboard over a fence to also serve as a bench.[21]

PRINT MEDIA ADVERTISING

Since the popularisation of the Internet, print media have suffered a decline in advertising investment, which in the case of Spain has started since 2007. With the exception of the Internet, ad expenditure has also declined in other media platforms in Spain. Newspapers, magazines and supplements in Spain saw their advertising revenue reduced by 13.5%, 19.1% and 25.6%, respectively, from 2012 to 2013, according to the 2014 study of advertising investment in Spain produced by InfoAdex.[22] If we compare the advertising investment from 2013 and 1999, the decline is 56.7% for newspapers, 55.2% for magazines and 64.4% for supplements.

However, print media still have great advantages from the point of view of advertising planning, such as audiences' high involvement with print content and the high discriminatory power of the thematic segmentation of print media, especially of magazines. Communication professionals are aware of the importance of creativity in promoting interaction beyond the reading of the advertisement in print media and, for this reason, they design ad formats in printed media that go beyond the space traditionally assigned to an ad.

As we have seen, in print media the advertising format can be used to communicate in a clear and direct manner the concept of the brand. An example is M&C Saatchi Stockholm's decision to introduce LG's OLED television, touted as one of the thinnest in the market, by advertising it on the spine of a magazine that had the same thickness as the product: four millimetres.

Beyond the creativity to use the advertising space in print media, advertisers can also use other elements to provide readers with some kind of interaction and achieve a greater impact and communicate the brand's idea better. To launch its Moto X smartphone series, characterised by a wide range of colours, Motorola placed in *Wired* magazine an interactive print ad made of polycarbonate foil and LED light tubes that allowed users to change the colour of the phone displayed by touching buttons of different colours.[23]

To advertise a scratch card, GPY&R Brisbane created an ad that allowed users to experience the use of the advertised product, since the entire ad piece could be scratched to show the benefits of winning.

In other cases, ads in print media offer readers some service or gift. DraftFCB Sao Paulo created for Nivea a magazine ad equipped with a wafer-thin solar panel and a phone plug that could be used for users to recharge their mobile phone with solar energy.[24]

Also in Brazil the ad agency JWT created for Ford a magazine ad equipped with a prepaid chip that let users get through a toll road for free, which materialised the brand's promise: "Go further".[25]

In collaboration with Forbes magazine, Microsoft made an ad that provided users free Wi-Fi. The ad included a micro router with a battery lasting 2–3 hours, capable of providing free Wi-Fi access for fifteen days.

NEW ADVERTISING FORMULAS IN CINEMA

Despite being the medium with the lowest percentage of advertising investment (0.5% of the total advertising investment in Spain in 2013, according to InfoAdex), cinema remains an advertising medium with great advantages, especially for the high spontaneous recalling rate that it generates.

The classic commercial spaces provided before the film starts in the movie theatre have allowed advertisers to develop attractive and surprising communication actions for viewers. For example, the ad agency Ireland/Davenport presented in a movie theatre in Johannesburg an advertising event to promote the launch of FOX Crime channel which involved a cinema ad whose protagonist comes out of the screen to the movie theatre which was equipped with UV lamps and fluorescent ink.[26]

In other cases the advertising ads shown at cinemas can also be designed to allow viewer interaction, as in the case of Mazda's, which turned two movie theatres in Canada into giant video game rooms to play the "Fast Lane" racing game, which people could play with their smartphones.[27]

Coca-Cola is one of the brands that have produced the largest number of cinema advertising campaigns. For the launch of Coca-Cola Zero, the agency McCann Ericsson Madrid carried out the "el cambiazo" ("the switch") advertising event in some movie theatres in Madrid. Viewers were given a glass of Coca-Cola Zero within a glass of normal Coca-Cola without knowing it, allowing the brand to test the new product and convey the message that Coca-Cola Zero tasted just like classic Coca-Cola. Before the movie started an ad was shown to tell the audience about the switch.[28]

CONCLUSIONS

This chapter has analysed the new forms of advertising in two very different areas: online marketing, including social networks and other Internet platforms, and the new forms of advertising that are presented in conventional media but break the traditional advertising formulas used in these media. So, how can we measure the audiences, impacts and return on investment of a campaign that combines all these resources and platforms?

With regards to digital media (digital television, Internet, mobile telephony, social networks, etc.) as potential platforms for interactive advertising, they provide much more concrete and precise possibilities for measurement and control than the rest of the media (Lamas, 2010).

What options do media agencies have to survive? What is their role in the new media and platforms landscape? On the one hand, they can become agencies that incorporate a high degree of creativity and propose campaigns similar to the ones described here to advertisers. However, this process would make the media agencies act almost like the advertising agencies from which they derived.

Another option is to develop a specific mechanism to measure both the audience and the impact of their proposals, such as the return on investment. Many agencies are already aware of this and have begun to do so.

Some authors argue that media planners still emphasise the measurement of audiences with traditional methods, and continue to ignore the possibilities and the need for the evaluation of consumers' behaviours and habits, which can facilitate the development of proactive and responsible measurement strategies, which subsequently would improve the validity of the agencies' choice of media and platforms. Thus, it is necessary for media agencies to replace their "media approach" or "consumer and audience approach" with one approach that integrates both perspectives (Cheong, 2009).

The need for media agencies to develop a new business strategy is highlighted in the professional sector as a solution. This strategy must include the new media, platforms and advertising forms, and for this it is necessary to carry out a major research effort to offer customers a differential value. The current tools and processes used in audience measurement are clearly insufficient to meet the needs of advertisers. On the other hand, it is necessary for media agencies to provide greater transparency in terms of measurement processes and billing services to advertisers. In the current climate it is necessary to offer the media, the advertising agency and advertisers access to the information system and data processes. The old system of the black box from which media solutions came out for advertisers must become a transparent box that benefits all stakeholders (BusinessDay Online, 2014).

Regarding the online media and platforms, an enthusiastic search has already begun for new indicators that respond to the particularities and needs of the new environment, beyond the classical metrics of coverage and frequency. As a result, today, website traffic analysis includes such indicators as visits, average session, click-through rates (CTR), referrals, landing pages, conversion rates, etc.

In the case of social networks, in addition to measuring effectiveness with the classical audience parameters, there are other factors more focused on engagement, influence, social relevance and even credibility (Lamas, 2010).

However, taking into account that, as shown in this chapter, the use of conventional media has also changed, how can these measurements be combined with those carried out in conventional media?

In this fragmented and complex media environment, advertisers have new needs and demand fully integrated communication strategies that are adapted to the new consumer habits, ensure the synergy of the planned actions, are creative, and focus on budget optimisation, increasing of coverage and making the greatest impact on the target audience with innovative formulas.

In this sense, the media agency will play a key role due to its extensive experience and deep knowledge of the whole media landscape: conventional and new, mass and one-to-one, above the line and below the line media.

Advertisers, often due to their lack of understanding of the methods used to measure the effectiveness of online media, opt for the measurement criteria provided by the World Federation of Advertisers (WFA). They emphasise the need for cross-media information and internationally comparable measurements. In particular, the document produced by the WFA establishes the following needs:

1- Be person-centric: start from a pre-defined universe.
2- Provide audience measures exclusively according to definitions and metrics pre-established and agreed upon at industrial level.
3- Describe the audiences with the same criteria commonly used in marketing and media research.
4- Perform and provide audience measures that are continuous, dated and timed.
5- Inform about key contact environmental information.
6- Inform, to the greatest possible degree, about other external indicators of contact environment (where it takes place: home, office, outside, etc.).
7- Deliver the information to subscribers in a timely manner and at a frequency compatible with the time-frame of decision-making processes.
8- Validate periodically the information it delivers, to make possible media choices, resource allocation, ROI projections and post-analyses, such systems should also be:

9- Structurally and technically ready to be integrated into larger "cross-media, consumer-centric, holistic" systems, through statistical fusion or other procedures. (WFA, 2009)

The integration of all measurement systems can be a solution, perhaps still far from being achieved undoubtedly due to the high costs of production.

Other researchers, on the other hand, have developed three new ways of measuring the complicated use of social media marketing campaigns: 1. The customer influence effect, which involves measuring the influence of a social network user on other social network users; 2. The stickiness index, which helps to identify those social network users that actively generate content about a brand, product or campaign; and 3. The customer influence value, that helps to calculate the economic benefits obtained by a company with a social media campaign, by calculating the influence of a user on purchases and the probability of purchase of other users (Kumar & Mirchandani, 2012).

With all this, it seems that the analysis of online audiences would not be a problem because the online medium largely provides the measurement and impact instruments for its different platforms. However, the website, the advertiser and the media agency (depending on the circumstances of the campaign, the specific platform and the type of advertising involved) can each obtain, analyse and interpret those results. What would be pending, however, is the integrated measurement of audiences, impact and ROI of a cross-media campaign.

As a conclusion, the researchers would like to point out that measuring systems within multiplatform advertising strategies in a changeable communicative context—as they happen nowadays—should take into consideration:

a) Variables related to the reached audiences (for instance, the audience in itself and audience measurement in the case of television or data views, and the number of reached viewers in the case of digital channels such as Facebook or YouTube), i.e., related to the circulation obtained from already planned communicative actions, particularly those connected with the target audience, namely coverage and frequency of exposure.
b) Variables derived from users' interactions on digital platforms as a consequence of those actions, such as:
   1-Comments, "Likes" and shared contents in the case of Facebook.
   2-"Likes", "Don't Likes" and comments in the case of YouTube.
   3-Mentions, retweets, favourites and use of hashtags when considering Twitter
c) Influence variables such as the ones mentioned above:
   4-Customer Influence Effect
   5-The Stickiness Index
   6-Customer Influence Value

The combination of all these variables will be essential to get to know and analyze the efficiency of advertising communication actions, since nowadays the results of these actions need to be complemented with those obtained from users' interaction.

d) Some specific measurement of the results from each action must be carried out. This means, to measure the consumer's behaviour from the perspective of the consumer and the audience approach. The way this specific measurement will be devised should fit the planned action and should have to be implemented *ad hoc* for that precise action.
e) The aim of the campaign:
Both the advertiser and the advertising agency or the media agency will check the initial aim of the campaign to assess eventually its success, efficiency and return on investment. The results of impact, audience, interaction, etc., are media results. Accordingly, the result of the campaign will be assessed as long as the initial aim of the campaign has been achieved.

Having stated all this, the measurement proposal the researchers devised could be summarised as follows:

Table 6.2. Measurement Proposal for a Multiplatform Campaign.

a)	Variables Audience	DataViews / Reached people (etc.)	Coverage (etc.)	Frequency of exposure (etc.)
b)	Variables Users' interaction	Comments Likes Shared (Facebook)	Likes Don't Likes Comments (YouTube)	Mentions Re-tweets Favourites Hashtags (Twitter)
c)	Influence Variables of customers	Customer Influence Effect	The Stickiness Index	Customer Influence Value
d)	Design of a measurement tool *ad hoc* for a developed communicative action: consumer and audience approach. To assess the degree of achievement of the specific aim of a certain action.			
e)	Initial aim of the campaign: To check the initial aim of the campaign, not only the media results, and assess the degree of achievement attained.			

Source: Compiled and elaborated by the authors of this research.

However, we go back to the starting point of this research study. Never in the history of commercial or advertising communications has there been such a proliferation of media and platforms, such a diversity of forms to achieve objectives and, above all, so much uncertainty about the future. What is for certain is that, in view of the situation we have described in this chapter, the need to combine different methods to measure audiences, media and different impacts will continue to be a reality.

Perhaps the future of the current media agency is: to be able to plan, develop and integrate different methods for each of the media and platforms, and to make them capable of measuring audiences, impacts and ROI for the advertiser. All this should be planned and executed in an integrated way, as is being done by the current advertising campaigns. Advertisers demand simplicity in the data provided to them to explain the results of their campaigns. Will the media agencies be able to meet this challenge? Only time will tell.

REFERENCES

Bermejo Berros, J. (2008). El receptor publicitario del siglo XXI en el marco de la interactividad: Entre el consumer y el prosumer. In M. Pacheco Rueda (Coord.), *La publicidad en el contexto digital* (pp. 49–78). Sevilla, Spain: Comunicación Social.

Bryant, J., & Miron, D. (2004). Theory and research in mass communication. *Journal of Communication, 54*(4), 662–704.

BusinessDay Online. (2014, March 4). Transparency by media planning agencies is solution to media debt. Retrieved from http://businessdayonline.com/2014/03/transparency-by-media-planning-agencies-is-solution-to-media-debt/#.U0VhAaiSynk

Castelló Martínez, A. (2010). *Estrategias empresariales en la Web 2.0: Las redes sociales online.* Alicante, Spain: Editorial ECU.

Cheong, Y. (2009, May). *Issues in media planning research from '99 to '03.* Paper presented at the annual meeting of the International Communication Association, Sheraton New York, New York City, NY [PDF]. Retrieved from http://www.allacademic.com/meta/p13608_index.html

Del Pino, C., Castelló A., & Ramos-Soler, I. (2013). *La comunicación en cambio constante: Branded content, community management, comunicación 2.0 y estrategia en medios sociales.* Madrid, Spain: Fragua.

Interactive Advertising Bureau Spain (IAB). (2013). *IV estudio anual redes sociales.* Retrieved from http://www.slideshare.net/IAB_Spain/iv-estudio-anual-de-redes-sociales

Kumar, V., & Mirchandani, R. (2012). Increasing the ROI of social media marketing. *Sloan Management Review, 54*(1). Retrieved from http://sloanreview.mit.edu/article/increasing-the-roi-of-social-media-marketing/

Lamas, C. (2010). Los medios interactivos y su publicidad. *Revista TELOS, 82.* Retrieved from http://telos.fundaciontelefonica.com/seccion=1268&idioma=es_ES&id=2010020409130001&activo=6.do

Marshall, D. (2004). *New media cultures.* London, UK: Arnold.

Negroponte, N. (1995). *El mundo digital.* Barcelona, Spain: Ediciones B.

Pérez-Latre, F. J. (2003). De la planificación de medios a la distribución de contenidos. In A. Arrese (Coord.), *Empresa informativa y mercados de la comunicación: Estudios en honor del Prof. Alfonso Nieto Tamargo* (pp. 305–325). Pamplona, Spain: Eunsa.

Pérez-Latre, F. J. (2011). *La publicidad y los medios*. Pamplona, Spain: Eunsa.
Regueira, J. (2011). *Big Brother is dead: El día que el consumidor hizo callar a las marcas*. Madrid, Spain: Esic.
Scolari, C. (2008). *Hipermediaciones: Elementos para una teoría de la comunicación digital interactiva*. Barcelona, Spain: Gedisa.
Scolari, C. (2013). *Narrativas transmedia: Cuando todos los medios cuentan*. Barcelona, Spain: Deusto.
Solana, D. (2010). *Postpublicidad: Reflexiones sobre una nueva cultura publicitaria en la era digital*. Barcelona, Spain: Postagencia.
Tomé, P. (2011). *Conecta! La empresa en la red social*. Barcelona, Spain: Libros de Cabecera.
Victoria Mas, J. S. (Coord.). (2005). *Reestructuras del sistema publicitario*. Barcelona, Spain: Ariel Comunicación.
World Federation of Advertisers (WFA). (2009). What advertisers want from online audience measurement. Retrieved from http://www.wfanet.org/pdf/med_documents/Whatadvertiserswant fromonlinemeasurement.pdf

NOTES

1. In Spain, according to data from InfoAdex, from 1999 to 2013 ad spend has fallen by 9.4%. 2011–2012 fall was 15.8%. Retrieved 10 February, 2014 from www.infoadex.es
2. IAB Spain, (2013), "Top Tendencias 2013". Retrieved from http://slidesha.re/11iltXC
3. The results of "Estudio Multitasking en España", published by Media Planning Group and Media Contacts, are available at http://bit.ly/1bpYOii (retrieved 10 February, 2014).
4. A video advertising of this app is available at http://youtu.be/XP5yySEZub8
5. Retrieved 19 February, 2014 from http://www.grupoconsultores.com/spa/files/contentscope13.pdf
6. Available for watching at http://youtu.be/_EDnMFJiv8U
7. Available for watching at http://www.youtube.com/user/heinekendropped
8. An example is available for watching at http://youtu.be/EJ1sMnlhWLc
9. Available for watching at http://youtu.be/z20CjCim8DM
10. Available for watching at http://youtu.be/-Cd523j3bx8
11. Available for watching at http://vimeo.com/80863708
12. Ad available for watching at http://youtu.be/AxPZj9x_Dsk
13. Ad available for watching at http://youtu.be/5k1fvMmfJxs
14. Examples available for watching at http://youtu.be/gKUfxL2AIAo and http://youtu.be/xgvX Zsgr9IQ
15. Cf. "Libro Blanco Digital Signage: La Cuarta Pantalla", edited by IAB Spain and available at http://www.iabspain.net/libros-blancos/
16. Ad of the campaign available for watching at http://youtu.be/W1RV7EjYSLM
17. Available for watching at http://youtu.be/JjVYVQOOJA8
18. Available for watching at http://youtu.be/ON8jLppE9-s
19. Several videos about different initiatives can be found on the following webpages: http://bit.ly/j2NobA and http://bit.ly/rxS6bj
20. Ad of the campaign available for watching at http://bit.ly/xjeFQV
21. Other examples of the campaign can be found at: http://youtu.be/4_oaWkXWujI
22. Study available at http://www.infoadex.es/
23. The video is available at http://youtu.be/iMrZmSPpIRw

24. Video of the campaign available at http://youtu.be/UYy1GmJgFXA
25. Video of the campaign available at http://youtu.be/1otLea8sG1s
26. Video of the event available at http://youtu.be/Qr16NmQV6dA
27. Video of the event available at http://youtu.be/1_2mrprtlqo
28. Video of the event available at http://youtu.be/ElWNtX0Tmgc

CHAPTER SEVEN

Media and the Creation of Brand Value in "Signification Advertising": Defining a Model and Case Studies: Muji, Moleskine, Bench

FELIP VIDAL

INTRODUCTION

THE MEDIA AND ADVERTISING: FROM THE CRISIS TO A NEW *PULL* ECOSYSTEM

The world of advertising is currently awash with a wide range of increasingly interactive and dynamic techniques, strategies, and tools, such as street marketing, advertainment, event marketing, and Point-of-Sale Advertising, indicating the enormous transformation that is taking place in the industry. However, this is not only —to paraphrase and combine two well-known books from a decade ago—the "Fall of Advertising" (Ries & Ries, 2002) "as we now it" (including the quotation marks) as an allusion to Zyman's Book "The End of Advertising As we Know it" (Zyman, 2002). It is also a new way of understanding the traditional market (Medina, 2010) and the methods used to create value through the semiotic creation of the brand (Caro, 2010, p. 190), which is in fact the main task of advertising.

Advertising has adapted to the changes taking place within the current social, technological, and economic context, whether these be the emergence of new forms of communication that are not strictly publicity based, the existence of new methods of communication, the appearance and growth of advertising in new media, or the fact that audiences are becoming increasingly critical of advertising. All of the above have created a great deal of complexity when it comes to determining the most effective combination of advertising media, techniques, and tools. As Joe Cappo states:

> the arena for the communications challenge of the future will be a battle for consumer attention. No single medium will dominate, as television did between the 1960s and 1990s. There will always be mass markets, but advertisers will not be able to reach them through mass communications, except for those few events that can draw a huge audience. This reality will require more emphasis on what were formerly below-the-line activities, such as direct marketing and sales promotion [...] here is what appears likely for other forms of marketing [...] place-based marketing [...] event marketing [...] sponsorship of public venues [...] co-branding and co-marketing [...]. (Cappo, 2003, pp. 242–243)

Figure 7.1, from 2010, shows the data for worldwide media advertising expenditures for the years 2007 and 2009 and a forecast (ZenithOptimedia, 2010) of a decrease in expenditures for the years 2011 and 2013, which the above company attributes to Internet competition. However, while investment in television advertising continued to grow in this period, the primary means of distribution, and consequently their advertising expenditure, decreased in favor of digital channels and video websites.

	2007	2009	2011	2013
Newspaper	130.744$	97.237$	93.019$	91.908$
Magazines	59.475$	43.844$	42.644$	42.300$
Television	181.322$	165.260$	191.198$	213.878$
Radio	38.697$	31.855$	32.580$	35.054$
Cinema	2.283$	2.104$	2.393$	2.681$
Outdoor	31.730$	28.120$	30.945$	34.554$
Internet	42.281$	54.209$	70.518$	91.516$
Total	486.532$	443.102$	463.297$	511.890$

Figure 7.1.

In 2013, when forecasting the evolution of advertising investment by 2016 (Figure 7.2), the same organization (ZenithOptimedia, 2013) observed that the Internet would continue to be the medium with the largest growth, largely due to the advent of mobile devices such as tablets and smartphones, while Internet advertising on computers would decrease.

	2013	2016
Television	40.2%	39.3%
Desktop internet	17.9%	18.9%
Mobile internet	2.7%	7.7%
Newspapers	17%	14.0%
Magazines	7.9%	6.3%
Outdoor	6.9%	6.9%
Radio	6.9%	6.3%
Cinema	0.5%	0.6%

Figure 7.2.

As Joe Cappo's predictions become reality, we now find an increase in Internet and alternative media investment (known as below-the-line media), to the detriment of conventional advertising. At the same time, we are also witnessing a growing complexity in advertising practices. New developments in marketing and communication techniques have emerged that include new tools and strategies, such as event marketing, experiential marketing, guerilla marketing, branded content, or social marketing. All of these have resulted in a new form of advertising characterized in recent years as neo-advertising (Bermejo, 2013) or post-advertising (Costa Solà-Segalés, 2007; Solana, 2010). As Jesús Bermejo states, new rhetorical strategies are emerging, resulting in a new kind of integrated advertising, neo-advertorials and self-referential advertising. This, in turn, takes the form of a simulated dialog with consumers, where push strategies take on a central role. Thus:

> New technologies capable of creating bi-directional links with the receiver take a step further towards the staging of a simulated dialog and therefore towards the communicative relationship between the advertiser and their target. Neo-publicity is another of the manifestations showing a current progressive advancement from traditional push strategies, characteristic of classic publicity, towards pull strategies. (Bermejo, 2013, p. 122)

The previous decrease in advertising investment reflected by data gathered in recent studies has been followed by growth due to the new distribution of the aforementioned investment to produce a new media ecosystem, one that tends towards multiple platforms in the search for new points of contact between brands and consumers. This highlights the importance of advertising as a tool for creating brand value, while also revealing new advertising methods where advertisers have redefined the most efficient combination of media as they adapt to new realities.

Thus, many traditional media outlets are now confronted with a significant decline in advertising revenue. This was initially due to a shrinking market, but subsequently also to two further factors: the loss of investment resulting from new tools that have made many of the traditional mass media less efficient, and an increase in below-the-line and Internet media, which has been accompanied by a change in advertising rhetoric.

The reason why the traditional media no longer monopolize advertising is that they no longer add value to brands, which are now turning their attention to "pull" strategies to attract the consumer rather than attempting to bring the brand to the consumer, as was the case with classic advertising using conventional methods.

As mentioned earlier, the advertising industry has evolved to adapt to the emergence of new forms and methods of communication, the appearance and growth of advertising in new media, and the fact that audiences are becoming increasingly critical of advertising. All of the above ultimately represent a media investment crisis for agencies and advertisers, which has led to new techniques, formats, and media being used that can be understood as new developments in "signification advertising". In the following section I am going to explore Antonio Caro's (1993) distinction between what he called *publicidad referential* and *publicidad de la significación*. I have translated the latter from Spanish as signification advertising.

The aim in these pages is to present and contextualize a conceptual toolbox for analyzing new developments in signification advertising resulting from a renewed semiotic production. Such production is characterized by the creation of a brand image in accordance with various shaping strategies that seek—through a simulation of the most authentic consumer experience possible—both to achieve the densification of brands which are becoming more and more virtualized and isolated from the product they represent, and to keep the nature of the brand's semiotic production invisible.

My objective in considering the new techniques, formats, and media being used in advertising and new developments in signification advertising is firstly to observe how brand value is currently being constructed through a renewed semiotic production materialized in three brand-shaping strategies: the creation of spaces, the construction of narratives, and the promotion of consumer activity. I then aim to provide what may be considered paradigmatic examples of these strategies through the description and analysis of the distinct cases of Muji, Moleskine, and Bench. And finally, I shall address the following question: What is the role of—and what are the challenges and opportunities presented by—the media in constructing new forms of brand value that operate under the three mechanisms described above within new developments in signification advertising?

SEMIOTIC PRODUCTION OF THE BRAND: OLD AND NEW PERSPECTIVES

Elaborating on the distinction made by Antonio Caro between referential advertising and signification advertising (Caro, 1993, pp. 92–96; 1994, p. 120; and Ibáñez, 1994, pp. 233–234), we may currently be witnessing not only the predominance of the latter, but also the appearance of new developments within it.

At the beginning of the 20th century, referential advertising, basically informative and product-centered, gradually gave way to signification advertising, oriented towards the construction or production of brand semiotics (Eguizábal, 2007, p. 129). Advertising, therefore, took on the most substantial part of the production and commercialization of any product or service, namely, the construction of the brand image, which assumes a depositary role for symbolic content until the product becomes known as "the tangible expression that supports the brand" (Caro, 1998, p. 685).

From this point onwards and for decades, creating brand value through the semiotic production of its image was based on the possibility of sustaining a referential illusion between the brand and its products. In other words, of keeping the logic of semiotic production hidden from the eyes of the consumer so as to avoid the brand's image standing as a sole reference and therefore not referring to anything but itself.

Advertising, to the extent that it has been more or less able to maintain this referential illusion, has likewise successfully created an emotional attachment in the consumer to the brand's image. The way that advertising has gone about trying to achieve this emotional attachment over time has shaped the unique evolution of signification advertising through to our current era, when such an illusion runs the risk of becoming seen as empty and insignificant, and leaves the advertising industry needing to respond to this threat.

There is now a plethora of new phenomena that can all be interpreted as new techniques and strategies aimed at maintaining the aforementioned referential illusion; such as the emergence of advertainment, advergaming, artvertising, new forms of publicity stemming from street marketing, event marketing, digital signage, techniques arising from interest in attention economy (Davenport & Beck, 2001) and neuromarketing (Lindstrom, 2008; Renvoisé & Morin, 2007), or from the changed role of the consumer, who takes the form of a prosumer in a context that is dominated by the Internet and Web 2.0 tools (Dwyer, Tabernero, & Tubella, 2008). They are new ways of creating brand value that have led to what can be considered new representations of signification advertising, produced according to the logic of a renewed semiotic production (Vidal, 2011).

Within the context of the economy of experience (Pine & Gilmore, 1999; Schmitt, 1999; Schmitt, Rogers, & Vrotsos, 2004), which is characterized by image being inflated via the semiotic production of the brand (Vidal, 2012), brands seek to create value through advertising. In doing so, they attempt to represent their image content through certain mechanisms consisting of diverse techniques and tools that conform to a renewed semiotics production of the brand, leading to new developments in signification advertising.

It is worth emphasizing in this regard that although the brand's autonomy is growing in relation to the material nature of the product and that, moreover, diverse circumstances are now seriously endangering maintenance of the referential illusion, this does not mean—as one might think at first glance—that the product has become irrelevant, nor that the brand is nothing more than a figment of the imagination. Rather, we have entered a new era in which it has become even more necessary to construct the signification of the brand's image through new means, techniques, and tools.

Such shaping mechanisms, which I detail in the following subsections, are materialized in: a) the use of distinct media and/or interfaces that may or may not be traditionally used for advertising, b) the resource of the brand's narrativization, and c) the embodiment of the brand through consumer activity. All of these mechanisms are aimed at constructing the brand through its materialization, while at the same time functioning as techniques that keep the consumer from seeing or recognizing how the brand's image has been constructed. In short, this involves closing off communication to allow the referential illusion between the product and the brand to be maintained. To put it in another way, the principal aim is to keep the logic of semiotic production hidden and not to reveal its constructed and fictional nature.

THE CREATION OF BRAND VALUE THROUGH RENEWED SEMIOTIC PRODUCTION

Shaping the brand through multiple supports and surfaces

In response to this first mechanism, a plethora of communication media, formats, techniques, and tools has emerged in recent years: guerrilla actions, event marketing or a Point-of-Sale Advertising that is becoming increasingly more dynamic. We find examples of this in outdoor advertising (increasingly more interactive) and in the construction of places (whether theme parks, flagship stores, or others) that serve as a physical anchor for the brand image, while constituting sites that encapsulate paradigmatic brand experiences.

Thus, through new developments in signification advertising the brand not only consists of producing semiotic constructions that add to, and in some ways replace, material productions. It has also ceased to be made up of visually represented image content, becoming instead three-dimensional, spreading throughout a multitude of media, platforms, practices, and techniques that seek to create a space for interaction between the company's identity and the identity of the target audience.

Accordingly, in modern-day adverts we are witnessing the extension of an increasingly more virtualized brand towards all areas of the consumer's life. The brand might be considered to have left the screen to expand physically, creating not only fictions of possible worlds, but also events or occasions, even authentic brand landscapes, or brandscapes (Klingmann, 2007), which in one way or another require the active participation of consumers to generate the projection of their own identity, resulting in their emotional adhesion.

Thus, the brand has become part of the commercial space, while the product itself has taken on a distinct central role. The retail space is not only a container for products, but rather a space that represents experiences where the product, beyond merely being shown, forms part of the scenography that contributes to the creation of the brand image and gives value to the consumer's experience. In this place, where product and consumer meet and exchange, the former has become an increasingly more relevant element to advertising, since its formal features greatly contribute (beyond the aesthetic component) to the creation of the signification behind the brand's image through its representation in space (Lipovetsky & Serroy, 2007, p. 110).

This evolution in the spaces where consumption takes place has been accompanied by an evolution in outdoor advertising due to its ability to complement other media, providing greater coverage and establishing interactive relationships with consumers through the digitalization of the exterior environment. Guerilla advertising or marketing (Dorrian & Lucas, 2006), street marketing actions, and geomarketing, among others, are habitually based on the unconventional use of exterior environments and represent a change in the advertising panorama in the sense that the brand has expanded into public and unconventional spaces with the goals of generating surprise, visibility, and interaction and stimulating virality.

In essence, it is safe to say that a renewed semiotic production situates its aims beyond the creation of the brand (or a valuable semiotic production based on the signification of the brand image) and goes one step further to be materialized in its expression on multiple platforms, seeking to specialize and expand to make the brand three-dimensional and to spatialize the product.

Shaping the brand through the use of narrative

It has been over a decade since Jensen (2001) forecast that by 2020 we would find ourselves in an era of dreams, where consumer culture would tell stories through the products we purchase. It seems that this era is already upon us. Storytelling is now a widely used technique (Nuñez, 2007; Salmon, 2007; Vincent, 2002) and it has existed as such for a long time without being defined and labeled (Jhally, 2000, p. 30; Kilbourne, 1999, p. 56).

Design, advertising, mass media, and fashion have all taken on a crucial role in current consumer culture as mediators and suppliers of the symbolic and discursive material by means of which consumers carry out the narrative self-construction of a constantly evolving identity. In this sense, brands are likewise constructions of identities that permit the consumer to create links with the values and lifestyles they represent, leaving room for the consumer to relate to and participate in the narratives that conform to the brand's image.

Brand image, in the construction of which narrative plays a fundamental role, allows new experiences to be transmitted to the consumer, thus facilitating both the projection of their own identity and their emotional attachment. In other words, the use of brand narratives as a mechanism for shaping the brand seeks to direct the consumer subject's projection of their own identity towards the brand image in order to achieve the experiential adhesion of the former to the world of the latter.

Through corporate identity and advertising communications, which is what creates connotative capacity in both the corporation and its products, associations with certain values and lifestyles are established. Advertising campaigns, within this symbolic system, represent and sum up these values and desires in such a way that the brand's symbolic image appears to the consumer subject as an ideal means of expression through which to represent him-/herself in a meaningful way. Advertising and consumption are vehicles for creating meaning through representation in the brand's identity. The consumer's identity is narratively constructed through the consumption of images and experiences that the brand provides as a "contract" related to genesis, origin, and authenticity (Remaury, 2004, pp. 85–86).

In particular, consumers are the ones who create their own narrative identity through a consumption experience contained within the brand's narratives, allowing them to control the projection of their own identity. Thus, it is interesting to observe how, throughout the evolution of the brand, emphasis has been redirected from the brand object to the consumer subject. If at first the product was represented in the brand, brands now project the consumer's image, as they have acquired the ability to demonstrate or represent the consumer subject, or rather the consumer subject is able to represent or project itself in the brand. In short, through new developments in signification advertising, consumers are represented in the brand by means of a product that makes them unique, while the brand does not so much represent the product as it does the consumer.

Shaping the brand through consumer activity

The current advertising industry has new devices available to it (primarily Web 2.0 tools, understood as a further materialization of what one might call "World 2.0") that permit the shaping of signification contained within the images of brands which lack any density beyond that provided by semiotic production through their embodiment in consumer activity. This is the case, for example, in campaigns that promote consumer-generated communicative content or personalization of the product consumers acquire, thus encouraging their participation in the creation of the brand's image.

All of these mechanisms, driven by Web 2.0 tools, allow the consumer not only to be a passive recipient of advertising communication, but also to contribute in a unique and meaningful way to the construction of advertising discourse. In what is clearly a growing trend, this leads to the generation of brand value via the co-creation of experiences (Prahalad & Ramaswamy, 2004). This, in turn, permits a deeper experiential adhesion to the brand through an act of consumption now expanded to other environments and activities that precede or follow the moment when the product is purchased.

As Ollé and Riu (2009) observe, nowadays branding cannot solely be based on making a sustained investment over time in order to construct an intangible differentiation in the medium term. Rather, branding should allow for consumers to contribute meaning to the brand in such a way that the market sustains a conversation (Levine et al., 2000) with the objective of engaging the consumer in one of the many opportunities (Sanders & Simons, 2009) for co-creation of brand value, be it through the co-creation of product design or through experiences.

Over time, value creation has been displaced, first from the product to the brand, and now from the brand to personalization of the consumer experience. Thus, User Generated Content (UGC) should be viewed within the context of self-made media, which is bringing about incredibly important change (Potts, Hartley, Banks, Burgess, & Cobcroft, 2008) due to the consumer's inclusion in value generation through the co-creation of value in their own consumption experience based on their emotional connection to the brand.

Moreover, one way or another, the brand seeks to be represented by and embodied in the consumer. Web 2.0 tools allow consumers to expand their projection of their own identity while playing a fundamental role in the fictional co-creation of authentic experiences as a brand value. This involves the consumer not only being a passive recipient of advertisements, but also contributing in a singular and meaningful way to the construction of the brand's image.

Thus, the consumer contributes to and participates in the construction of advertising discourse as well as the brand's image by adding meaning and value to it. It could be argued that this has led to value creation being displaced from the product to the brand and from the brand to the personalization of the consumption experience and the creation of a discourse on authenticity.

A study of three paradigmatic cases

Below, I provide an analysis of three brands (Muji, Moleskine, and Bench) in order to illustrate the mechanisms presented in the previous section. This is not intended as an exhaustive examination of the commercial or marketing policies of each of these brands, but rather as an overview of the practices that help to generally illustrate—though the nuances of each will be described below—the three shaping mechanisms.

It should be borne in mind that these three mechanisms are not isolated nor mutually exclusive but rather mutually compatible and constructed on each other. Thus, if we wished to extrapolate the analysis presented here, we would in all likelihood find brands where it is difficult to clarify each of these mechanisms as they are not, in practice, clearly outlined, nor do they always have the same influence. This is mainly due to the array of possibilities presented by Web 2.0 tools, but also the increasingly complex 360° advertising campaigns. Therefore, as evidenced by each of the three shaping mechanisms in all three of the brands analyzed here, the focus of the discussion has been trained on the most characteristic element of each mechanism, or that which distinguishes them from the others.

Muji

The Japanese brand Muji consists of a "no-brand brand" (Aaker, 2011) that masterfully combines specialization of the product with making the brand three-dimensional. This is done in such a way that its image is unequivocally represented in its products and sales displays, while associating its value with a certain lifestyle concept that allows the consumer to be the protagonist.

The wide range of Muji products, from stationery to common kitchen utensils, places emphasis on the brand's concepts such as products being recyclable, their simple casing, and minimum waste. Additionally, in place of a logo—Muji comes from the expression *Mujirushi ryohin*, meaning unbranded quality—the package design and label embody the brand image while emphasizing the product.

Muji aims to create an atmosphere of natural simplicity as a counterpoint to the fast pace of today's world. Product design is not merely packaging but also infuses the brand's values, and is aimed at providing functional products free from superfluous features. In this way, it appears as if the brand, rather than retreating and disappearing, has been dispersed within its products, becoming a formative part of them, becoming "spatialized".

The sales displays are branded areas characterized by their austerity, simplicity, and organization that seek to connect with the idea of natural simplicity through the use of unvarnished wooden furniture. The original display, which was used as a prototype for other stores, is considered to be "a perfect personification of Muji's image" (Yangjun & Jiaojiai, 2007, p. 8), and has been translated into the construction of not only pre-fabricated houses but even a Muji Village—a town with Muji houses—or Camp Muji. There are also future plans to "construct Muji hotels throughout the world" (Yangjun & Jiaojiai, 2007, p. 225).

Firstly, Muji constructs the brand's values on the idea of authenticity. In the brand's history, emphasis is placed on highlighting the company's honesty when looking to come up with new products. Muji emerged in 1980 as a unique strategic response to a market dominated by generic brand, price-driven products that did not pay attention to the consumer's perception of the brand, and additionally as an antithesis to the consumerist and brand-driven habits derived from the economic prosperity of that time. Later, in July 1991, Muji went international with the inauguration of its first store in London. Then, from 2000 onwards, the brand continued to expand its product portfolio, marketing sunglasses, stationery, clothing, shoes, beauty products, bicycles, furniture, household appliances, and even houses and summer camps, all while continuing its international expansion throughout the world.

Secondly, the brand is characterized by how it values authenticity, not only in the use of materials, but also in the connection it creates between Japanese and Western traditions, to the extent that this value not only stems from the brand's history, but is also created through its products. For example, oak is used in the Real Furniture line with the goal of manufacturing furniture that can be used for a very long time. The brand has implemented simple designs that appear to form part of the architecture of the space and have a concept that is similar to that of a traditional Japanese home, where flat surfaces can have various uses.

Furthermore, Muji connects with Western tradition and history when it produces redesigns of major design icons (which similarly implies an act of co-branding) as is the case with model nº14 of the Thonet chair, or Steel Chair, designed by Marcel Breuer, one of the most representative objects of the Bauhaus movement.

The third brand shaping strategy is accomplished in two ways: customization of the product, and communication of the brand. These would of course appear to be more of a development strategy for the future, once the brand has achieved a standardization of fundamental products that are used daily. The company has started to develop a *do it jibunde* (Do It Yourself) line that allows consumers to create their own designs of Muji's products using thread, ribbons, etc. with the goal of personalizing them.

Ultimately, Muji represents a return to the product once the brand has become virtualized to the point that it is no longer directly represented. This would perhaps represent a post-brand that is embodied in the product just as it is in the sales displays, while at the same time creating a setting where the unique and individual lifestyle of each of its consumers can take shape.

Therefore, despite Muji being a no-brand, and not directly represented in its products, the brand connects with the consumer. It has gone from representing the product to representing the consumer, to the extent that consumers participate in the brand image.

Moleskine

While the brand Moleskine has its origins in a famous notebook, as noted on its website, it can nowadays be defined as a brand that "is made of a family of nomad objects dedicated to our mobile identities: notebooks, diaries, agendas, bags, writing tools and reading accessories, dedicated to our mobile identities. Objects that follow us wherever we go and that can identify us in any part of the world". Thus, although the notebook is its star product, the company has developed a brand image that has expanded to include different products, such as writing sets, glasses, and backpacks.

Undoubtedly, Moleskine's history is, first and foremost, one of notebooks used by artists and intellectuals such as Vincent Van Gogh and Pablo Picasso, Ernest Hemingway and Bruce Chatwin. Hence it appears to be so closely tied to the consumption of cultural products, professional activities, and free time. It is aimed at a creative and professional public, to whom it provides, from a history based on the "legendary notebook", a connection to the past that is conveyed through a brand image defined by culture, travel, memory, imagination, and personality.

Nevertheless, even though it might appear that the narration of the notebook's history has a target audience made up of artists who commemorate the past through their participation in a tradition of using high-quality products, the brand is not solely aimed at professionals, although they do fall within the specialized and creative-minded audience. Moleskine products in fact embody romanticism, utility, history, functionality, transversality, identification, and movement in such a way that when Moleskine consumers buy one of the brand's products they do not acquire a "relic", a vestige from another era, but something that is useful in the present.

While the predominant shaping mechanism is related to the brand's narrativization, it also has exceptional relevance with regard to the third aforementioned mechanism, shaping the brand by means of its embodiment in consumer activity.

Thus, the brand's history is intended for consumers to construct their own identifying narratives. Moleskine does not only make a brand history available, but it uses very resourceful instruments to create stories about the consumers themselves. Moleskine presents a narrative that allows for consumers to project their own identity, giving them the opportunity to participate in the brand's values, which then form part of the construction of their own identity.

In the age of access (Rifkin, 2000), when it is not only important to have the experience, but also its posterior narrative, Moleskine provides the tools necessary to construct a narrative about ourselves, the ideal canvas for consumers to chart their experiences as memories within the context of an identity narrative. Thus, in their product portfolio we find notebooks for recording different kinds of wine or movies, as well as notes on exhibitions or other artistic gatherings that we may have attended.

Another representation of the third mechanism emerges in the use of social networks such as Facebook, blogs like moleskinerie.com, or on the Moleskine corporate website, all created with the objective of promoting consumers' participation in their virtual communities. This allows for the integration of multiple media, such as video and photography, which move beyond the confines that might exist between the real and the virtual. Given these conditions, it is as equally possible to create a digital notebook as it is to add videos to a printed notebook that has already had notes jotted down in it. Or to simply take notes or make sketches in a notebook and later digitize them using the application Evernote, which combines digital and analog inputs to allow the integration of paper and touch screen, resulting in a smart notebook.

In this way, Moleskine products help to fill the consumer's surroundings with physical content, whereby the shaping of the brand, through the use of multiple canvases and surfaces, is not so much done via the construction of physical spaces—with the exception of the displays located in multi-brand stores—but rather as a result of the customization and involvement of consumers who provide physical content for their own environment.

Consumers are not only able to customize more generic notebooks, but also to obtain specialized notebooks that can be customized for specific needs. However, it is also interesting to observe how the ability to create and customize a virtual Moleskine notebook produces a connection between the mobility and travel values of the brand, not just by way of different physical locations, but also through different media. Moleskine products are, so to speak, cross media, in the sense that they provide different platforms and possibilities: notebooks for different situations, bags, laptop covers, glasses, etc.

Moleskine is not a mere product, but a brand that has succeeded in situating its value in the experience it provides for the consumer, clearly applying the three aforementioned shaping mechanisms to its communication strategies. Thus, it is a brand that has an ever-growing product portfolio (first mechanism), was built upon a history, has its own narrative (second mechanism), and allows consumers to create identity narratives about themselves that are intimately linked to the brand and its embodiment (third mechanism) through participation and customization. This results, via consumers' projection of their own identity, in their experiential adhesion to the brand's image.

Bench

Bench, launched in Manchester in 1989, is a brand dedicated to fashion that defines itself as a "global lifestyle brand". It holds a contest called Made Yourself, which is geared towards "people who are making things happen" (meaning all kinds of cultural creators and intermediaries). The winners are given a monetary prize to fund their own project, in addition to the visibility they receive from their interviews on the corporate website and in a book-catalog called Self Made Book.

The contest has the following structure: those interested sign up using a profile created on Facebook, where it is noted that "you can win an experience money can't buy". Contestants are then asked to explain their project in 500 words or less, and a jury selects the winner.

The profile of the target audience for the contest is particularly interesting. If we analyze the texts that appear on the website and in the Self Made Book arising from the first edition of the contest, we clearly see that both publications use similar terms to express their ideas. In other words, the characteristics used to describe the profile of the ideal candidate are the same as those the website uses to define the identity of the brand, thereby demonstrating an attempt to identify the history of the brand with that of the participants. For example, according to the website the contest is aimed at:

> The people who don't wait for things to be handed to them. The people who go out there and do it themselves. This is Bench Self-Made [...] the hard-working and multitalented guys and girls with vision and ambition. The ones who aren't afraid to get their hands dirty. The ones crafting their own futures and changing the faces—and the streets—of the cities they live in.

Meanwhile, within the same text, the company identifies itself with the expression Self Made in the following way:

> A self-made success in its own right, Bench has evolved from a group of friends selling their t-shirt designs in Manchester to a global lifestyle brand. So we recognize and admire the determination and commitment needed to take on the world. Self-Made sets out to explore, document and inspire.

This is all particularly evident when we observe how the Self Made Book is divided into two parts: the presentation of the contest (Self Made) and the presentation of the brand itself (Self Made History), which turn out to be nearly identical in their content and the way they are written.

We must bear in mind, however, that the majority of the brand's consumers do not participate in the contest or generate content, which leads to two questions: first of all, what is the real reach of Web 2.0 tools? And secondly, to what extent can we say that this campaign makes a contribution that is effective and relevant to the construction of an advertising discourse and the brand image?

We find two kinds of target audiences for the campaign: those that participate by creating content later used for interviews in the *Bench Self Made Book* and on the website; and receptors, who visit the website and read or peruse the book, but remain passive. It is worth pointing out that the originality and effectiveness of the tools and strategies analyzed here lie not in the mass participation of the audience in the advertising campaign but rather in the (co)creation (through the use of Web 2.0 tools, which turn out to be ideal for this purpose) of a discussion about creating authentic experiences as a brand value.

To this end, the brand pursues the significant participation of a few consumers to generate, as if it were a point of contact, a supposed convergence between cultural intermediaries. Thus, while the brand represents itself (through the narration of its own history) with the identity traits characteristic of its cultural intermediaries (creativity and innovation) it provides support and a platform for the promotional and dissemination activities of artist and creators, even beyond the Self Made contest, through a Concept Store where a great variety of cultural events take place.

Furthermore, the sensation of authenticity does not originate only from the presentation and convergence of or similarities in life narratives, but also through brand representation and spectator identification. Thus, the photographs that show the winners of the contest carrying out everyday activities in their workshops or even in their bedrooms give an effect of recognition between supposed equals (protagonist/winner of the contest and passive spectator) as an identification of the brand's way of operating.

In other words, the visibility of the contest winners provides, in part, an embodiment of the brand and moreover generates a recognition effect. In this way, the brand, in lieu of its own physical image, is represented through the consumer's activity. Not only does this showcase the brand through the construction of narratives, but it also seeks to encourage the consumer's projection of, or empathy with, the brand image based on a call for connectivity as an element of recognition on the part of other potential consumers. We might therefore observe that the Bench Self Made campaign creates authentic experiences that are discursive in nature and lead to adhesion to the brand image by creating and sustaining a recognition effect in which even the passive public participates.

Based on this analysis of the Bench Self Made campaign, we could interpret that the brand looks to the aforementioned shaping mechanisms in order to materialize the meaning contained within the brand's image: be it through a book-catalogue, the corporate website, or the Concept Store (first mechanism), a wide range of narratives (second mechanism), or, finally, promoting consumers' projection of their own identity, which creates the image of the brand through the recognition effect on the part of other potential consumers as a result of the Self Made contest (third mechanism).

A "PULL" MEDIA ENVIRONMENT FOR NEW DEVELOPMENTS IN SIGNIFICATION ADVERTISING: CHALLENGES AND OPPORTUNITIES

The past few years have seen an evolution in signification advertising as a result of a renewed semiotic production that has focused on the creation of brands. Within this, the brand equity, which in referential advertising was attributed to the intrinsic characteristics of the brand or imaginary content created by seduction, fascination, and all kinds of predominantly emotional persuasive rhetorical resources, has moved almost exclusively to the experience the consumer's participation brings to the brand's image.

This renewed semiotic production aims to facilitate the consumer's adhesion to the brand's image. Therefore, new forms of advertising attempt to create brand spaces and stories while fostering participation through Web 2.0 tools, all of which is aimed at densifying and hiding the nature of semiotic production from the eyes of the consumer.

Using the description and posterior analyses of distinct cases that might be considered paradigms as a departure point, we have observed that today the creation of brand value is achieved, in reference to advertising, through three brand shaping mechanisms that determine the brand's renewed semiotic production. These new ways of constructing and creating brand value present enormous challenges for the traditional media, which no longer wield their unchallenged power in advertising.

Thus, with new developments in signification advertising brands are turning towards pull strategies to attract the consumer. Given this environment, the media should try to incorporate tools that create the opportunity for simulated and open dialog, where consumers contribute meaning and value to their own consumption experience and ultimately to the brand.

The media, in other words, face the challenge of determining which tools will allow them to contribute to the semiotic construction of brands. Brands that are expanding and being disseminated through a multitude of practices, and techniques aimed at creating physical spaces of interaction, while also leaving room for the narrative appropriation of the brand's image and not making consumers passive recipients but allowing them to personalize the consumption experience.

This means finding those tools which facilitate consumers' projection of their own identity in order to achieve an emotional adhesion to the brand's image, given that this is where the creation of brand value ultimately lies.

BIBLIOGRAPHY

Aaker, D. (2011). Muji: The no-brand brand. *Marketingpower*. Retrieved from http://www.marketingpower.com/ResourceLibrary/Publications/MarketingNews/2010/1_30_10/ Aaker.pdf

Bermejo, J. (2013). Nuevas estrategias retóricas en la sociedad de la neopublicidad. *Icono14*, *11*(1), 99–124.

Cappo, J. (2003). *The future of advertising: New media, new clients, new consumers in the post-television age*. Chicago, IL: McGraw-Hill.

Caro, A. (1993). *La publicidad de la significación (marco, concepto y taxonomía)*. Madrid, Spain: Servicio de Publicaciones de la Universidad Complutense de Madrid.

Caro, A. (1994). *La publicidad que vivimos*. Madrid, Spain: Celeste D.L.

Caro, A. (1998). La marca como mito. In T. Blesa (Ed.), *Mitos: Actas del VII Congreso Internacional de la Academia Española de Semiótica* (tomo I; pp. 683–689). Zaragoza, Spain: Asociación Española de Semiótica y Universidad de Zaragoza.

Caro, A. (2010). *Comprender la publicidad*. Barcelona, Spain: Universitat Ramon Llull.

Costa Solà-Segalés, J. (2007). Pospublicidad: La era de la comunicación global. *Pensar la Publicidad. Revista Internacional de Investigaciones Publicitarias*, *1*(1), 41–54.

Davenport, T. H., & Beck, J. C. (2001). *The attention economy: Understanding the new currency of business*. Boston, MA: Harvard Business School Press.

Dorrian, M., & Lucas, G. (2006). *Guerrilla advertising: Unconventional brand communication*. London, UK: Lawrence King.

Dwyer, V., Tabernero, C., & Tubella, I. (2008). *Internet y televisión: La guerra de las pantallas*. Barcelona, Spain: Ariel.

Eguizábal, R. (2007). *Teoría de la publicidad*. Madrid, Spain: Cátedra.

Fukasawa, N., Hara, K., Kanai, M., Koike, K., & Sugimoto, T. (2010). *MUJI*. New York, NY: Rizzoli.

Harkin, J. (2012). *Niche: Why the market no longer favours the mainstream*. London, UK: Abacus.

Himpe, T. (2007). *Advertising is dead: Long live advertising!* London, UK: Thames & Hudson.

Ibáñez, J. (1994). *Por una sociología de la vida cotidiana*. Madrid, Spain: Siglo XXI.

Jensen, R. (2001). *The dream society: How the coming shift from information to imagination will transform your business*. London, UK: McGraw-Hill.

Jhally, S. (2000). Advertising at the edge of the apocalypse. In R. A. Andersen & L. Strate (Eds.), *Criticical studies in media commercialism* (pp. 27–39). Oxford, UK: Oxford University Press.

Kilbourne, J. (1999). *Can't buy my love*. New York, NY: Touchstone.

Klingmann, A. (2007). *Brandscapes*. Boston, MA: MIT Press.

Levine, R., et al. (2000). *Cluetrain manifesto*. New York, NY: Basic Books.

Lindstrom, M. (2008). *Buyology: Truth and lies about why we buy*. New York, NY: Broadway Books.

Lipovetsky, G., & Serroy, J. (2007). *L'ecran global*. Paris, France: Seuil.

Medina, A. (2010). *Bye, bye, marketing: Del poder del mercado al poder del consumidor*. Madrid, Spain: Pirámide.

Nuñez, A. (2007). *¡Será mejor que lo cuentes!*. Barcelona, Spain, Empresa Activa.

Ollé, R., & Riu, D. (2009). *El nuevo brand management: Cómo plantar marcas para hacer crecer negocios*. Barcelona, Spain: Gestión 2000.

Pacheco, M. (2008). Street marketing: El espectáculo está en la calle. In M. Pacheco (Coord.), *La publicidad en el contexto digital: Nuevos retos, nuevas oportunidades* (pp. 145–160). Sevilla, Spain: Comunicación Social.

Pine, B. J., & Gilmore, J. H. (1999). *The experience economy: Work is theatre and every business a stage*. Boston, MA: Harvard Business School Press.

Potts, J., Hartley, J., Banks, J., Burgess, J., & Cobcroft, R. (2008). Consumer co-creation and situated creativity. *Industry and Innovation, 15*(5), 459–474. Retrieved from http://eprints.qut.edu.au/18073/1/c18073.pdf

Prahalad, C. K., & Ramaswamy, V. (2004). Co-creation experiences: The next practice in value creation. *Journal of Interactive Marketing, 18*(3), 5–14.

Remaury, B. (2004). *Marques et récits: La marque face à l'imaginaire culturel contemporain*. Paris, France : Editions du Regard.

Renvoisé, P., & Morin, C. (2007). *Neuromarketing: Understanding the "buy button" in your customer's brain*. Nashville, TN: Thomas Nelson.

Ries, A., & Ries, L. (2002). *The fall of advertising and the rise of PR*. New York, NY: HarperCollins.

Rifkin, J. (2000). *The age of access: The new culture of hypercapitalism, where all of life is a paid-for experience*. New York, NY: Tarcher/Putnam.

Salmon, C. (2007). *Storytelling: La machine à fabriquer des histoires et à formater les esprits*. Paris, France: La Découverte.

Sanders, L., & Simons, G. (2009). A social vision for value co-creation in design. *Open Source Business Resource*. Retrieved from http://timreview.ca/article/310

Schmitt, B. H. (1999). *Experiential marketing: How to get customers to SENSE, FEEL, THINK, ACT and RELATE to your company and brands*. New York, NY: Free Press.

Schmitt, B. H., Rogers, D. L., & Vrotsos, K. (2004). *There's no business that's not show business: Marketing in an experience culture*. Upper Saddle River, NJ: Financial Times Prentice Hall.

Solana, D. (2010). *Postpublicidad: Reflexiones sobre una nueva cultura publicitaria en la era digital*. Barcelona, Spain: Índice Arts Gràfiques.

Vidal, F. (2011). La producción semiótica ante la significatización de la economía (O ¿cómo lograr una publicidad efectiva en la era del capitalismo virtual?). *Pensar la Publicidad. Revista Internacional de Investigaciones Publicitarias, 5*(1), 75–97.

Vidal, F. (2012). La inflación de lo emocional en la actividad publicitaria: ¿Constituye un cambio de paradigma? *Pensar la Publicidad. Revista Internacional de Investigaciones Publicitarias, 6*(2), 173–197.

Vincent, L. (2002). *Legendary brands: Unleashing the power of storytelling to create a winning market strategy*. Chicago, IL: Dearborn Trade.

Yangjun, P., & Jiaojiai, C. (2007). *MUJI*. Barcelona, Spain: Maomao.

ZenithOptimedia. (2010). *Steady recovery in global ad expenditure to continue for at least three years.* Retrieved from http://www.optimedia.de/fileadmin/pdf/presse/2010-12-06-AEF_ENGLISH.pdf

ZenithOptimedia. (2013). *Resumen ejecutivo: Previsiones de la inversión publicitaria—Diciembre 2013.* Retrieved from http://www.slideshare.net/ZenithES/resumen-ejecutivo-previsiones-de-inversin-publicitaria-zo-diciembre-2013

Zyman, S. (2002). *The end of advertising as you know it.* New York, NY: Wiley.

CHAPTER EIGHT

Engagement Is the Name of the Game: *Gamification* as a Communication Strategy in Advertising and Public Relations

ELISENDA ESTANYOL, MIREIA MONTAÑA, AND FERRAN LALUEZA

INTRODUCTION

The research undertaken aims to determine how gamification is being applied in advertising and public relations through the study of recent campaigns. Gamification is an emerging concept in the field of the academic disciplines that concern us. Indeed, this term—understood as "the use of game design elements in non-game contexts" (Deterding, Dixon, Khaled, & Nacke, 2011)—was coined as recently as 2008.

The methodology we used in our analysis is based on case studies of advertising and PR campaigns conducted between 2009 and 2013 (Nike, McDonald's, Axe, Adidas, Volkswagen and Marriott). A data matrix was constructed in order to pinpoint the following categories and items in the campaigns in the sample: *game mechanics*, *game dynamics*, *target audience*, *medium*, *degree of virality* and *level of engagement*. The analysis of various communication campaigns with gamification components was complemented by in-depth interviews with the marketing and communication directors of some of these companies, specifically, the director of advertising of Volkswagen Spain and the marketing manager of Axe Spain.

To provide a framework for the case studies, data from the World Internet Project (WIP) Spain 2013 study on use and evaluation of Internet and video games were analysed. This study is based on 1,600 interviews conducted on the telephone with individuals aged 16 and older, resident in Spanish homes with landlines. The fieldwork was carried out between the 2nd and the 20th of December 2013.

The results show that a characteristic feature of the campaigns analysed is the search for engagement with the targets. The campaigns often use an outdoor medium or digital environments. Through these strategies, brands and organizations are able to differentiate themselves from competitors, foster the interactive participation of the target and extend their reach thanks to social networks. The study concludes that the application of gamification in advertising and PR offers the opportunity to establish new links with stakeholders, who are invited to take part in a creative game and fun-focused experience.

Gamification is attracting growing interest in different spheres of society beyond the video games industry. Indeed, according to a number of studies, thanks to the spread of mobile technology, gamification will become a significant trend in the next few years (BBVA, 2012; Deloitte, 2012). It is estimated that in 2015 more than 50% of organizations that manage innovation processes will gamify these processes (Gartner, 2011).

On a marketing level, there is evidence that gamification helps companies increase user participation, loyalty and brand recognition, as well as aiding in the training of employees (Meloni & Gruener, 2012). In advertising and PR, it is essential to establish links between brands, organizations and targets in order to reinforce loyalty. Therefore, it is not surprising that the sector is already applying gamification techniques. This research focuses on the study of some of the campaigns that reflect this trend.

THEORETICAL FRAMEWORK

Key concepts

Academic disciplines such as education, psychology, economics and technology have paid the most attention to gamification. These disciplines served as a basis for the close examination we have made of some of the key concepts of gamification.

Gamification

The term "gamification" was coined as recently as 2008 and it did not become generally used until 2010 (Paharia, 2010). So gamification is an emerging concept, and consequently its definition is subject to different interpretations. Even so, there is a certain consensus that it refers to "the use of game design elements in non-game contexts" (Deterding et al., 2011).

Huotari and Hamari (2012) emphasize that one of the objectives of gamification is to make these non-game contexts more fun and engaging. The Deloitte study (2012) stresses that the purpose of gamification is to exploit the essence of games: fun, participation and passion. Kapp (2012) defines gamification as an attitude, a learning strategy and a movement; an all-in-one, whose ultimate objective is the creation of positive results, while users feel motivated and committed.

Play

The American psychologist Bruner (1984) defines play as "a way of using mind, or better yet, an attitude toward the use of mind. It is a test frame, a hot house for trying out ways of combining thought and language." The Dutch historian Huizinga (1938) also proposes a definition of play as "a free action subject to rules." For his part, Caillois (1958/1986) states that play must have the following characteristics: it must be *free* (a game one is forced to play ceases to be play), *separate* (play is established within the limits of time and space), *uncertain* (the end of play is not established), *unproductive* (it does not generate goods or wealth), *governed by rules* (rules are established which have to be abided by), and finally, *make-believe* (a parallel reality is established in which play develops).

According to McGonigal (2011), all games have four defining traits: a goal, rules, a feedback system and voluntary participation. Gamification is structured on game mechanics and dynamics. According to Kapp (2012), *game mechanics* are the different actions, behaviours, techniques and control mechanisms that are used to turn an activity into a game. These mechanics create an attractive experience that is easy for the player to become involved in. The mechanics include: points, levels, prizes, virtual goods, classifications, challenges, missions and gifts.

For their part, *game dynamics* are the effect, motivation and desires pursued by users, which are based in turn on a human being's fundamental needs (see Maslow, 1943; Reiss, 2004): reward, status, achievements, expression or self-expression, competition and altruism.

Flow

In the view of McGonigal (2011), understanding flow is essential to generate motivation and to understand how games function. Flow was defined by Csikszentmihalyi (1996) as "a state of spontaneous pleasure in which the person is fully involved in a task thanks to profound motivation." A state in which the individual is at the perfect level of their skills: neither under-challenged (boredom) nor over-challenged (anxiety and frustration).

Intrinsic motivation

Linked to the concept of flow, we find what cognitive psychology has defined as *extrinsic motivation* and *intrinsic motivation*. Whereas the former is determined by the environment and is a motivation directed toward meeting an external goal such as recognition or reward, *intrinsic motivation* leads the individual to perform an activity for its own sake, because it is interesting and satisfying in itself (Amabile, 1997). In gamification activities, these two motivations play a very important role, although intrinsic motivation is essential to securing the engagement of the participant.

Engagement

Engagement refers to an involvement, a link, a relationship of commitment. May, Gilson, & Harter (2004) drew a distinction between three levels of engagement: cognitive, emotional and physical. In turn, in the world of video games, three types of engagement are identified: *direct engagement* (when users interact with the product, service or process), *individual engagement* (when the user autonomously explores the environment), and *communal engagement* (when links, dialogues and interactions are established among the community taking part in the game) (Meloni & Gruener, 2012).

GAMIFICATION IN ADVERTISING AND PR

Although some work can be found on gamification in marketing (see, for example, Hamari & Lehdonvirta, 2010; Huotari & Hamari, 2012), the attention paid to this subject area by scientific literature specializing in advertising and PR remains scant. Contributions on how gamification can be applied in communication campaigns and actions come mainly from the professional world (articles published on the websites of professional associations, in sector-based publications and on the corporate blogs of the agencies and consultants themselves).

Gamification in advertising

The beginnings of the use of games in advertising can be found in what Oliver Pérez (2012) calls *participative narrative*, open advertising stories, full of questions, intrigue and ambiguities, which require the participative involvement of the viewer (commercials such as *Amnesia* for Volkswagen Golf).

According to *AdExchanger*,[1] gamification creates new advertising opportunities, thanks to a number of benefits: it increases the level of user-consumer commitment, creates stronger emotional connections with him/her and achieves higher virality.

At the same time, gamification provides data about new consumers which is of great value to brands: more nuanced information about their motivations, levels of commitment and response times. As a result, an involvement is created in each stage of the customer's life cycle: *acquisition* (fostering the exchange of content and recommendations, which increases the social component), *commitment* (enabling greater levels of interaction thanks to challenges and rewards) and *retention* (creating a more frequent dialogue that helps to retain communities and increase their commitment).

We also find other concepts related to gamification, such as advergaming (games expressly created by a brand, to which access is gained via the website of the brand or its Facebook and Twitter profiles) and in-game advertising (advertisements inserted into video games).

Gamification in PR

According to Zuk (2012), through gamification expectation is created, messages can be transmitted and the results of PR actions can be evaluated. Along these same lines, the WPP website[2] and the PR Newswire[3] and Lewis PR[4] blogs claim that gamification helps to increase the level of involvement between audiences and organizations, a type of relationship resembling that described by Kent and Taylor (2002) as dialogic engagement.

For his part, Kay (2012) emphasizes the importance of studying the target audiences of organizations, and in gamification he sees an opportunity to gain greater insight into their different personalities, preferences and attitudes. According to Holtz Communication,[5] the use of games in corporate communication initiatives proves extremely positive, and companies feel encouraged to create games linked with PR actions that offer the opportunity for virality through social networks, highlighting the importance of endorsement.

Beyond marketing communication, gamification can be incorporated into various PR techniques (See Knightly & McKie, 2012). In this respect, Lager (in Kay, 2012) proposes gamifying the training of spokespeople with role-playing exercises, while Choe, Jang, and Song (2011) advocate gamifying corporate events. Moreover, initiatives such as Toobeez[6] and Lego Serious Play[7] are being successfully applied in teambuilding and internal communication activities.

METHODOLOGY

The methodology used is based on case studies, a technique by means of which units can be analysed in depth and holistically, on account of their interest and intrinsic value (Stake, 2005). In the study, in this case of gamified communication campaigns, the characteristics of gamification defined in the theoretical framework are illustrated with examples, and it can be seen how these have been adapted for the purposes of advertising and PR. Thanks to this methodology, it is possible to observe the similarities and differences between the various cases (Daymon & Holloway, 2010), and an in-depth analysis can be made of the problem to be investigated (Hernández Sampieri et al., 2010).

The study sample is based on campaigns conducted between 2009 and 2013 by Nike, McDonald's, Axe, Adidas, Volkswagen and Marriott. A data matrix was constructed in order to pinpoint the following categories and items in these campaigns: *game mechanics* (points, levels, prizes, virtual goods, classifications, challenges, gifts), *game dynamics* (desire for reward, status, achievement, expression, competition, altruism), *target audience*, *medium*, *degree of virality* and *level of engagement*. The starting point for determining these variables has been the games mechanics and dynamics identified by Kapp (2012), whose theoretical contribution has been considered a benchmark with respect to gamification indicators.

Documentary analysis has been completed with in-depth interviews with the director of advertising of Volkswagen Spain, Pedro Soldevilla (conducted on 21 October 2013), and the marketing manager of Axe, Sara Molina (conducted on 15 April 2014).

As a framework for the case studies, data from the World Internet Project (WIP) Spain 2013 study on use and evaluation of Internet and video games were analysed. These data were drawn from 1,600 digital interviews with individuals aged 16 and older, resident in Spanish homes with landlines. The fieldwork was carried out between the 2nd and the 20th of December 2013.

The WIP is an international project (World Internet Project International network) led in Spain by the Internet Interdisciplinary Institute (IN3) Communication and New Media research group, and its purpose is to study the social, political and economic impact of the Internet and other digital technologies such as video games and mobile telephones. The WIP works with data from its own survey conducted every two years among the population of Spain.

RESULTS

The target

The report containing the results of the WIP Spain 2013 study provides us with relevant data on the use, knowledge and evaluation of Internet and video games in Spain. From the responses obtained, the data have been filtered to focus on the target audience for the gamification actions analysed, young people aged from

16 to 25, and then by sex. We should remember that, for example, both Volkswagen and Axe target a male audience.

The main conclusions obtained are that young people like using the Internet to look for material that is funny and entertaining. This applies to 47% of boys, decreasing to 23% in the case of girls. Thirty-one per cent of boys, compared with 12% of girls, report using the Internet as a platform for playing video games. Another significant data item is that 41% of young males say they play video games on a regular basis, compared with 18% of girls and 12% of the population.

What most interests these young men is that video games offer the opportunity for collaboration. This applies to 69% of boys, compared with 48% of girls. Competition is also valued highly by boys, 61% of whom state that they like this, whereas this figure drops to 19% for girls. Another characteristic to be taken into account when designing games for this target is that 80% of boys and 63% of girls prefer video games that are played in the company of others.

When asked about the device they most like to play with, 78% of boys and 44% of girls say they prefer to play from a fixed device at home.

Although 75% of boys and 76% of girls believe that video games are addictive, they assert that these games help them to release stress (56% of boys and 44% of girls).

CASE STUDIES

Volkswagen

According to the director of advertising in Spain, Volkswagen's investment in gamification as part of its communication strategy is representative of the brand's tendency to run campaigns "in quite a different way from our competitors" and with a strong commitment to innovation. In this respect, this executive stresses that actions with gamification components must be suited to a specific product and target, in the case of Volkswagen, car models aimed more at young people, and that these initiatives cannot just be applied on a massive scale to any product. He observes: "We try to surprise people three or four times a year with this type of content," adding that they will continue to invest in these types of actions because they are satisfied with the results, having noted that "people like it when you do things differently."

For the Volkswagen brand, the changes that have taken place in the field of communication and advertising media have obliged them to change their strategies, above all when the aim is to reach young people: "Up until recently, brands launched content that was one-way, [...] you would say: this car, this price. Now, however, the most important thing is to generate a conversation with the people who are the targets of your message."

The Fun Theory[8]

The Fun Theory was an idea developed by Volkswagen, which organized an online competition in search of ideas to demonstrate that, by introducing elements of fun, some activities can become more effective. Subsequently, some of these ideas were put into practice:

- ***Speed camera lottery:*** this initiative, which was supported by the Swedish National Road Safety Organization, took place in Stockholm in November 2010. Drivers who respected the speed limit were automatically entered into a lottery. As a result, drivers' speeds dropped by 20%.
- ***Piano stairs:*** in September 2009, with the aim of increasing the number of people who use the stairs rather than the escalator in the underground, the stairs were turned into the notes on a giant piano, which sounded when users stepped on them. As a result, the number of people who took the stairs increased by 66%.
- ***Have fun recycling:*** through a project christened *Global Bank Arcade*, in October 2009 a recycling container was turned into a gaming machine, which gave a prize to everyone who correctly separated cardboard and plastic packaging.

With respect to these actions, Burke (2013), an analyst at Gartner, is of the opinion that they became successful cases of applied gamification, precisely because they manage to strike a chord with the interests of the public, while their design gives centre stage to the player rather than the brand. Created by DDB Stockholm, these actions actually fall within the category of what in PR is defined as Corporate Social Responsibility (CSR). Furthermore, they gained considerable media coverage, so media relations skills were also successfully applied. For example, Volkswagen's initiative was covered by national media, but also many international media, including BBC television from Britain and ABC from the US. Additionally, in terms of impact achieved, the actions went viral, with 20 million visits on YouTube. To top it off, Volkswagen eventually won a Cannes Cyber Grand Prix for a Digitally Led Integrated Campaign.

The # Polowers[9]

This action was developed in Spain in May 2012 to present the new Volkswagen Polo. The campaign was aimed at a very specific target: digital natives. A competition was created via Twitter, along with a microsite. Internauts competed by sending tweets with the hashtag *#polowers*, and the more messages they sent, the further their virtual car moved forward on the microsite, with the incentive that the winner would receive a Polo. The campaign reached 10% of Twitter users in Spain. This initiative was rounded off with branded content on the television programme *El Hormiguero* on Antena 3, but according to Pedro Fondevilla, head of advertising for Volkswagen Spain, in this case television airtime is not what is pursued most, for it makes the campaign a little less credible, given that "I can be on there today, but then tomorrow it will be somebody else." Fondevilla said that the main campaign was conducted on Twitter, because as a medium it is a little younger than Facebook: "The truth is, the profile we're looking for, a young person of 18, spends more time on Twitter than on Facebook" and this campaign was designed for a young target. Fondevilla continued: "Given that 50% of young people in Spain are unemployed, let's make things a little easier for them. Let's make an ad that's fun and give them a good time, but also offer them something different that they can play with, be entertained by and finally give them the chance of winning a car. In the end, it's a little bit about hitting on what they want."

Ecuación Polo[10]

For its part, *Ecuación Polo* (Polo Equation) was another Twitter-based action developed by Volkswagen in Spain in October 2013, in which a mathematical problem had to be solved in order to win a Polo. The problem was worded as follows: *In Finisterre, literally meaning 'the end of the earth', in Galicia, we find Aranga. He is an Anglo-Arabian horse, 8 years of age and weighing in at 400 kilos. His fuel? 7 or 8 kilos of forage and 2 kilos of cereals a day. Aranga has taken part in several races, coming second in the 90 km race. Although you need to bear one thing in mind: he needs to take a 30-minute rest after each 25–30 kilometres he runs. On the other side of Spain, in Cap de Creus, Catalonia, we have a brand new Volkswagen Polo with the key in the ignition. The equation is simple. At what point will they meet? If you are able to indicate where, as exactly as possible, you will take away the Polo as a prize. Sorry, the horse already has an owner.* To take part, users had to register online. The presentation of the problem was accompanied by an explanatory video. (http://www.youtube.com/watch?v=0ry0nfHRfDU). According to data announced by Volkswagen, this campaign yielded 270,000 tweets. Communication was complemented by guerrilla marketing action at several universities, where Post-its were put up and messages were left on blackboards encouraging students to take part in the competition. According to the brand managers, there are three keys to the success of these campaigns: (1) speak the same language as the digital natives and do so in a digital setting that they are familiar with and feel comfortable in, creating an online experience that, rather than focusing on getting a prize, is fun in itself; (2) integrate the communication channels (graphics, advertisements on Twitter, outdoor, banners and branded content on television programmes) to create expectation; and (3) go for multi-platform communication, understanding that the target of these actions connects to Twitter via smartphones and tablets, as well as from a computer.

In the preparation of this campaign, Volkswagen asked various agencies to tender, eventually choosing Carrots. Fondevilla said: "Sometimes the smaller agencies help you to make the creativity just a little fresher, above all with the online and social media side of things." He confirmed that, especially for the Polo brand, they are committed to creating games. According to his data, the *Ecuación Polo* campaign was a resounding success, since as a result Volkswagen became an organic trending topic for the first time in Spain.

In short, at Volkswagen they are extremely satisfied with campaigns like this one, since "they can reach a potential client that watches less and less television. To boost their interest in our brand, what we do is give them content. And gamification forms part of this content: games that we create in which we lay down a challenge and they have to compete. In the end, this gives us good results." Despite the fact that gamification is very productive for Volkswagen, it should be noted that in 2013 it was only assigned 300,000 euros, representing just 9.5% of the overall advertising budget.

In summary, in the case of the two gamification actions carried out recently by Volkswagen Spain, and as the director of advertising seeks to stress, they were focused on the Polo model. This was because the Polo is aimed more than any other of the company's vehicles at a young target group. In this respect, Fondevilla emphasizes that the actions developed are indeed very closely linked with social networks and the online environment, since

> through online media you can capture a type of client that you don't get with other [more traditional] media. And in our case, using actions [...] with which we have been able to reach a young target. In the end, we move to the tune of our audience. If our audience is an online consumer, then we will invest more in online, which is the only medium not on the decline. What we do is reduce investment in offline and shift it to online. We run a lot of campaigns on social media, on Facebook and Twitter. People want you to do different things. Gaming is a very broad field, but in the end it is all about user participation.

McDonald's

McDonald's interactive billboard[11]

In London, McDonald's set up some giant screens with which passers-by could interact and win free products at McDonald's restaurants. Participants just had to use their camera or smartphone to capture the image of one of the products (an ice cream, a cake...) which appeared on the giant screen, camouflaged among images of other objects. All the images were moving to make the game more complicated. Once the image of the product wanted had been captured, clients simply had to show the screen with the snapshot at the nearest McDonald's restaurant.

McDonald's Pick 'n' Play[12]

This time, giant screens were erected in Stockholm. Passers-by could play ping-pong with their smartphone and watch the game on the giant screen. The only requirement was that players should register beforehand on the *Pick 'n' Play* microsite.

Adidas

Adidas myCoach[13]

A campaign run in 2013 in which users could download an app to their smartphone (*myCoach Running* and *myCoach Football*). The app has a coach who not only trains the user, but also his/her virtual avatar. The sporting efforts made by the user are transferred to his/her avatar, with which the user can play online, competing with the avatars of other users. At the same time, training results can be shared and compared with those of friends, and they appear in a world ranking. Users can also train at home, playing the game with Xbox Kinect. During training there are different levels and programmes (speed, endurance, strength and so on).

Nike

Nike+[14]

In 2010, Nike developed an application called *Nike+*, which allowed runners to monitor their races and their results. In addition to following the steps suggested, burning calories, and calculating distance and duration, users could compare their efforts with those of friends, creating a community, and keep up their motivation with virtual competitions, trophies, medals and congratulations with sports icons.

Axe/Lynx

Even angels will fall[15]

Based on their ad, which won a Grand Prix at the 2012 Cannes Festival, Axe (Unilever) ran a global campaign with local actions. In the Netherlands, angels literally fell from the sky and gathered in a mansion. By using all kinds of social media, users could gain access to the mansion villa, and through gamification they competed to win an actual visit.

As part of the same global campaign, Axe (Lynx in the United Kingdom) staged an outdoor action in London's Victoria Station based on augmented reality. Travellers were invited to interact with 'virtual angels' who landed next to them while they were waiting at the station, and they could see the result on a giant screen.

Axe Apollo Space Academy (AASA)[16]

In 2013, Axe launched a worldwide competition aimed at a male target audience. The international team wanted Axe to go where only a few and the very best have gone: space. Axe was going to give young people the opportunity to have a unique life experience: a trip into space. For this purpose, Axe created the Axe Apollo Space Academy (AASA) together with one of the first men to set foot on the Moon: Buzz Aldrin. In 2015, this academy would give 22 young people the opportunity to travel into space with the Space Expedition Corporation (SXC) space agency. In the most ambitious launch of its 30-year history, Axe reached young men and women in 60 countries, in 45 different languages, encouraging them to create their astronaut profile at www.axeapollo.com and tell the world why they deserved to travel into space. The most voted candidates faced the challenge of various tests in their own countries, and the best of them won a place at the Axe Global Space Camp in Orlando (Florida). There, having completed a number of space simulation tests, the 22 candidates were chosen who would travel into space. This campaign was designed bearing in mind that Axe's target audience is young lower- or middle-class individuals aged 17–25, who are still studying or beginning their professional careers, who like going out at night with seduction in mind, and who are up-to-date with the latest trends in music, games, sport and urban culture.

As the director of marketing of Axe Spain explains, "We had to look at how we were going to activate the launch at a local level: define the mechanics or activation process to be followed in order to find the most suitable candidate to travel into space, define how we would generate noise about this activation and generate engagement with the consumer [...] First of all, we understood how a cool brand connects with consumers. We learnt that the consumers who connect with cool brands are those for whom brands transcend the point of sale, giving them and their friends experiences and fun by means of digital platforms and alternative media."

In Spain, participants were recruited through a genuine brand experience, "by means of a space simulator that we took to universities and points of sale" backed up by the advertising campaign on television. Different classification stages were organized, first in Madrid and later in Ibiza, where the Axe Space Jump event was held. At this last stage of the nationwide competition, two participants were selected who would travel to the AASA in Florida for the final stage of the competition. There, specific tests for astronauts (high performance flight, zero gravity and G force) awaited them, before a decision was made on who would travel into space in 2015.

In terms of results, Axe announced that 17,000 young men took part. Internationally, 1,000,000 people participated. According to the director of marketing in Spain, the introduction of gamification strategies into the communication campaigns of the Axe brand is very positive, since this is "a phenomenon that is enjoying a boom [...]; what the brands are looking for is to interact with consumers to gain a higher degree of loyalty, given how competitive the market is. This aspect is an important one with a view to successfully creating *love brands*, brands with which consumers strongly identify."

Marriott

My Marriott Hotel Facebook Game[17]

A game launched on Facebook with the aim of recruiting new employees, with a similar format to Farmville and The Sims. Users try out different professional positions at the hotel, and as they win points, they are promoted.

Comparative Analysis of the Campaigns Analysed

Analysis of the campaigns shows that game mechanics and dynamics have been applied in all of them (see Table 8.1). In some cases, the reward available is a gift linked with the product (desserts and coffees at McDonald's or a Volkswagen Polo in the case of *Polowers* and *Ecuación Polo*) or it may be an exclusive experience (*Axe Apollo Space Academy*). In other campaigns, the challenges and competitions themselves attract users despite there being no material prizes. In this respect, they appeal to the intrinsic motivation of the user, encouraging them to better their own performance (*Nike+*, *Adidas myCoach*).

It can be seen that the higher the level of engagement, the higher the degree of virality. Furthermore, in those cases in which the target is more clearly defined, a community is successfully created. Examples here would be *Adidas myCoach* and *Nike+*, which offer runners the opportunity to make contact with other sportsmen and women to compare their personal records and improve their training.

With respect to the media employed, it is very common to find outdoor media with integrated technology (augmented reality, giant digital screens, etc.) and applications for smartphones, microsites and games on Facebook and

Twitter (Marriott, Volkswagen Polo). Actions based on events are usually reinforced with traditional advertising (Axe), leading to integrated communication campaigns.

The component of fun, characteristic of gamification, is very clearly observed in actions such as *The Fun Theory*, which have a strong element of surprise and make boring activities attractive and exciting. The cases of Axe and McDonald's also include touches of humour. This element attracts passers-by, encourages participation, and at the same time promotes virality, since participants want to share their experience on social networks.

The following table describes the game mechanics and dynamics analysed.

Table 8.1. Game Mechanics and Dynamics Applied in the Campaigns Analysed.

	Game mechanics	*Game dynamics*	*Target audience*	*Medium*	*Degree of virality*	*Level of engagement*
Nike +	Levels, classifications, challenges and competitions	Reward, status, self-expression and competition	Runners	Microsite+iPod/smartphone+special sports equipment	High	High
McDonald's	Challenge of skill and gifts	Reward and achievement	Passers-by with a camera or smartphone	Digital billboard in outdoor setting	Low	Low
Axe	Points, levels, classifications, challenges, competitions and gifts	Status, achievements, self-expression and competition	Young men	Microsite + augmented reality event	High	High
Adidas myCoach	Levels, classifications, challenges	Reward, status, self-expression and competition	Runners and footballers	Website+iPod/smartphone+special sports equipment	High	High

	Game mechanics	*Game dynamics*	*Target audience*	*Medium*	*Degree of virality*	*Level of engagement*
Volkswagen (*The Fun Theory*)	Challenges	Achievements, expression, altruism	Passers-by	Electronic game in outdoor setting (stairs, cardboard recycling container, digital billboard)	Low	Low
Volkswagen (*Polowers*)	Gift	Reward, competition	Digital natives	Game on Twitter linked to microsite	High	High
Volkswagen (*Ecuación Polo*)	Gift	Reward, competition	Digital natives	Microsite	High	High
Marriott	Levels, challenges, mission	Reward, status, achievement, self-expression	Candidates for jobs	Game on Facebook, closer to advergaming	High	High

Source: Compiled by authors.

CONCLUSIONS

Against a background in which investment in traditional advertising has decreased, it is increasingly common for brands and organizations to look for new ways in which to connect with consumers and other key audiences (employees, associations, etc.). These audiences are becoming ever more hyper-connected and hyper-segmented, and now they are joined by digital natives.

Thanks to digital technology and smartphones and tablets with a permanent Internet connection and geolocation services, communication campaigns can be personalized according to the time and place where the target audience is to be found. At the same time, ease of access to social networks means that advertising and PR campaigns can be created that target a user who is no longer passive, but takes part in the communication process. This makes it possible for a dialogue to be established with consumers, for them to live an experience and for a community to be created. Video games, now accessible from mobile devices, are a tool that some brands are beginning to use to communicate with a young target. In this respect, it is interesting to note that, according to the WIP Spain 2013 report, 41% of young men play video games on a regular basis (well above the figure of 18% for young women). Brands such as Volkswagen Polo and Axe are aware of this when they come to design gamification actions aimed at this target.

For brands like Volkswagen, Nike, Axe, Adidas, McDonald's and Marriott, gamification has become a new way of contacting key audiences in a setting in which a lack of effectiveness is beginning to be detected in traditional advertising. Through communication campaigns that apply game mechanics and dynamics, these brands have succeeded in increasing expectation when launching new products, as well as generating virality and the active participation of key target audiences (young digital natives). With respect to the planning of gamification actions, data from the WIP 2013 report suggest that these may be useful for brands that wish to target the 16–25 age bracket: young people prefer games that involve collaboration, competition (more popular with boys than girls) and playing in the company of others.

In short, gamification opens up a new opportunity to create new links between consumers and brands and, more generally, between organizations and stakeholders. In gamified campaigns such as those studied here, in which the line between advertising and PR becomes blurred, the aim is to surprise, entertain, encourage the active participation of users, increase engagement, promote virality and boost brand notoriety.

It remains to be seen whether in the future these actions will also form part of campaigns for other types of product aimed at broader target audiences, and whether a way will be found to create attractive games for targets that are considerably less familiar with video games. What does appear to be certain is that, as the marketing and communication executives observe, any action that applies gamification in its strategy needs to offer the user a meaningful experience if it is to be successful.

ACKNOWLEDGMENTS

The research presented in this chapter is part of the project Ludoliteracy (Ludic Culture, Digital Literacy and Learning) CS02014–57302-P funded by the Spanish Government (Ministerio de Economía y Competitividad).

BIBLIOGRAPHY

BBVA. (2012). *Gamificación: El negocio de la diversión*. Innovation Edge, 3. Bilbao, Spain: Fundación BBVA.

Bruner, J. (1984). *Acción, pensamiento y lenguaje*. Madrid, Spain: Alianza Editorial.

Burke, B. (2013, June). *When we align the player, goals and the company, we all win.* Paper presented at the Gamification World Congress 2013, Madrid, Spain. Retrieved from http://www.gamificationworldcongress.com/2013/05/08/brian-burke-when-we-align-the-player-goals-and-the-company-we-all-win

Caillois, R. (1986). *Los juegos y los hombres: La máscara y el vértigo.* Mexico, DF: FCE.

Choe, S. P., Jang, H., & Song, J. (2011, May). *Roleplaying gamification to encourage social interactions at parties.* Paper presented at CHI 2011, Vancouver, Canada.

Cole, A. (2012). *Gamification is good: How winning is changing the Web.* Retrieved from http://www.adexchanger.com/ad-agents/gamification

Csikszentmihalyi, M. (1991). *Flow: The psychology of optimal experience.* San Francisco, CA: Harper Perennial.

Daymon, C., & Holloway, I. (2010). *Qualitative research methods in public relations and marketing communications.* New York, NY: Routledge.

Deloitte. (2012). *Tech trends 2012: Elevate IT for digital business.* Retrieved from http://www.deloitte.com/assets/DcomUnitedStates/Local/Assets/Documents/us_cons_techtrends2012_013112.pdf

Deterding, S., Dixon, D., Khaled, R., & Nacke, L. (2011). From game design elements to gamefulness: Defining "gamification." MindTrek '11. In *Proceedings of the 15th International Academic MindTrek Conference: Envisioning Future Media Environments* (pp. 9–15). New York, NY: ACM.

Duch, J., & Tejedor, H. (2011). *Introducción a los videojuegos.* Barcelona, Spain: Editorial UOC.

Estanyol, E., Montaña, M., & Lalueza, F. (2013). Comunicar jugando: Gamification en publicidad y relaciones públicas. In K. Zilles, J. Cuenca, & J. Rom (Eds.), *Breaking the media value chain.* VII International Conference on Communication and Reality (pp. 109–117). Barcelona, Spain: Blanquerna School of Communication, Ramon Llull University.

Estanyol, E., Montaña, M., & Lalueza, F. (2014, January). *La gamification como apuesta comunicativa: El caso Volkswagen.* Presented at the IV International Congress of the Spanish Association of Communication Research (AE-IC), Bilbao, Spain.

Eysenck, M. W. (1982). *Attention and arousal: Cognition and performance.* New York, NY: Springer-Verlag.

Game Marketing. (2012). *Estudio 2012. Gamificación. Expectactivas y grado de adopción en España.* Retrieved from http://www.gamkt.com

Gartner. (2011). *Gartner gamification report 2011.* Retrieved from http://www.gamification.org/wiki/Gartner_Gamification_Report_2011

Hamari, J., & Lehdonvirta, V. (2010). Game design as marketing: How game mechanics create demand for virtual goods. *International Journal of Business Science & Applied Management, 5*(1), 14–29.

Hernández, R., Fernández, C., & Baptista, P. (2007). *Fundamentos de metodología de la investigación.* Madrid, Spain: McGraw-Hill.

Huizinga, J. (1938). *Homo ludens.* Madrid, Spain: Alianza Editorial.

Huotari, K., & Hamari, J. (2012). Defining gamification: A service marketing perspective. MindTrek '12. In *Proceedings of the 16th International Academic MindTrek Conference* (pp. 17–22). New York, NY: ACM.

Kapp, K. (2012). *The gamification of learning and instruction.* San Francisco, CA: Pfeiffer.

Kay, J. (2012, February 24). Block out the hype and rethink gamification. *BrandRepublic.* Retrieved from http://www.brandrepublic.com/research/1117125/block-hype-rethink-gamification

Kent, M., & Taylor, M. (2002). Toward a dialogic theory of public relations. *Public Relations Review, 28*(1), 21–37.

Knightly, S., & McKie, D. (2012, July). *Gaming for greater engagement and PR.* Paper presented at BCN Meeting Com 2012, Barcelona, Spain.

Maslow, A. H. (1943). A theory of human motivation. *Psychological Review, 50*(4), 370–396.

May, D. R., Gilson, R. L., & Harter, L. M. (2004). The psychological conditions of meaningfulness, safety and availability and the engagement of the human spirit at work. *Journal of Occupational and Organizational Psychology, 77*(1), 11–37.

McGonigal, J. (2011). *Reality is broken: Why games make us better and how they can change the world.* London, England: Penguin Press.

Meloni, W., & Gruener, W. (2012). *Gamification in 2012: Market update on consumer and enterprise trends. Technical report.* Encinitas, CA: M2 Research.

Paharia, R. (2010, December). *Who coined the term 'gamification'?.* Retrieved from http://www.quora.com/Who-coined-the-term-gamification

Pérez, O. (2012). El valor del juego: 'Ludificación' en la narrativa audiovisual contemporánea. *Telos: Cuadernos de Comunicación e Innovación, 93,* 23–33.

Reiss, S. (2004). Multifaceted nature of intrinsic motivation: The theory of 16 basic desires. *Review of General Psychology, 8*(3), 179–193.

Stake, R. E. (2005). *Qualitative case studies.* London, England: Sage.

Zuk, R. (2012). *How communicators can leverage gamification.* Retrieved from http://www.prsa.org/Intelligence/Tactics/Articles/view/9591/1044/How_communicators_can_leverage_gamification

NOTES

1. *AdExchanger* [Online]. *Gamification Is Good: How Winning Is Changing the Web.* April 23, 2012. Retrieved from http://www.adexchanger.com/ad-agents/gamification/
2. *WPP* [Online]. *Gamification.* Retrieved from http://www.wpp.com/wpp/marketing/publicrelations/gamification.htm
3. *PR Newswire* [Online]. *Lessons for PR: Think Like a Gamer.* Retrieved from http://blog.prnewswire.com/tag/gamification/
4. *Lewis PR* [Online]. *Gamification as the Holy Grail of Engagement?* Retrieved from http://blog.lewispr.com/2012/10/gamification-as-the-holy-grail-of-engagement.html
5. *Holtz Communication* [Online]. *Gamification of PR Messages Could Be a Game Changer.* Retrieved from http://holtz.com/blog/gamification/gamification-of-pr-messages-could-be-a-game-changer/3820/
6. *Toobeez* [Online]. Retrieved from http://www.toobeez.com
7. *Lego* [Online]. *Lego Serious Play.* Retrieved from http://www.seriousplay.com/
8. *The Fun Theory. VOLKSWAGEN.* [Online]. Retrieved from http://www.thefuntheory.com/
9. *The #polowers. VOLKSWAGEN* [Online]. *Volkswagen Spain Fuels Engagement With Digital Natives on Twitter.* Retrieved from https://business.twitter.com/en/optimize/case-studies/vw/
10. *Ecuación Polo* [Online]. *¡Resuelve la #EcuaciónPolo y Gana un Polo! VOLKSWAGEN.* Retrieved from http://www.blogocio.com/ecuacion-polo-resuelvela-y-el-polo-es-tuyo
11. *YouTube* [Online]. *McDonald's Interactive Billboard.* Retrieved from http://www.youtube.com/watch?v=CIzLd8zRwXw

12. *YouTube* [Online]. *McDonald's Pick n Play*. Retrieved from http://www.youtube.com/watch?v=7u0ij9D5S4Y
13. Adidas My Coach [Online]<https://www.micoach.adidas.com>
14. *Nike* + [Online]. Retrieved from http://www.nike.com/es/
15. *YouTube* [Online]. *Even Angels Will Fall*. Retrieved from http://www.youtube.com/watch?feature=player_embedded&v=rFuUFeQIdpk
16. *Axe Apollo Space Academy* [Online]. Retrieved from https://www2.axeapollo.com/es_ES/
17. *My Marriott Hotel Facebook Game* [Online]. Retrieved from http://apps.facebook.com/mymarriotthotel/

Part Three:
Traditional Television Teams Up With the Social Networks

CHAPTER NINE

Value Changes in Television Audiences: From the Traditional Audience to the Social Audience

ANA GONZÁLEZ-NEIRA AND NATALIA QUINTAS-FROUFE[1]

INTRODUCTION

This study is an investigation into the behaviour of the social audience in Spain. Viewing habits are analyzed with the aim of identifying any similarities that exist between the traditional and the social audiences and which broadcast formats are most successful on Twitter.

The introduction offers a glance at the new media ecosystem. This is followed by data collated for traditional and social audience viewing figures in Spain covering the period from February 2013 to January 2014, from which conclusions about the social audience in the country have been drawn.

The changes in the traditional media (the press, radio and television) resulting from digitization have altered not only the viewing dynamics of their users but also the assessment of these viewing habits by the advertising industry. One of the most recent changes in this process is the advent of *social television* that has arisen from a combination of social networks and television. Viewers are able to add their voices via social networks to discussions about any television programmes they watch, creating a collective: the *social audience*. In reality this is a fragmentation of the traditional audience according to their use of social networks.

This phenomenon of a second screen has become so commonplace that nowadays all broadcasters take it into account when launching programmes, or add new and innovative strategies to the programming to increase their success on such platforms.

Without doubt, the spread of mobile devices has contributed to the success of social television, since viewers become prosumers by posting comments on social networks about television programmes from their tablets or smartphones whilst viewing. In this way, the audience can influence or actively participate in the development of a programme.

Although the data derived from social television contains biases, as it only refers to those people who participate via social networks, it does provide television broadcasters with valuable qualitative information on the formats that are most popular with the audience, as well as on the most suitable time slots for broadcast. Furthermore, studies have shown a correlation between an increase in tweets and audience size (Nielsen, 2013).

Viewers can also enhance their viewing experience by interacting with the bonus content that the programmes themselves produce for social networks as part of their *transmedia* strategy, at the same time as interacting with other viewers. This produces bi-directional vertical interactivity between the traditional broadcaster (the television programme) and the recipient (the audience), and horizontal activity among viewers, creating a community of users (in which the fans of the programme play a central role).

Scientific research into this new reality has focused primarily on the specific experiences of certain programmes (Claes, Osteso, & Deltell, 2013; Coates Nee, 2013; Highfield, Harrington, & Bruns, 2013; Larsson, 2013). Some of the studies carried out under the Cost Transforming Audiences, Transforming Societies initiative (2010–2014) have also dealt with this subject (Bredl, Ketzer, Hünniger, & Fleischer, 2014). Significant contributions have been made by Harrington, Highfield and Bruns (2013), Deller and Hallam (2011), Wohn (2013) and Wohn and Na (2011) with regard to the influence of comparative audiences; between programmes (Fernández, 2014; Quintas-Froufe & González-Neira, 2014) and even between countries (Echegaray, 2013).

This new reality requires new research methodologies and measures in order to collate more information about who is behind comments on social networking sites and to research more deeply into the trend for personalized television. For the first fifty years of broadcasting, the media was in control of its relationship with the public; however, social networks have altered this relationship by conferring more power on the public. In this way the concept of active audiences will be perfected.

It is therefore necessary to adapt the methods used for measuring viewing figures in order to take these new realities into account. While until recently programme makers and advertising agencies only took traditional viewing figures into account, they must now also incorporate quantitative and qualitative data about the social audience into their research. They should monetize the economic value of users who become fans of a programme via social networks. Likewise, it is also important to take into consideration the level of consumption of the dozens of *apps* for mobile devices that television channels have set up to enhance and complement the viewing experience.

Various media analysts, including the giant Nielsen, the multinational Kantar Media and Spain's Global In Media, have attempted to quantify the scope of this social audience. However, they have not reached a consensus concerning methodology, nor have they established a single standardized system, as exists for measuring traditional viewing figures. The ubiquity of this audience creates new challenges for its measurement. Whilst initial focuses were on gathering quantitative data, attempts are now made to reach qualitative conclusions in order to learn more about viewers on social networks. Nevertheless, the use of complex algorithms can never grasp nuances such as irony, sarcasm or ambiguity contained in many tweets. Such nuance makes analysis more complex and the resulting data less accurate.

Spain is the main focus of this report, as it is the European leader in social television and ranks among the top five in the world (The Wit, 2013). This research could provide useful insight into the behaviour of social audiences in other countries where this phenomenon is, as yet, not so widespread. The reason for Spain's position in this ranking is its high consumption of television: having one of the highest per capita proportions of viewing minutes per day, surpassed only by Portugal and Italy. It also has the highest number of mobile devices per capita in Europe (Deloitte, 2013a, 2013b; Phocuswright, 2013). At the present time, social networks are mostly accessed via mobile devices (IAB, 2014). According to the Zenith 2014 report, 78% of users access Twitter via mobile devices.

METHODOLOGY

This research aims to investigate the behaviour of the social audience in Spain in order to discover which programmes and formats awaken the greatest interest and contrast these with those with the highest audience figures in order to identify any causal relationship between them.

The research objectives are as follows:

1) Determine if there is any relationship between the three programmes with the largest combined number of viewers and the three programmes with the largest social audience in each of the months during which the analysis was carried out.
2) Analyze the formats of those programmes with the highest traditional and social audience figures.

3) Discover which channels are followed most loyally by both the social and traditional audiences.
4) Establish the peak viewing times and those with the greatest social media impact in order to determine whether these periods coincide or not.

This research focuses solely on the social networking site Twitter, as it is the platform on which the majority of conversations about television programmes are held. Due to the way it operates it also has the fastest update rate. According to TwitterLabs, 60% of Twitter users use their mobile devices while watching television and one in three search for information about what they are watching.

In order to analyze both aspects of the audience, data on the most viewed (in relation to number of viewers and audience share) and the most followed (those with the highest number of social viewers and generated comments) programmes were compiled. The data relating to the social audience was obtained from Tuitele. Recently acquired by the multinational Kantar Media it is one of the main gauges of social audiences in Spain. The data for the traditional audience was taken from the audience rankings published in the monthly reports of the audiovisual consultancy Barlovento Comunicacion. These rankings give the most viewed programmes according to their actual real-time viewing figures. The period of analysis selected was the twelve months from February 2013 to January 2014.

Subsequently, two data sets were created for one of the dimensions of the audience in which the following data was compiled: that concerning the traditional audience included the names of the three most viewed programmes, the channel, format, broadcast time (day and time), and the viewing figures as both the audience share and the total number of viewers. The dataset for the social audience includes the name of the three programmes with greatest social impact, the channel, format, broadcast time and day, the number of comments generated and the number of social viewers.

RESULTS

The results obtained from the analysis are presented in this chapter, with one table for each month containing the basic data for each audience (programme, channel, format, time, indicator[2] and size of traditional and social audience).

In February no similarity between the two audiences was observed. Traditional audience figures are dominated by sports programmes (two football matches), whereas the programmes with the highest social impact (*Goya Awards*, *Gran Hermano 14* and *El Barco*) were of three different formats (award ceremony, reality show and series). It appears that the preferences of television viewers are more homogeneous than those of the social audience. It is worth noting that two TVE1 programmes made it onto the most viewed list (the movie of the week and the Oporto–Malaga football match) and one onto the list of most followed programmes (*Goya Awards*).

Table 9.1. Traditional and Social Audience in February 2013.

Audience	Programme	Channel	Format	Time (Day/Time)	Indicator	No. of viewers
Traditional	Football Copa del Rey: Seville–At.Madrid	T5	Sports programme	Wednesday 27 22:00–23:49	23.1%	4,721,000
	Movie of the week "Robin Hood"	TVE1	Movie	Sunday 24 22:15–00:21	23.3 %	4,611,000
	Football Champions League: Oporto–Malaga	TVE1	Sports programme	Tuesday 19 20:45–22:34	22.1%	4,432,000
Social	Goya Awards	TVE1	Award ceremony	Sunday 17 21:59–01:14	398,551	121,755
	Gran Hermano 14	T5	Reality show	Monday 11 22:23–01:48	430,054	91,396
	El Barco	A3	Series	Thursday 21 22:42–00:47	262,766	51,819

Source: Tuitele/ Barlovento Comunicacion.

The following month, traditional audiences demonstrated an even stronger tendency to view sports programmes, with the three most viewed programmes being football matches. Spain's qualifying match for the World Cup was the most viewed programme of the month, attaining an unusually high audience share of 52.5%, more than ten million viewers. This football match was also one of the three most followed programmes by the social audience, coming second in the ranking. The viewing of this match by the social and traditional audience meant that the channel Telecinco was included in both audience rankings, heading the list for the traditional audience and occupying second place for its social audience. Furthermore, the broadcast of the World Cup match and *Gran Hermano 14* placed Telecinco as leader for social audience in March, whilst TVE1 came out on top of the ranking for the traditional audience as a result of its broadcast of the two football matches.

Table 9.2. Traditional and Social Audience in March 2013.

Audience	Programme	Channel	Format	Time	Indicator	No. of viewers
Traditional	Football World Cup classification: Spain–France	T5	Sports programme	Tuesday 26 21:00–22:50	52.5%	10,522,000
	Football Champions League: Manchester–Real Madrid	TVE1	Sports programme	Tuesday 5 20:45–22:36	45.4%	9,785,000
	Football Champions League: Barcelona–Milan	TVE1	Sports programme	Tuesday 12 20:45–22:34	41.7%	8,884,000
Social	Splash !	A3	Contest	Monday 4 22:41–01:11	318,738	77,710
	Football World Cup classification: Spain–France	T5	Sports programme	Tuesday 26 21:00–22:50	199,761	75,050
	Gran Hermano 14	T5	Reality show	Monday 18 22:31–01:46	256,517	68,489

Source: Tuitele/ Barlovento Comunicacion.

In April, the traditional and the social audience figures were both clearly dominated by sports programmes (UEFA Champions League matches). On Tuesday 30th April the traditional and the social audience both opted for the same television content: the UEFA Champions League football match (Real Madrid vs. Borussia).

It is worth noting the presence of a news programme among the most viewed programmes in April; this is most likely due to its inclusion in the half-time break of the football. This *dragging effect* on the audience means that it obtained a much higher share than normal for a news programme (43.1%).

Table 9.3. Traditional and Social Audience in April 2013.

Audience	Programme	Channel	Format	Time (Day/Time)	Indicator	No. of viewers
Traditional	Football Champions League: Real Madrid–Borussia	TVE1	Sports programme	Tuesday 30 20:45–22:38	49.9%	9,492,000
	Football Champions League: Bayern–Barcelona	TVE1	Sports programme	Tuesday 22 20:45–22:33	43.0%	8,226,000
	News 2	TVE1	News	Tuesday 30 21:32–21:42	43.1%	8,116,000
Social	Football Champions League: Real Madrid–Borussia	TVE1 / TV3	Sports programme	Tuesday 30 20:45–22:38	273,052	119,023
	Football Champions League: Borussia–Real Madrid	Canal+ Champions League	Sports programme	Wednesday 24 20:45–22:38	236,795	88,029
	Gran Hermano 14	T5	Reality show	Monday 8 22:42–01:48	291,541	75,957

Source: Tuitele/ Barlovento Comunicacion.

May saw an almost identical viewing pattern to the previous month for both audience types. Sports programmes (*Copa del Rey* and UEFA matches) once again dominate both the social and traditional audiences. *News 2* on TVE1 was once again among the three programmes with the highest number of viewers (7,993,000).

The three most viewed and two of the most followed programmes were broadcast on the channel TVE1 (*Copa del Rey* match and *Eurovision*). It is striking that the *Eurovision Song Contest*, which traditionally gets good results in the case of the traditional audience, does not feature among the most viewed programmes although it makes the list for the most followed ones, with 91,574 social viewers.

Table 9.4. Traditional and Social Audience in May 2013.

Audience	Programme	Channel	Format	Time (Day/Time)	Indicator	No. of viewers
Traditional	Football Extra time Copa del Rey: Real Madrid–Atletico	TVE1	Sports programme	Friday 17 23:21–00:07	57.8%	11,499,000
	Football Copa del Rey: Real Madrid–Atletico	TVE1	Sports programme	Friday 17 21:30–23:21	51.1%	10,062,000
	News 2	TVE1	News	Friday 17 22:16–22:26	40.3%	7,993,000
Social	Football Copa del Rey: Real Madrid–Atletico	TVE1	Sports programme	Friday 17 21:30–00:07	418,405	190,610
	Football Champions League: Barcelona–Bayern	Canal+ Cham-pions League	Sports programme	Wednesday 1 20:45–22:38	252,257	146,091
	Eurovision 2013	TVE1	Award ceremony	Saturday 18 21:00–00:30	238,995	91,574

Source: Tuitele/ Barlovento Comunicacion.

In June, the Confederations Cup match broadcast by Telecinco achieved unusually high traditional audience rates (67.9%). However, the social audience did not follow this broadcast as had been observed in previous months, choosing instead other content types such as reality shows (*Un Principe Para Corina* and *Gran Hermano 14*). It is also worth noting that a non-football sporting event, the Roland Garros tennis tournament, featured among the most followed programmes, but not among the most viewed.

The broadcast of sporting events (the Confederations Cup match and Roland Garros) and of *Gran Hermano 14* made Telecinco both the most viewed and the most followed channel in June. It is important to highlight the fact that the viewing figures reflect what is essentially one football match as three separate programmes (Extra-Time, Penalties, and Post-match Analysis) and that these three programmes occupy the top three places on the list.

Table 9.5. Traditional and Social Audience in June 2013.

Audience	Programme	Channel	Format	Time (Day/Time)	Indicator	No. of viewers
Traditional	Football Penalties Confed. Cup: Spain–Italy	T5	Sports programme	Thursday 27 23:32–23:47	67.9%	13,355,000
	Football Extra Time Confed. Cup: Spain–Italy	T5	Sports programme	Thursday 27 22:50–23:32	60.3%	11,966,000
	Football Post-Confed. Cup: Spain–Italy	T5	Sports programme	Thursday 27 23:47–23:53	58.9%	10,662,000
Social	Gran Hermano 14	T5	Reality show	Tuesday 18 22:36–01:46	560,243	115,628
	Roland Garros	T5/ Canal+ Sports	Sports programme	Friday 7 13:14–17:51	199,110	95,067
	Un Principe Para Corina	Cuatro	Dating show	Monday 3 22:35–00:35	254,540	78,750

Source: Tuitele/ Barlovento Comunicacion.

In July *MasterChef* achieved the highest traditional and social audience figures, establishing a clear correspondence between the two audiences, making this the second time in the first six months of the study that one programme achieved top ranking for both the social and the traditional audience.

Even so, the programmes with the highest traditional audience were still sporting events, in this case Formula 1 races broadcast on Antena 3. The broadcast of both races (Germany and Hungary G.P.) achieved a large number of viewers (4,214,000 and 3,997,000 respectively), an outstanding success taking into consideration that they were broadcast at midday on a Sunday, a time when audiences tend to be significantly smaller. However, it is surprising that two programmes *Un Principe Para Corina* and *Pulseras Rojas*, broadcast on the same day and at the same time, garnered the greatest number of followers and comments.

Table 9.6. Traditional and Social Audience in July 2013.

Audience	Programme	Channel	Format	Time (Day/Time)	Indicator	No. of viewers
Traditional	MasterChef	TVE1	Talent show	Tuesday 2 22:31–00:38	33.1%	5,524,000
	Formula 1: G.P. Germany	A3	Sports programme	Sunday 7 14:00–15:45	38.5%	4,214,000
	Formula 1: G.P. Hungary	A3	Sports programme	Sunday 28 15:03–15:46	36.4%	3,997,000
Social	MasterChef	TVE1	Talent show	Tuesday 2 22:31–00:38	254,540	98,304
	Un Principe Para Corina	Cuatro	Dating show	Monday 8 22:38–00:37	237,645	97,787
	Pulseras rojas	A3	Series	Monday 8 22:40–00:21	316,109	69,259

Source: Tuitele/ Barlovento Comunicacion.

In August, another sports event (the Super Cup final, shown on August 28th) gained the first place for both audiences. It is significant that the three most viewed and commented on programmes on Twitter were football matches, and that they coincide in four cases for both audiences.

The channel TVE1 broadcast the most viewed and commented on programmes in August, followed by Antena 3.

Table 9.7. Traditional and Social Audience in August 2013.

Audience	Programme	Channel	Format	Time (Day/Time)	Indicator	No. of viewers
Traditional	Football Super Cup: Barcelona–At. Madrid	TVE1	Sports programme	Wednesday 28 23:00–00:51	37.9%	5,688,000
	Football Super Cup: At. Madrid–Barcelona	TVE1	Sports programme	Wednesday 21 23:01–00:49	38.4%	4,930,000
	Football Penalties Super Cup: Bayern Munich–Chelsea	TVE1	Sports programme	Friday 30 23:19–23:30	31.4%	4,368,000

Audience	Programme	Channel	Format	Time (Day/Time)	Indicator	No. of viewers
Social	Football Spanish Super Cup: Barcelona–At. Madrid	TVE1 / TV3	Sports programme	Wednesday 28 23:00–01:00	412,965	294,852
	Football Santiago Bernabeu Trophy	A3	Sports programme	Thursday 22 22:37–00:23	289,535	122,798
	Football European Super Cup: Bayern Munich–Chelsea	TVE1 / TV3	Sports programme	Friday 30 20:45–22:45	175,782	78,360

Source: Tuitele/ Barlovento Comunicacion.

In September, the figures for only one programme coincided for both audiences; a European competition football match. Whilst the traditional audience for the football match achieved first place, it dropped to second place for the social audience, as the first episode of *La Voz* talent show captured the most social viewers. It is also worth mentioning that the Neox Fan Awards show, aimed at a younger audience (coinciding with the demographic which is most active on social networks), was ranked the third programme of the month in terms of social viewing figures. This is one of the rare occasions when a minority TDT channel appears among the leaders for social audience. Again, it should be noted that News 2 was the second most viewed programme for the traditional audience, most likely due once again to the dragging effect of the football match, as it was broadcast during the half-time break.

Table 9.8. Traditional and Social Audience in September 2013.

Audience	Programme	Channel	Format	Time (Day/Time)	Indicator	No. of viewers
Traditional	Football Champions League: Galatasaray–Real Madrid	TVE1	Sports programme	Tuesday 17 20:47–22:42	36.1%	6,140,000
	News 2	TVE1	News	Tuesday 17 21:39–21:49	31.3%	5,413,000
	Challenge Champions	TVE1	Sports programme	Tuesday 17 20:16–22:43	33.0%	5,134,000

Audience	Programme	Channel	Format	Time (Day/Time)	Indicator	No. of viewers
Social	La Voz	T5	Talent show	Monday 16 22:30–01:45	435,530	117,299
	Football Champions League: Galatasaray–Real Madrid	TVE1 / TV3	Sports programme	Tuesday 17 20:45–22:45	199,991	104,615
	Neox Fan Awards	Neox	Award ceremony	Tuesday 24 22:02–00:31	267,014	60,435

Source: Tuitele/ Barlovento Comunicacion.

In October, broadcast football matches still achieved first place for traditional audience figures and second and third place for social audience figures. However, these figures were not achieved by the same matches (as shown in Table 9.9) so there is no relationship between the two audiences. *La Voz* was leader in terms of social audience, as it achieved a greater number of social viewers than the European competitions and the League football matches.

As in the previous month, the second news bulletin on TVE1 appeared among the most viewed programmes due to the dragging effect of the football.

Table 9.9. Traditional and Social Audience in October 2013.

Audience	Programme	Channel	Format	Time (Day/Time)	Indicator	No. of viewers
Traditional	Football World Cup classification: Spain–Georgia	T5	Sports programme	Tuesday 15 21:01–22:51	34.2%	6,587,000
	Football Champions League: Milan–Barcelona	TVE1	Sports programme	Tuesday 22 20:46–22:37	32.6%	6,333,000
	News 2	TVE1	News	Tuesday 22 21:33–21:44	27.7%	5,369,000

Audience	Programme	Channel	Format	Time (Day/Time)	Indicator	No. of viewers
Social	La Voz	T5	Talent show	Monday 28 22:39–01:25	208,752	70,709
	Football League: Real Madrid–Seville	Canal+ League / Goal TV	Sports programme	Wednesday 30 22:00–23:45	227,410	61,686
	Football Champions League: Real Madrid–Juventus	Canal+ Champions League	Sports programme	Wednesday 23 20:45–22:45	178,578	59,646

Source: Tuitele/ Barlovento Comunicacion.

As in the previous month, sports programmes still achieve first place for both audiences with the European football competitions and the World Motorcycle Championship. The only non-sports programme on the list was the television premiere of the multi-award winning movie *Avatar* on Telecinco, which became the second most viewed programme of the month.

Likewise, it is worth noting that the World Motorcycle Championship was leader for the social audience on Telecinco, despite its unpopular Sunday morning time slot.

Table 9.10. Traditional and Social Audience in November 2013.

Audience	Programme	Channel	Format	Time (Day/Time)	Indicator	No. of viewers
Traditional	Football Champions League: Juventus–Real Madrid	TVE1	Sports programme	Tuesday 5 20:45–22:35	36.3%	7,091,000
	Cinema Avatar (2nd part)	T5	Movie	Wednesday 13 22:30–00:00	32.2%	6,250,000
	Football post-Champions League: Juventus–Real Madrid	TVE1	Sports programme	Tuesday 5 22:35–22:38	29.3%	6,173,000

Audience	Programme	Channel	Format	Time (Day/Time)	Indicator	No. of viewers
Social	World Motorcycle Championship (race)	T5	Sports programme	Sunday 10 11:01–14:47	205,284	92,253
	Football Champions League: Juventus–Real Madrid	TVE1 / TV3	Sports programme	Tuesday 5 20:45–22:35	230,261	84,006
	Football Champions League: Real Madrid–Galatasaray	Canal+ Champions League	Sports programme	Wednesday 27 20:45–22:45	168,893	66,023

Source: Tuitele/ Barlovento Comunicacion.

Traditional audience viewing figures for football continued to lead in December, whilst they achieved third place for the social audience. December demonstrated a notable variety of formats, a change from the uniformity seen in the preceding months, there being only one programme that coincides for both audiences. In both cases there are award ceremonies among the first places; A New Year's Eve Party with the bell chimes at midnight for the traditional audience, and the *40 Principales* Awards for the social audience. As was the case in September, this last programme is aimed at the audience which is most active on social networks, hence the impact of this event on Twitter. Even so, the final show of *La Voz* became the most commented on Spanish television programme of the month, and of the entire year (with 689,256 comments).

Table 9.11. Traditional and Social Audience in December 2013.

Audience	Programme	Channel	Format	Time (Day/Time)	Indicator	No. of viewers
Traditional	Football Champions League: Copenhagen–Real Madrid	TVE1	Sports programme	Tuesday 10 20:46–22:34	27.4%	5,304,000
	New Year's Eve Party	TVE1	Gala	Tuesday 31 23:46–00:03	37.9%	5,261,000
	El Tiempo Entre Costuras	A3	Series	Monday 16 22:45–00:26	26.5%	4,877,000

Audience	Programme	Channel	Format	Time (Day/Time)	Indicator	No. of viewers
Social	La Voz	T5	Talent show	Wednesday 18 22:38–01:50	689,256	129,444
	40 Principales Awards	Divinity	Gala	Thursday 12 19:02–20:20	326,980	78,367
	Football Champions League: Copenhagen–Real Madrid	TVE1 / TV3	Sports programme	Tuesday 10 20:46–22:34	129,128	61,047

Source: Tuitele/ Barlovento Comunicacion.

In the last month to be analyzed, third place coincided for both audiences: the *Copa del Rey* match. It is striking that this month was the only one in which a Spanish-produced drama series (*El Tiempo Entre Costuras*) achieved first and second place for the traditional audience, whereas for the social audience these positions were taken by a football match and the final of *MasterChef Junior*.

Table 9.12. Traditional and Social Audience in January 2014.

Audience	Programme	Channel	Format	Time (Day/Time)	Indicator	No. of viewers
Traditional	El Tiempo Entre Costuras	A3	Series	Monday 20 22:43–00:11	27.8%	5,536,000
	El Tiempo Entre Costuras	A3	Series	Monday 13 22:45–00:10	25.2%	5,014,000
	Football Copa del Rey: Levante–Barcelona	A3	Sports programme	Wednesday 22 21:59–23:46	22.8%	4,699,000
Social	Football League: Betis–Real Madrid	Canal+ League / Goal TV	Sports programme	Saturday 18 16:00–17:45	47,027	141,517
	MasterChef Junior	TVE1	Talent show	Monday 6 22:13–00:15	48,009	123,495
	Football Copa del Rey: Levante–Barcelona	A3 / TV3	Sports programme	Wednesday 22 21:59–23:46	45,680	115,768

Source: Tuitele/ Barlovento Comunicacion.

DISCUSSION AND CONCLUSIONS

The following conclusions have been derived from the results obtained based on the objectives established above:

a) There is only a partial correspondence between the programmes with the highest viewing figures and those with the greatest number of comments on social networking sites. There is usually only one programme in the top three in which the highest viewing figures and the largest social audience coincide, even if they do not appear in the same position. In all cases (except during July) the number one programme was a football match. The only programmes that manage to achieve the top of the rankings for both the social and traditional audiences were the football match between Real Madrid and Borussia in April and the *MasterChef* talent show in July, probably because July was the only month without football matches.

February, June and October demonstrate no similarity between the two audience figures. August is the month with the greatest similarity, since two of the programmes with the highest viewing figures are also those that received the most comments, sports programmes in both cases.

b) The second research objective was to see which formats have the largest social and traditional audiences. The data reveals that the traditional audience views fewer genres than does the social audience. In general, live events such as award ceremonies and sports programmes were found to be the most successful formats with the social audience.

Sporting events, principally football, occupy the first position for both audiences; to the extent that there is no month in which this type of programme does not appear among those with the highest viewing figures and the greatest number of comments. According to the data on the traditional audience, of the 12 months analyzed, on 10 occasions a football match was the programme with the highest viewing figures, a demonstration of the power of such programmes to attract an audience. These football tournaments (*Copa del Rey*, The Confederations Cup, UEFA Champions League and the World Cup classification matches) have very high audience shares (with up to double the traditional share of a successful programme). These viewing figures would be impossible for an average prime-time programme to achieve, as these normally take around 20–24% of the audience. It is worth noting that in most cases these were matches involving Real Madrid or FC. Barcelona.

In the case of the social audience, although sports events are almost always among the first three positions in the rankings, they achieve first place on only four occasions (April, May, August and November). *La Voz* talent show stands out, as it managed to break social audience records, during the months it was broadcast (except November), receiving the most comments of any programme on social networking sites, beating even the football matches.

News programmes only make an appearance in the traditional audience figures, and on just four occasions. In all of these cases the news was broadcast during the half-time break of a football match, so, in fact, their figures can be attributed to the dragging effect of the sports programme. Likewise, there is a difference between the two audiences when it comes to certain formats such as quiz shows or contestant participation shows, talent shows and reality shows, which are highly popular with the social audience (*La Voz*, *MasterChef*, *Gran Hermano 14* and *Un Principe Para Corina*). With the exception of *MasterChef* in July, such shows fail to make the list for the traditional audience.

Drama series do not make it to first place for either the most viewed or commented on programmes, except *El Tiempo Entre Costuras*, which dominated the traditional audience in all the months during which broadcast output was analyzed; *El Barco* and *Pulseras Rojas* each appeared once in the top three programs in the case of the social audience. It is also striking that programmes which traditionally have high audience shares (*Goya Awards* or *Eurovision*) no longer manage to occupy any position among the most viewed programmes, but they are among the most followed on the social networks.

c) The conclusion is reached that TVE1, followed by Telecinco and Antena 3 are the channels with the greatest traditional audience following. TVE1, followed very closely by Telecinco, also leads the classification for the social audience.

For both cases, the audience is concentrated on the mainstream channels, with the exception of two award shows broadcast by Neox and Divinity, which were among the most commented on programmes in September and December, respectively; something that should be taken into account by advertising and media strategy agencies.

It is interesting that the subscription broadcaster Canal+ had shows in the data for the greatest social audience on six occasions (as it broadcast a number of football matches), but does not have any programme on the list for the traditional audience.

d) Both the most viewed and the most commented on programmes are usually broadcast in the same time slot: between 20:45 and 00:30, coinciding with prime-time in Spain. The six exceptions to this were sporting events such as Roland Garros, Formula 1 (two programs), the World Motorcycle Championship Race, the Football League Betis–Real Madrid match and the *Los 40 Principales* show, whose broadcast times were not set by the channels. It has been observed that for both types of audience the top positions in the rankings are generally occupied by programmes broadcast during the week, with some exceptions such as *Eurovision* or the *Goya Awards* that are shown at the weekend.

The results obtained in this study reveal that the behaviour of the social audience has a different dynamic from that of the traditional audience. It turns out that the same formats do not necessarily appeal to both audiences, nor is there a precise parallel between the most viewed programmes and those with the greatest number of followers or comments on social networking sites.

Future research in this area should refine and standardize methodologies to address these new realities in television viewing habits. It should also include new strategies to gauge not only the values of the traditional audience, but also those on social networking sites, especially bearing in mind that the adults of the future are the greatest current users of the social networks. This would allow television channels to access a much greater amount of information to aid them in making their shows more profitable.

REFERENCES

Bredl, K., Ketzer, C., Hünniger, J., & Fleischer, J. (2014). Twitter and social TV: Microblogging as a new approach to audience research. In G. Patriarche, H. Bilandzic, J. L. Jensen, & J. Jurisic (Eds.), *Audience research methodologies: Between innovation and consolidation* (pp. 196–211). New York, NY: Routledge.

Claes, F., Osteso, J. M., & Deltell, L. (2013). Audiencias televisivas y líderes de opinión en Twitter: Caso de estudio: El Barco. *Estudios sobre el Mensaje Periodístico, 19*(1), 347–364.

Coates Nee, R. (2013). Social TV and the 2012 election: Exploring political outcomes of multiscreen media usages. *Electronics News, 7*(4), 171–188.

Deller, R., & Hallam, S. (2011). Twittering on: Audience research and participation using Twitter. *Participations: Journal of Audience & Reception Studies, 8*(1), 216–245.

Deloitte. (2013a). *The state of the global mobile consumer, 2013: Divergence deepens.* Retrieved from https://www2.deloitte.com/content/dam/Deloitte/global/Documents/Technology-Media-Telecommunications/dttl_TMT-GMCS_January%202014.pdf

Deloitte. (2013b). *Survival of the fastest: TV's evolution in a connected world.* Retrieved from https://www2.deloitte.com/content/www/global/en/pages/technology-media-and-telecommunications/articles/survival-of-the-fastest.html

Echegaray, L. (2013). *El análisis de audiencias en la televisión social: El uso de Big Data en los mercados americano, británico y español.* Retrieved from http://www.portalcomunicacion.com/monograficos_det.asp?id=262#sthash.lR47LCoN.dpuf

Fernández, P. E. (2014). La audiencia social desde la televisión Argentina: Tecnología y optimización de las redes sociales. *Redes.com, 9*, 377–395.

Harrington, S., Highfield, T., Bruns, A. (2013). More than a backchannel: Twitter and television. *Participations: Journal of Audience & Reception Studies, 10*(1), 405–409.

Highfield, T., Harrington, S., & Bruns, A. (2013). Twitter as a technology for audiencing and fandom. *Information, Communication & Society, 16*(3), 315–339. doi: 10.1080/1369118X.2012.756053

IAB. (2014). *V Estudio anual de redes sociales.* Retrieved from http://www.iabspain.net/wp-content/uploads/downloads/2014/04/V-Estudio-Anual-de-Redes-Sociales-versi%C3%B3n-reducida.pdf

Larsson, A. O. (2013). Tweeting the viewer: Use of Twitter in a talk show context. *Journal of Broadcasting & Electronic Media, 57*(2), 135–152. doi: 10.1080/08838151.2013.787081

Nielsen. (2013). The follow back: Understanding the two-way causal influence between Twitter activity and TV viewership. Retrieved from http://www.nielsen.com/us/en/newswire/2013/the-fol low-back--understanding-the-two-way-causal-influence-betw.html

Phocuswright. (2013). España cuenta con la mayor penetración móvil de smartphones en Europa con un 66%. Retrieved from http://www.tecnohotelnews.com/2014/02/espana-cuenta-con-la-may or-penetracion-movil-de-smartphones-en-europa-con-un-66/

Quintas-Froufe, N., & González-Neira, A. (2014). Audiencias activas: Participación de la audiencia social en la televisión. *Comunicar*, *43*, 3–90. doi: 10.3916/C43-2014-08

The Wit. (2013). 10 trends for social TV in 2013. Retrieved from http://www.my-mip.com/RM/RM_MIPWORLD/2013/documents/pdf/resourcecentre/whitepapers/miptv-mipcom-the-wit-ten-trends-social-tv-2013-whitepaper.pdf?v=634946493438778738

Wohn, Y. (2013). History of social television. Retrieved from http://yvettewohn.com/2013/01/11/history-of-social-television/

Wohn, Y., & Na, E. (2011). Tweeting about TV: Sharing television viewing experiences via social media message streams. *First Monday*, *16*(3). Retrieved from http://firstmonday.org/ojs/index.php/fm/article/view/3368/2779

Zenith. (2014). *Panorama digital, mayo 2014*. Retrieved from http://blogginzenith.zenithmedia.es/estudio-zenith-panorama-digital

NOTES

1. Jorge Vazquez Herrero, the research grant holder from the Department of Humanities at the University of Coruña, collaborated on this research.
2. A specific indicator was chosen for each type of audience. For the traditional audience, the specific indicator is the audience share, whereas for the social audience it is the number of comments.

CHAPTER TEN

Towards a History of Media Conjuncture: *The Daily Show*, Audience and the "Revolution"

BORIS RUŽIĆ

INTRODUCTION

When reading about new media today, one can often find himself lost amidst overly deterministic renditions of our everyday technologies (optimistic and pessimistic). In this chapter I hope to display an approach akin to cultural studies while trying to analyze the specificities of media practices. Thereby, I hope to lay out a reading of television and the internet as a productive space for both the so-called producers of the information in the media value chain, as well as the receivers. Moreover, I hope to undermine not only the notion of a binary relation of the producer and the receiver (as has been done by Hall and Morley), but to show how exactly the modern media ecology can benefit from this new, fragmentary "public anonymous" that inhabits the contemporary mediasphere. Drawing from two main examples (a comedy show, *The Daily Show With Jon Stewart*, and the 2014 Ukrainian revolution) I will propose that the new media perspective and the appropriation of technology (internet) have modified the nature of the dissemination of information. Also, I propose to relinquish the notion of "breaking the media value chain" in favor of the concept of media "conjuncture", a term used by Antonio Gramsci and subsequently Stuart Hall. Through a series of anecdotes and theoretical widening in the introduction, I will set the methodological and theoretical framework for the specific analysis of contemporary culture and its discontents.

In 2010 Slavoj Žižek gave an interview for a journal, *Psychoanalysis, Culture and Society*, where he mentions an interesting anecdote from the communist Romania of the 1980s. The dictator Nicolae Ceaușescu wanted to build a river beneath the already existing river in the town of Bucharest "so that underneath there would be all the dirt, and the upper level would be clean for people to enjoy" (Žižek, 2010). The infamous leader was completely aware of the troubles with which his country was faced: external debt, food rationing, failed politics, corruption. But nevertheless, he had a perverted sense of power—although his people were starving and dirty, he wanted the facade of his city to stay clean. Almost as though it didn't matter what was happening beneath the surface, as long as the face of things looked normal for the outside spectator. The second anecdote from Žižek's famous 2008 book, *The Sublime Object of Ideology*, is somewhat different, but instructive nevertheless. He retells a well-known joke about a Jew and a Pole in a train, underlining the political incorrectness intrinsic to the supposed "Jew and Pole" dichotomy:

> 'Tell me, how do you Jews succeed in extracting from people the last small coin and in this way accumulate all your wealth?' The Jew replied: 'OK, I will tell you, but not for nothing; first, you give me five zloty [Polish money].' After receiving the required amount, the Jew began: 'First, you take a dead fish; you cut off her head and put her entrails in a glass of water. Then, around midnight, when the moon is full, you must bury this glass in a churchyard…' And: the Pole interrupted him greedily, 'if I do all this, will I also become rich?' 'Not too quickly' replied the Jew; 'This is not all you must do; but if you want to hear the rest, you must pay me another five zloty!' After receiving the money again, the Jew continued his story; soon afterwards, he again demanded more money, and so on, until finally the Pole exploded in fury: 'You dirty rascal, do you really think I did not notice what you were aiming at? There is no secret at all, you simply want to extract the last small coin from me!' The Jew answered him calmly and with resignation: 'Well, now you see how we, the Jews….' (Žižek, 2008, p. 68)

For Žižek, the joke is important because it shows that the Jew is not deceiving the Pole. He is showing him exactly the process of accumulating the Jews' wealth *in situ*. He goes on to say that the Pole's mistake is his perspective: "He looks forward to the 'secret' being revealed somewhere at the end; he situates the Jew's narration as a path to the final revelation of the 'secret'; but the real 'secret' is already in the narration itself" (Žižek, 2008, p. 69).

What can we learn from these two anecdotes in relation to the proposed topic of the chapter? I contend that the debate on media values and on the future of digital culture is twofold. On the one hand, various debates on new media society in the western world (and increasingly in the rest of the world) too often regress to the nostalgic views on dominant economical and political structures of modernism, lamenting the inability to engage with today's contemporary culture. Take the work of cultural critics Jean Baudrillard or Paul Virilio as example, or the work of Nicholas Carr and Andrew Keen which is more oriented towards popular writing. For example, Paul Virilio engages in techno-deterministic accusations of new technology, especially photography and its contemporary successor—the *virtual image*, as he calls it. In his debate, *The Vision Machine*, through citing Rodin he asserts: "It is the art that tells the truth and photography that lies" (Virilio, 1994, p. 2). Later, he will call upon the "automation of perception" as being responsible for the absence of a "viewer" (1994, p. 54)—delegating the interpretation of the visual world to the machine. In other words, Virilio claimed that analogue technology did not succumb to what he called *paradoxical logic* (although photography had its predicaments) because it was dependant on material techniques and means of production (photographic film, for example, which supposedly displayed only that which was "possible"). The development of the digital technologies for Virilio meant that reality becomes more suitable for total manipulation, for it has no relation to the material world anymore. This digitalized "industrialization of vision" renders image completely automatized in its perception of the world. These machines depersonalize the act of looking, and the subject is no longer an ocular witness. He goes on to say: "In the face of such representational open slather, the philosophical questions of plausibility and implausibility override those concerning the true and the false" (1994, p. 70). Debating this kind of technological reductionism is of paramount importance.

The body of work described here has a tendency of invoking a historical time and discourse that never really existed *par excellence*. For example, those lamenting the supposed shallowness of media forget Georg Simmel's work stemming from 1903 in which he describes his contemporary culture as "the rapid crowding of changing images, the sharp discontinuity in the grasp of a single glance, and the unexpectedness of onrushing impressions" (Charney & Schwartz, 1995, p. 279). Contemporary media theory, by this account, is becoming increasingly autistic—by invoking the nostalgic experience of "previous times", techo-deterministic media theorists are at the same time invalidating specificities and cultural significances that were in effect in a particular context and cultural frame. More specifically, the lamenting portion of new media theory sometimes resembles Ceaușescu's proposed river: while trying to pretend as though the surface of the media today is almost uniform (either techno-optimistic or techno-pessimistic), today's proponents of the mediasphere are sweeping much of the ambiguities of the discourse under the rug, i.e., beneath the clean river of Bucharest.

On the other hand, some of the scholars that engage more readily with sometimes insurmountable problems and challenges of the modern media act as though there is a great secret that eludes us, but should be revealed if we are to enact a grand description of today's society. Just like the joke from the beginning warns us, the aim of this chapter is to propose a middle ground between the notions that:

a) there is a great secret that needs to be brought to light if we are to understand the grand theory of societal intricacies of media and;
b) we need to go back to the time where information "didn't want to be free"[1]—the time of mainstream, dominant media systems.

In this chapter I am proposing the relinquishing of the notion of "breaking the media value chain" in favor of the concept of media conjuncture, a term used by cultural theorists Antonio Gramsci and subsequently Stuart Hall.

In order to draw from Hall's insights into popular culture, one needs to turn to the work of Italian theoretician Antonio Gramsci first, as he was a notable influence not just for the field of cultural studies and the study of ideology in general, but he influenced Stuart Hall in particular.

THE RETURN TO THE NEW

Antonio Gramsci, a well known Italian Marxist whose work in the first half of the 20th century is best recognized for the popularization of the concept of hegemony, innovated an approach to the analysis of contemporary society that does not use the doctrine of economics to account for all the specificities of a culture. Through his reading, it is clear that in Marxist terms economy all too often already encompasses the planes of culture and politics. Instead, he claims that "the three mentioned planes exist in mutual correlation" (Jones, 2006, p. 5). For Marx, the economic base is the foundation and the most potent dimension of social life that "brings the superstructure into being and which gives it its character. In turn, the superstructure works to maintain the existing economic structure and to disguise or legitimize the real conditions of economic exploitation" (Jones, 2006, p. 29). To be a revolutionary in Marxist terms, one needs to change the economic base (for example, take control of the means of production). For Gramsci, this reading was not sufficient for the analysis of contemporary culture. He proposed a model of "conjunctural thinking" that represented the kernel of his notion of hegemony—a more useful term than "dominance" because it took into consideration the part that the subordinated play in the propagation and circulation of power/authority. In other words, Gramsci knew that social power is not solely related to the dominance of one privileged group over the other (presumably, the subordinated). In today's society, Gramsci writes, the "privileged group" dominates precisely through consent of the subordinated group. He goes on to say that the notion of power is put forward "as what appears to be a free expression of their own interests and desires" (Jones, 2006, p. 4). But at the same time, capitalism as the dominant economic and cultural system appears to represent a space of deep and "incurable problems which he calls its 'organic' crisis" (Jones, 2006, p. 95). It is precisely here that the mentioned conjunctural qualities of Gramsci's thinking come to fruition as he uses it to describe temporary forms of political and cultural mobilization in popular culture. His notion of popular culture as a place of hegemonic struggle greatly influenced Stuart Hall, who, a couple of decades later proclaimed that popular culture is a "contradictory space", a site of continuous negotiation (Procter, 2004, p. 25).[2] Hall later described conjuncture as "a period in which the contradictions and problems and antagonisms, which are always present in different domains in a society, begin to come together. They begin to accumulate, they begin to fuse, to overlap with one another" (Hay, Hall, & Grossberg, 2013, p. 16).

Hall argues that the orthodox view on Marx's theory by which the economic base affects the superstructure is not sufficient, as contemporary culture mirrors a more dynamic process of change. For him, "if popular culture is not fixed, or guaranteed in advance by the economic base, then its meaning and function can be negotiated and reconfigured through cultural intervention" (Procter, 2004, p. 18). This strategy of conjuncture is twofold: on the one hand it recognizes the multitude of discursive practices embedded in the everyday culture (and, by the same account, media), admitting to the structural complexities of ideological, economic and cultural power relations, thereby rendering the concept of "breakage" (e.g., the clear-cut transformation of discursive practices) insufficient. At the same time, it opens up a challenge of an in-depth analysis of those relations. The goal of this chapter is precisely in the center of those two leverages, proposing that the concept of "breaking the value chain" refers to the almost clear-cut transitions within various discourses that are not sufficient in analyzing today's new media paradigm. Through the analysis of *The Daily Show* (most notably), I hope to outline precisely the strength and pertinent character of the theoretical framework described so far.

It may be strange to propose a return to the likes of Gramsci and Hall when analyzing today's functioning of specific media occurrences—after all, political, economic and cultural circumstances have changed in the last 50 years. Gramsci himself was often used as a common denominator when talking about political struggle, sometimes without much-needed context. Richard Bellamy, for example, "argues that Gramsci's work has been misinterpreted as a general theory of ideological power in western democracies" (Jones, 2006, p. 122). Insofar, historicism is an important intellectual movement that insists precisely on the mentioned importance of context when debating relevant theories. Media studies today often succumb to a "presentism" of sorts; they forget to employ a diachronic perspective when analyzing particular effects in the media. Steve Jones, in regards to that, writes:

> Gramsci developed a flexible historicism that could encompass the relationship between past, present and an uncertain future. We might recall that his description of common sense is not some fully formed and immobile philosophy, but a series of 'disjointed and episodic' layers. (Jones, 2006, p. 123)

How does what has been said translate to the specific analysis of media texts? When confronted with new means of communication and dissemination of information, media often take a recursive step to the same denominator when describing those changes: one of the "revolution". Revolution is the usual denominator, especially with regards to the new media: almost every development is revolutionary, and every product "game-changing". Not only did Marshall McLuhan coin the term "global village" which was appropriated by internet activists through the nineties to designate the supposed ability of technology to traverse great distances and atone for social inequalities, U.S. senator and Vice-President Al Gore gave a notable speech on what he called the "information superhighway". Maybe the most famous indicator of the overly optimistic and ahistorical view on the rapid technological development came not from cultural theorists, but from stock markets in the form of the "dot-com bubble". It showed how speculation about the effects of technology and faith in the power of something "new" can produce a crisis situation, not "a revolution", as the stock markets fell drastically following speculative growth the new technologies and the internet supposedly brought throughout the nineties. This is precisely why the rest of the chapter will propose a review of the concept of the "revolution" in the media chain as constitutive and productive for media conjuncture by appropriating its original Latin meaning of "circling" or "returning", and not of relinquishing or breaking. Just as much of the work in the field of cultural studies tried to overcome economic reductionism in describing the all-encompassing changes in British culture of the 1970s, I will try to show how the *economical model* of engaging with the new media is practically too recursive and outdated.

In the following section I will analyze a couple of significant media occurrences that portray possible directions for new media strategies (most notably, a comedy show, *The Daily Show With Jon Stewart*, and the 2014 Ukrainian revolution). In that light, my main goal is to propose that the new media perspective and the appropriation of technology (internet) have modified the nature of the dissemination of information. New media provides a new perspective in which the user is almost always the arbiter of informational usefulness. The functioning of today's media institutions as "objective" and universal becomes dead weight as the idea of information as semantically ambiguous provides new, interesting possibilities for contemporary media theory. By that account, my analysis will try to show the possible trajectory of new media thinking towards the notion of "information with a face". Therefore, the "crisis of media" which is often called upon as a contemporary problem could be averted by abandoning the idea of an unidirectional dissemination of information from the "producers" to their receivers in favor of "nomadic hierarchy" by which the information sphere is always intersubjective (through internet-decentralized participation). Therefore, the question of *which contents are users willing to pay for* in the age of social networks should be remade into that of *which specific content is media willing to disseminate* in the age of informational ubiquitousness.

CALL ME SUBJECT. RENDER ME ABSENT

As we have seen, views that emerged in part as a reaction to technological developments of the modern era rendered the discursive field of *media studies* loaded with different highly ambivalent (to the extent of contradictory) theoretical approaches. One particularly pertinent approach to the study of media stems from the field of cultural studies that arose as (anti)discipline in Birmingham in the 1960s. At first concerned with political and economical specificities of the United Kingdom, scholars quickly became interested in a broader media investigation, seeing it as part of a greater discourse of popular culture. Building on Marxism, scholars such as Hebdige, Hoggart and Hall innovated an approach to the study of culture that involves "exposing the relations of power that exist within society at any given moment in order to consider how marginal, or subordinate groups might secure or win, however temporarily, cultural space from the dominant group" (Procter, 2004, p. 2). The crucial message from the quoted sentence is sometimes forgotten in the analysis of contemporary media: Stuart Hall knew—just like the joke from the beginning tells us—there is no big secret at the end of the story. Rather, the process of narration is the secret itself. Conveyed to the field of cultural studies, he claimed that every analysis is at the same time fragmentary and specific, and culture was a process over which we must struggle. There is no easy way to describe such a big entity, because we are always describing a dynamic and not static, monolithic structure with its presumably intrinsic properties.

The aim here is to provide a similar gesture through the investigation of specific contemporary media practices and their particular effects on a cultural and political habitus. As has been stated in the beginning of the chapter, through an approach that takes into account the specificities of media practices, my aim is to analyze particular media practices as productive space for both the so-called producers of the information in the media value chain, as well as the receivers.

One of the most notable cultural theorists, John Fiske, in his seminal study, *Television Culture* (2001), stated that the existence of television in historical terms is not shaped only by technology-specific discourses. Instead, he argued that important approaches such as Marxism, semiotics, (post)structuralism and ethnography widened and contextualized analysis of everyday mediated life. Because of that, everyday life (he calls it "reality") is always already encoded by the culture in which we are immersed. If the role of media technologies such as television is to participate in (or create) everyday culture, its functioning must be coded accordingly. Otherwise, it would render disseminated information useless and unintelligible (Fiske, 2001, pp. 4–13). Therefore, if our everyday culture is shaped by the codes that the dominant culture produces, by this account cultural reality becomes determined by the way people decode produced signs. In other words, it becomes the purpose of ideology to impose certain practices of interpretation with the goal of naturalization of everyday life. Although Fiske had valuable insights into the functioning of media practices, practical analysis should include historical specificities of various media instances, which can be carried out though the reading of Hall's famous essay, "Encoding/Decoding" (2012). For Hall perhaps the biggest question was that of what is popular, why, and how it becomes popular. Seemingly simplistic, his investigation had thorough consequences on the theory and practice of cultural studies. That which is popular "is not a 'thing' we can confidently point to, like a can of Coke on the supermarket shelf; it can only be understood in relation to the cultural forces within which it is caught at any particular moment" (Hall, 2012, p. 139). This moment of convergence with Gramsci (for whom the objects of culture do not stand for themselves, but in relation to power and other objects) points to the important part of the problem of media theory today that needs to be underlined. Gramsci's conjunctural quality, or the "ability to locate his thinking within a particular historical moment or set of conditions" (Procter, 2004, p. 49), enabled Hall to depart from the more usual structuralist view. Incidentally, Hall is not interested in concepts as such, but in the relations these concepts constitute between themselves, which he famously expressed in the already mentioned essay, "Encoding/Decoding".

Influenced by Gramsci's notion of "common sense",[3] Hall presupposed that every story is dependant on (but not confined to) the "preferred meaning". He claimed that the dominant media systems were specifically devoted to the creation and repetition of various narratives by which they were trying to enact "common sense". His theoretical efforts were aimed at deconstructing this monolithic view of the dissemination of information and its presupposed manipulative qualities. He famously proposed three divergent readings of dominant media systems: dominant-hegemonic position, negotiated position and oppositional position. If one side of the ideological spectrum refers to the traditional notion of a hierarchical medium that controls the flow of information from the producer to its receiver, the other side underlines the importance of "audience" as constitutive for the interpretation of messages. In other words, the same permissiveness that enables dominant media structures to influence a wide array of people through cultural hegemony, at the same time makes space for the *oppositional* and *negotiated* reading of the same media value chain. In this way, studies of media practices took into account not only the (hegemonic) nature of dominant structures, but also the *habitus* of the audience who now had the opportunity not to be subjected to a particular kind of reading. Race, culture, class, ethnicity, geography and such were all part of necessary conditions that should be considered when talking about media production and values.

Hall's intervention in the usual media value chain paradigm was at the same time a serious departure from the common Marxist view on ideology which Slavoj Žižek explained in *The Sublime Object of Ideology* via the famous utterance "they do not know it, but they are doing it" (2008, p. 24), i.e., false consciousness. By the seventies, Louis Althusser in his essay, *Ideology and Ideological State Apparatuses* (1970), advanced this view on ideology. We cannot explain it only as false consciousness, he claims—there is a finer interplay of relations at hand. Althusser asserts that it is the role of the regime to recreate the conditions in which the production of the subject in the social structure can be seen as natural. The process of interpellation—the constitution of the subject—was dependant precisely on the production of cultural codes exerted in particular contexts. The constitution of the subject through power-relations (or hegemony) was of paramount importance to the Frankfurt School's notion of ideology. If the nature of information is contained in the value it receives upon its production, can there be any means of escaping the ideological power embedded in it? Hall's reading of divergent modes of the reception expands precisely on this question. Althusser was aware that culture is a site of struggle and not a false consciousness, a "system of representations (images, myths, ideas or concepts) through which we live, in an imaginary way, our real conditions of existence" (Procter, 2004, p. 45). Nevertheless, Hall in part criticized this view on ideology as the one which denies agency and the possibility of political intervention. Trying to advance and deconstruct at the same time this structuralist notion of ideology, Hall sees popular culture as "not necessarily a capitalist instrument" (Procter, 2004, p. 18). This view is particularly instructive to the study of media occurrences, because it situates the viewer in the center of the media value chain.

THE DAILY SHOW AND THE "MOMENT OF ZEN"

It seems as though what is sometimes lacking in the modern investigations of media is the very participant (not the "viewer"). Contemporary renditions of media theory sometimes forget to look beyond the usual ideological critique of the viewer which usually consists of two extremes:

a) on the one hand, we have a traditional, passive viewer who cannot escape the clutches of dominant media systems. For example, Marco Senaldi in his essay, "Tele-Aesthetics: Between Television and Art", calls the television viewer "interpassive" (2008). Senaldi sees a spectator of a television programme as interpassive because his activity is not required, the programme is completed without his involvement. He builds upon Debord and Situationists to explain the supposed passivity of a viewer.
b) on the other hand, techno-eschatologists call upon the new media paradigm as the omnipotent force of the participant/creator of information. Early transhumanists and entrepreneurs/thinkers such as Raymond Kurzweil were at the forefront of this media utopism.

In the next couple of sections I hope to lay out two rather divergent examples in order to elucidate the need for productive thinking about the participant in the media value chain: the television show, *The Daily Show With Jon Stewart*, and the cultural and political struggle of Ukraine in late 2013 and through 2014.

The television show, *The Daily Show With Jon Stewart*, is one of few examples in mainstream media that stands its ground when confronted with the production of information through dominant media. Although packed with humor, sarcasm and entertainment (at times expected of a commercial cable network), *The Daily Show* often undergoes serious analysis of mainstream media reporting. When the Deepwater Horizon oil spill emerged in 2010, headlining most newspapers with the reports of death, injuries and wildlife damage, Jon Stewart saw through the need of the mainstream media to build upon the disaster to create a narrative similar to those of blockbuster movies (which, as even Pierre Bourdieu showed a couple of decades ago in his study of television, are one of the pillars of viewership retention). Stewart, unlike the mainstream media which drew almost exclusively on the spectacular side of the disaster, underwent a deep reading of British Petroleum's tainted past, their faulty safe mechanisms for dealing with the disaster and, most importantly, the mainstream media's inability to deal with breaking news with any traces of depth, context and the production of information (rather than perpetuation that was taking place).

The Daily Show mirrors the exact same difference from mainstream television (CNN or Fox News, for example) as the abovementioned differences between the study of dominant media structures between various theoretical approaches. Take, for example, the marriage of Chelsea Clinton, the daughter of the former U.S. President Bill Clinton from 2010. Although the family took all needed steps to secure their personal event from media coverage (rendering the small town practically unavailable to the journalists), all of the major broadcasting companies gathered in an attempt to cover the wedding ceremony. Confronted with a pure flow of time, journalists had nothing to report on: there was no story, the daughter and the President were not there, the streets were practically empty. Yet, the media conglomerates did not give up: they were making up news, trying to buy some time hoping to get a glimpse of the actual wedding that never really happened as a media event—it went unrecorded. Jon Stewart was—in his usual criticism of dominant media reporting—particularly accurate in describing this (non)event.

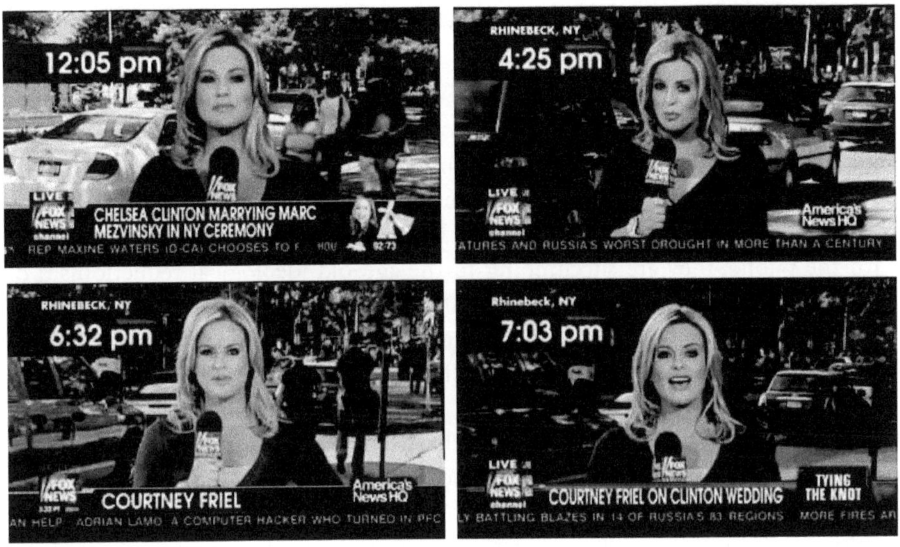

What was happening in this instance was not a communication between the producer and the receiver of information, but rather a complete *ecstasy of communication*: communication about the communication itself (Andrew Murphie & John Potts, 2003, p. 16). CNN's coverage of the death of the famous singer Whitney Houston furthered the paradigm of the inability to communicate. In the new media age when almost every *simple* bit of information can be found online, CNN thought it needed to reinvent the paradigm of media broadcasting. They had a reporter on the streets of the city stopping people saying:

> CNN: "News just broke. It's…ehm…not so good news. Whitney Houston has died."
> Random person 1: (shocked) "Oh my god…"
> Random person 2: "She did?! What?! You're kidding me?"
> CNN: "No, just happened."

For a moment, it looked as though CNN had completely abandoned the idea of reporting, succumbing to Twitter-esque 140-characters impressions. The people on the streets were the same as those in front of their screens: a market they must try to feed with short impressions to stay relevant.

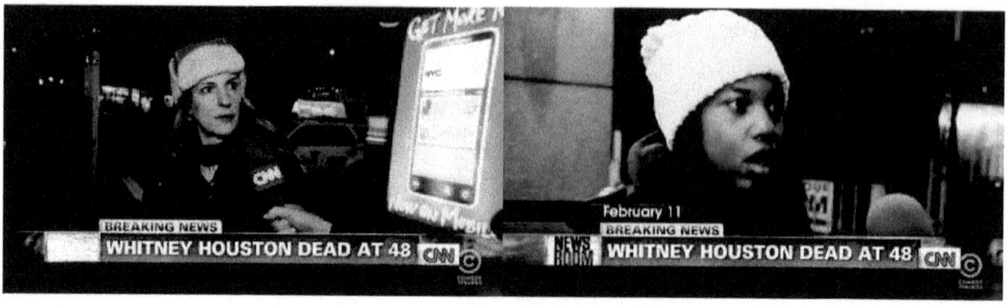

Taking into account what has been said already, dominant media structures too often communicate to the viewer, and not with the viewer. The point of convergence of Hall's theories inspired by Gramsci (and Vološinov) lies exactly at the point at which the mainstream media make the exact same mistake of already mentioned economical reductionism of the public sphere. By talking to, and not with the public, they are succumbing to the age-old ideological reductionism of identities to immobile structures of a culture. Jon Stewart's perhaps most memorable public outburst can be traced to October of 2004, on the same programme he usually criticizes: CNN's since-cancelled show called *Crossfire*. In the segment that is now remembered as the one that broke the usual chain of command and sequence of TV programming, Stewart chastised modern media reporting and its pseudo-journalistic punditry at great and not-so-humorous length. Needless to say, the hosts of *Crossfire* were stunned, as they were probably expecting a highly humorous and mildly intelligent guest (that was, after all, expected of a host of a *comedy* programme), but they were confronted with highly eloquent bashing. What was the problem? *The Daily Show* functions as a comedy show, fake news and entertainment, but through the years it has proven to be one of the most pertinent satires and commentaries on contemporary society, politics and media. The reporting of the mainstream media mostly operates through the concept of a firm "interface" or format. In other words, there is a formal boundary through which communication cannot be explored accordingly towards the public, as that public is viewed as a rather static audience with defined interests and tastes. Hall described it like this: "the dog in the film can bark, but it cannot bite!" (2012, p. 139). In other words, every utterance is limited by the discursive field of the language, ideology and the interface of a media-specific practice. Stewart, in CNN's show, found objectionable precisely the enslavement of the format via two pundits who were not ready to discuss existing complexities in the society, but were exerting only spectacular binarisms of discourse. They were already envisioned in a specific format (to bark, and not to bite, so to speak). In a way, it seems as though mainstream television programming is limited to two options: either it will be "informative" through a format that is not dialogical, but normative; or it will employ an illusion of dialectics of meaning through spectacular debates on various topics only to perpetuate the *image* of the subject, and not to elucidate its complexity.

Gerald J. Erion in his article, "Amusing Ourselves to Death With Television News: Jon Stewart, Neil Postman, and the Huxleyan Warning", tries to connect this limitation of an interface with the techno-pessimistic philosophy of Neil Postman. He mentions Postman's example of a smoke that can transmit threat signals (basic communication), but it cannot be used for philosophical inquiries. Therefore, he concludes, "*The Daily Show* functions along the lines of Postman's philosophy, as it reflects the restrictions placed by our contemporary electronic media (including television) upon their content" (Erion, 2007, p. 6). While it is true that one of the basic principles of Jon Stewart is enshrined in detecting the inability of mainstream media to reorganize their medium of communication for more efficient and content-driven reporting, Erion's referring to Postman is too simplistic. The reading of Jon Stewart's satire leads directly to Stuart Hall's notion of conjunctural thinking. Why was *The Daily Show*'s host so angry at *Crossfire*'s hosts? Stewart believed that the structure of CNN's show can enable a serious discussion on relevant everyday topics, and yet, Stewart's comedy show undertook serious analysis more often than *Crossfire*.

It was exactly Hall who tried to advance the view on audience with the already mentioned "conjunctural" thinking. For Hall, the process of articulation always connotes a sort of stepping out of the given framework. Procter goes on to say:

> This process of linkage is not fixed or final. Articulations can only be made under a specific set of circumstances or, to adapt one final theoretical concept used by Hall, at a particular historical *conjuncture*. Hall's theorizing is conjunctural in the sense that it is always informed by and articulated as a response to, events at a particular moment. (2004, p. 54)

In other words, Hall is trying to circumvent the usual modernism/postmodernism division. In an interview, "On Postmodernism and Articulation: An Interview With Stuart Hall", he clearly states that the postmodernist project is one of

> absolute rupture with the past, the beginning of a new global epoch altogether.... If you are within the same epoch—the one which opens with the age of imperialism, mass democracy, mass consumption and mass culture from about 1880–1920—you have to expect that there will be continuities and transformations as well as ruptures and breaks. (Grossberg, 1986/2005, p. 133)

This situation of already mentioned "presentism" Hall addresses as "another version of that historical amnesia characteristic of American culture—the tyranny of the New" (Grossberg, 1986/2005, p. 133). My point of contention between some of the traditional mainstream media occurrences I mentioned and *The Daily Show* is precisely in the way they treat contemporary cultural practices. The first is—by trying to win over the audience with their presumable understanding of contemporary media culture—postmodern in their historical amnesia and the lack of serious analysis. The latter is "modern" through satire: it is able to produce various serious readings of popular culture by avoiding the pitfalls of modern media communications. To put it bluntly, on the one hand, traditional media outlets such as CNN often use the postmodern fragmentariness of today's society in order to render the political and ideological struggles of our times irrelevant—they are converting complex stories to Twitter feeds. On the other hand, *The Daily Show* uses fragments of our cultural reality to try to build a mosaic of relevant commentary of our culture. Hall very prophetically addresses this problem in an interview he first gave in 1986 (Grossberg, 1986/2005). While answering a question about the popularity of postmodernism in the US, Hall returns to Walter Benjamin's seminal essay about the denigration of *aura*. He asserts that although our era:

> breaks the one, true meaning into fragments and puts one in the universe of the infinite plurality of codes, it does not destroy the process of encoding, which always entails the imposition of an arbitrary 'closure'. Indeed, it actually enriches it, because we understand meaning not as a natural, but as an arbitrary act—the intervention of ideology into language. Therefore, I don't agree with Baudrillard that representation is at an end because the cultural codes have become pluralized. (Grossberg, 1986/2005, p. 137)

Jon Stewart's show very similarly tries to negotiate with today's modern media situations, critiquing their inability to address the pertinent cultural problems and the viewers at the same time, succumbing to the vortex of fragmentary information. Let us look at one recent example of *The Daily Show*, that was aired September 17, 2013, amidst the so-called Washington Navy Yard Shooting that occurred the day before. Stewart has a habit of a dialectization of other news organizations, revealing their contradictions, inconsistencies and (at times) malevolence.[4] Stewart is cynically analyzing, as he often does, failed coverage of the shooting by the mainstream media.

Stewart:	"It's times like these we require the context and clarity that only these noble dormant cable giants can provide."
Fox News:	"I don't want to speculate but…"
Stewart:	"I'm sorry, did I say context and clarity? I meant speculation. Yes, for every all too familiar American tragedy you can be sure the news will exacerbate it with yet another force 5 'wrongnado.'

After the brief segment, Stewart goes on to list a number of news sources (MSNBC, CNN, Fox News…) that speculated on the whole story as it was happening, with CNN doing their "Clinton's daughter's wedding" fiasco, where they reported for hours on—nothing. At one point, CNN's Wolf Blitzer asks on air: "The fact, Tom, this individual is described as someone that is dressed in a black top, black jeans…what does that say, if anything, about a possible motive or whatever? Can we begin to draw any initial conclusions? [...] Sometimes these initial conclusions can obviously be very very wrong." Stewart quickly responds in two equally significant ways:

a) He points to Blitzer's colleague, Anderson Cooper, who is in a photo wearing a black top and black jeans. This resort to his colleague is not at all banal. It points to the dialectical potential of *The Daily Show* because it establishes a sort of denaturalization of cultural positions mainstream media often occupy. In the words of Karim, "in the moment when a historical event passes under the sign of discourse, [...] it is subject to all the complex formal 'rules' by which language signifies. To put it paradoxically, the event must become a 'story' before it can become a *communicative event*" (quoted in Procter, 2004, p. 64). In other words, to presuppose without any evidence that black jeans could be related to crime is highly ideological and loaded with fallacies.
b) Stewart points out the feebleness of mainstream media reporting by saying: "this speculation...it's like a compulsion! I know you think that saying 'this could all be wrong' makes it ok to say it, but it doesn't make it ok! No one else in the world is allowed to operate that way. And that's when I realized...All of yesterday's confusion and the reporting: it's not a mistake! [...] So my final, not initial conclusion is: this is deliberate. The chaos they vomit onto the screen. The very thing we thought the news organizations were created to clarify is a feature, not a bug."

This kind of coverage done by *The Daily Show* completely turns on its head the notion of "interpassivity" I mentioned through Senaldi's reading of spectatorship. The real potential of intertextuality lies precisely in this "fragmentary" but alert analysis. On the one hand, the viewers, to be able to understand the satire, must be educated about topics the show is reacting to. On the other hand, *The Daily Show* isn't just "negative" news, but through the reading of our everyday culture, it *is* news, loaded with (not fake) information. Gerald J. Erion (2007) writes about a study from 2004 by the Annenberg Public Policy Center which "found that viewers of *The Daily Show* were *better* informed about the positions and backgrounds of candidates in the 2004 US Presidential campaign than most others." Nevertheless, Jason Zinser (2007), in the paper, "The Good, the Bad and The Daily Show", criticizes the show on the grounds of "dilution". Basically, he is afraid that *The Daily Show* adds to the ongoing complexity of the informational sphere where real news is sometimes undistinguishable from fake news. The internet is, of course, the main suspect. But at the same time he fails to acknowledge at least one main point of the show's credibility: its use of the new media technologies not to obfuscate, but to illuminate various ideological and political tensions in our everyday culture.

Stewart uses the multiplicity of sources like users on the internet often do: he compares and confronts. Fragmentariness here isn't all that bad: it is a prerequisite for the show's functioning. By being fragmentary—to retreat to the beginning—the show is not undermining information. On the contrary! The "multivocalization" of *The Daily Show* enables the deconstruction of the exact media structures that maintain the false illusion of ideologically "complete" truth. This isn't a retreat to relativism. It is a complex demand to take the notion of a viewer or participant of the mediasphere not as a complete and static individual, but to include him as part of the societal and media reality that surrounds him. Even for Hall, identity isn't endlessly wandering just because it's complex: "every identity is placed, positioned, in a culture, a language, a history.... It insists on specificity, on conjuncture. But it is not necessarily armor-plated against other identities. It is not tied to fixed, permanent, unalterable oppositions" (quoted in Procter, 2004, p. 121).

THE *FACE* OF THE INTERNET

New media technologies and the internet in the recent decades took the main stage for media theorists around the world as a discursive field of struggle over the notion of their political and cultural potential against the mainstream (often described as hegemonic) media, and rightly so. Centralized production of information (uniformity of content) of mainstream old media gives place to a new mode of production on the internet, still taking into account the traditional viewer, as well as the new media agent. As much as traditional media dissemination is limited to its interface that enables almost exclusively communication from the sender to the receiver in the media value chain,[5] the internet turns that strategy on its head. Precisely because of the inversion of the producer-receiver relationship, the internet is a place of two extremes: on the one hand it is celebrated as a utopian space without a master, abundant in "democracy"; and on the other, it is characterized as a space of banality, amateurism and false freedom. I argue neither of the accounts is right. My second example will try to make way for a more dialectical notion of new media as a place of dialogue and negotiation with the information.

The Ukrainian crisis in late 2013 and continuing in 2014 was riddled with reports not just from traditional media outlets but was a big part of the new media sphere.[6] The Ukrainian crisis is an excellent example of today's synchronic functioning of the information sphere. On the one hand, divergent dominant media reporting can be divided most loosely into three separate spheres: Ukrainian, Russian and western.[7] They all had at least three similar characteristics:

1. Media reporting on the Ukrainian crisis was often strikingly simplistic. Therefore, information conveyed through the dominant media was regularly condensed into "one minute reports" that touched upon virtually nothing but the perpetuation of the basic informational dimension.
2. Censorship that emerged from the dominant media was partly the result of precisely this neoliberal ideological approach to the news. Unlike the examples from textbook totalitarian or ideological censorship that emerged as a reaction to the "inadmissible" reports of individuals, I believe the more dangerous forms of censorship lie within the realm of almost "accidental" self-censorship that finds its roots in the first characteristic described above. The inability to report on the news or events informationally heterogeneous or semantically challenging is not the result of the ideological leanings of the broadcasting companies towards any particular side of the conflict, but is the result of the neoliberal aspiration to "please" the audience with simplistic information, evading the everyday complexities of political struggles.
3. Nevertheless, actual censorship cannot be disregarded, as it can be visible on both sides. For example, Russian television channel Russia Today (abbreviated RT) was under heavy criticism for its alleged one-sided reporting on the Ukrainian Crisis. During March of 2014, an RT news anchor, Liz Wahl, even resigned her position because she could not handle the alleged censorship and one-sidedness, saying she's "proud to be an American and believe in disseminating the truth."[8] Of course, her position as conveyor of truth was mythologized to the level of the nation, regardless of various instances of western censorship throughout the decades.[9] The USA had (and still has) a plethora of cases when the censorship in that country was not only visible, but was a part of a national agenda.

Although the magnitude of actual censorship has yet to be determined, it seems clear that the analysis of contemporary media cannot restrict itself only to traditional as well as clear-cut media occurrences. On the contrary, it needs to be reiterated that the power of ideology lies not only in one-sided reporting, but in the very lack of information. In a sense, the real danger of censorship is not in its visible effects, as we have seen in the third example, but in the very neutrality and ideological autism mainstream media often tries to represent.

It is often said that the traditional media (television, radio or newspapers) are unidirectional agents of communication from producer to receiver, although the field of cultural studies with Stuart Hall and David Morley (to name a few) very provocatively questioned that notion. The Ukrainian crisis crystallized a need for the development of a relation between the producer and the receiver of information in a digital age. We cannot talk about authenticity or credibility in terms of "telling the truth or lying." On the contrary: today users can verify information by contrasting traditional media, or by autonomous investigation on the internet. In that manner, the information is rendered semantically ambiguous.

I claim that new media opens up a possibility of real intersubjectivity, where the public sphere need not be a part of mainstream media. Isn't the public (and private) online sphere the embodiment of this gesture? The intersubjective process exerted in a decentralized cyberspace denaturalizes the position of an all-knowing subject towards a user, who can compare, check, analyze, comment and improve on the information found online. The process of signification on the internet becomes of central value. While editors of daily newspapers or news anchors sometimes hide behind institutions while producing information (which *The Daily Show* masterfully shows), online users are almost always subjected to the process of individualization. The crisis that is evident in contemporary media mirrors this sentiment. The process of intersubjectivity cannot always be adopted by mainstream "old" media because it would nullify their authority as creators of objective reality. Take, for example, the Ukrainian crisis and the visual systems employed. As we have seen, traditional, as well as online media participated in the coverage of the Maidan protests and the ouster of President Viktor Yanukovych. Twitter erupted in activity after the civilians swarmed his already abandoned presidential estate. One of the more popular tweets was a photograph of President Yanukovych's alleged golden bathroom toilet. The legend below the photo was of the same form as legends describing photographs from various instances in dominant media. Almost every news outlet in Croatia (but also internationally!) provided the same photograph of the tweeted toilet as a synecdoche for the unfair and corrupted life of the president. A couple days later, I found out on the internet that the toilet is an old image, dating at least to 2012, of a random luxury apartment. Traditional news broadcasts in Croatia never really confuted their reports. One had to find that out online, amidst the supposed dystopia of the information sphere.

CONCLUSION

Media theory today stands out as one of the most dynamic disciplines in the social sciences and humanities. The present study constitutes a modern reading of the enduring cultural theory of the 20th century, taking into consideration analyses that can encompass the relationship between past, present and future. As a media scholar, I firmly stand on the side of cultural analysis that is grounded in the canon represented by the works of Adorno and Horkheimer, as well as Habermas and

Stuart Hall on the questions of the public sphere, industrialization of everyday life, and dialectics of ideology. Nevertheless, exciting new approaches to pertinent problems of contemporary culture can be seen in works not necessarily related to emerging disciplines such as digital humanities or big data studies, which tend to overquantify and generalize specific questions of (cultural) politics. Conversely, the emancipatory potential of future research can be seen precisely at the intersection of the aforementioned theoretical backbone that is rejuvenated and enhanced by media occurrences that are in need of political and cultural contextualization: the so-called new media revolutions and protests that, methodology-wise, are often treated uniformly. New research by Clay Shirky, Geert Lovink and even Slavoj Žižek (to name a few) offers new possibilities in reading cultural dynamics not as an uniform structure, but as a complex set of relations between classes, material and virtual space, politics and economy.

Deep structural changes in the mediasphere are only reaffirming the age-old questions of power relations between culture, economy and information, and their dialectic can be properly viewed only through systemic analysis of their complex historicities. Media institutions must adapt to these new complexities of conjuncture, as the fact that their power of controlling the market and information has decreased substantially proves to be a revolutionary potential in the era of information. Stuart Hall, in an already mentioned interview, detects these complexities that are relevant even today. He argues: "I think we are in a period of infinite multiplicity of codings [...]. We have all become, historically, fantastically codable encoding agents. We are in the middle of this multiplicity of reading and discourses and that has produced new forms of self-consciousness and reflexivity" (Grossberg, 2005, p. 137). Television shows such as *The Daily Show* should not be easily dismissed, as their complexity is a witness to the new arena in which political, economic and cultural questions are intensified through the production of popular culture. Further research is needed on the intersection between popular dominant systems (television) and the internet. How can "traditional" media benefit from the nominally democratized digital social space? How can we use the tools of 20th-century cultural theory and apply them to the digital age which is, as I have demonstrated, based on the same old relations of economy, politics and ideology?

In this chapter I have tried to show how media paradigms of today cannot hope to encompass the study of an audience by means of a general theory of society or culture. Market specificities, as well as the complexity of our culture, require innovative approaches to the public which is increasingly fragmentary in light of digital media developments. Nevertheless, in investigating these non-totalizing approaches to the political and ideological struggles of our everyday lives, theory should not be in awe of these new technologies. Theories of Antonio Gramsci and subsequently Stuart Hall's approach to cultural studies even today stand firm with relation to the analysis of cultural hegemony and power struggles. *The Daily Show With Jon Stewart* and the political crisis in Ukraine show us how the audience—regardless of the medium—requires attention as the creators of the public sphere. To be truly revolutionary today means traveling back and investigating—partly in a way proposed here—how the age-old dynamics of ideological struggles can be of use today in a media value chain that often thinks communication to the audience is increasingly hard. Through my analysis, I have tried to show how to advance the notion of communicating *to* the audience towards the notion of communication *with* the audience.

REFERENCES

Althusser, L. (1970). Ideology and ideological state apparatuses. In L. Althusser, *Lenin and philosophy and other essays* (pp. 127–186). New York, NY: Monthly Review Press.

Charney, L., & Schwartz, V. R. (1995). *Cinema and the invention of modern life*. Berkeley, CA: University of California Press.

Erion, G. J. (2007). Amusing ourselves to death with television news: Jon Stewart, Neil Postman, and the Huxleyan warning. In J. Holt (Ed.), *The Daily Show and philosophy* (pp. 5–16). Oxford, UK: Blackwell.

Fiske, J. (2001). *Television culture*. New York, NY: Routledge.

Grossberg, L. (Ed.). (2005). On postmodernism and articulation: An interview with Stuart Hall. In D. Morley & K.-H. Chen (Eds.), *Stuart Hall: Critical dialogues in cultural studies* (pp. 131–150). London, UK: Routledge.

Hall, S. (2012). Encoding/decoding. In M. G. Durham & D. Kellner (Eds.), *Media and cultural studies: Keyworks* (pp. 137–144). Oxford, UK: Wiley-Blackwell.

Hay, K., Hall, S., & Grossberg, L. (2013). Interview with Stuart Hall. *Communication and Critical/Cultural Studies, 10*(1), 10–33, doi:10.1080/14791420.2013.768404

Jones, S. (2006). *Antonio Gramsci*. London, UK: Routledge.

Morley, D., & Chen, K.-H. (Eds.). (2005). *Stuart Hall: Critical dialogues in cultural studies*. London, UK: Routledge.

Murphie, A., & Potts, J. (2003). *Culture and technology*. Houndmills, UK: Palgrave Macmillan.

Peović Vuković, K. (2014). Democracy and revolution on the Internet. *Crisis and Critique, 1*, 90–115.

Polk Wagner, R. (2003). Information wants to be free: Intellectual property and the mythologies of control. *Columbia Law Review, 103*(4), 995–1034.

Procter, J. (2004). *Stuart Hall*. London, UK: Routledge.

Senaldi, M. (2008). Teleestetika. *Tvrđa*, 1–2, 83–93.

Virilio, P. (1994). *The vision machine*. Bloomington, IN: British Film Institute and Indiana University Press.

Zinser, J. (2007). The good, the bad and *The Daily Show*. In J. Holt (Ed.), *The Daily Show and philosophy* (pp. 41–55). Oxford, UK: Blackwell.

Žižek, S. (2008). *The sublime object of ideology*. London, UK: Verso.

Žižek, S. (2010). Unbehagen and the subject: An interview with Slavoj Žižek. *Psychoanalysis, Culture & Society. 15*(4), 418–428. doi:10.1057/pcs.2010.22

NOTES

1. The trope, "information wants to be free", "is a well-known techie-activist rallying cry, typically invoked against any efforts to limit access to or charge money for information" (Polk Wagner, 2003, p. 999). It was first uttered by a techno-optimistic activist, Stewart Brand, more than 50 years ago, and from that moment onwards, became a sort of a popular battle cry for the tech-savvy.
2. For example, Hall continues the work of Dick Hebdige and the analysis of subcultures. He asserts that the sites of continuous negotiation between the dominant and subordinated are maybe best seen in the rebellious nature of subcultures which can be appropriated and "tamed" by capitalism.
3. For Gramsci, "common sense" is—to put it simplistically—a mode of conformist thinking, signaling consent to the dominant order.
4. This habit, as I hope to demonstrate shortly, is maybe closest to the idea of the internet-enabled communication any television programme has achieved.
5. Although, as I've shown with *The Daily Show*, mainstream media is still hugely relevant for the study of audience and ideology.
6. The first "real" revolutions that happened online were a part of the so-called Arab Spring in 2010. For more information see Katarina Peović Vuković (2014), "Democracy and Revolution on the Internet", *Crisis and Critique*, *1*, 90–115.
7. Taking into account the immense political and cultural complexity of the situation in Ukraine, I will defer from making universal or simplistic claims about it, and will instead focus on media perspectives and their difficulties in reporting on this event.
8. Retrieved May 10, 2014 from http://www.thedailybeast.com/articles/2014/03/05/exclusive-rt-today-anchor-liz-wahl-explains-why-she-quit.html
9. For instance, television host Phil Donahue managed to get his show cancelled on MSNBC. On February 25, 2003 MSNBC cancelled the show, citing his opposition to the imminent invasion of Iraq by the United States military.

Part Four: Inter-Continental Corollaries of Breaking the Media Value Chain in Journalism

CHAPTER ELEVEN

The Disruption of the Portuguese Media Democracy? Economic Crisis and Media Ownership

RITA FIGUEIRAS AND NELSON COSTA RIBEIRO

INTRODUCTION

In the last years many media companies, particularly those operating in the press business, have entered into crisis leading to newspaper closures, reduction of pages per edition and newsroom downsizing. This has led several publications to lose not only journalists but also resources that are important so that investigative work can be conducted. Against this background, a new series of concerns about the role of journalism have reemerged and the ability of the press to monitor "the activities of economically and politically powerful groups" (Franklin, 2012, p. 3) is being seriously questioned. While some cases, namely *The New York Times*,[1] have created international awareness about the alterations taking place inside many newsrooms, the scenario seems not to be much different in most Western countries, which is the result of a rapid decline in press advertising, along with a decrease in the number of readers, many of whom now simply access information available on the internet, via content aggregators and micro blogs which have become available not only on computers but also on smartphones and other portable devices. Additionally, in Western countries, in the last few years, several companies operating in the communication and media sector, mostly involved in print, have been acquired by new investors that were not traditionally involved in the media and communication business. One of the most visible cases is the *Washington Post*, acquired in 2013 by the founder and executive director of Amazon, Jeff Bezos.

Within this framework, the chapter analyzes the recent alterations that have been taking place in the Portuguese media system and discusses how the economic crisis that became more evident in 2008 has led to severe transformations in the media sector, namely business models, ownership and funding. Following the country's loan from the IMF, the European Central Bank and the European Commission, Portugal entered into a severe recession which has had a significant impact on media companies whose revenue dropped quite drastically due to the retraction of the advertising market. Several media groups entered into financial strangulation and started looking for new investors mostly coming from countries with autocratic regimes, such as Angola.

The investment by Angolan companies in the Portuguese telecommunication and media companies started in 2008 with the acquisition of influential stakes in some of the most important Portuguese companies operating in the media and telecommunication sectors. Moreover, these same investors also started to have dominant positions in other strategic businesses such as banking, oil and construction.

Besides describing and analyzing how these ownership changes are reconfiguring the Portuguese media market, the chapter will also discuss the fact that some of these acquisitions took place without even being clear who were the new owners. One explanation for this is that despite the fact that the Portuguese constitution states that an independent administrative entity shall guarantee the non-concentration of ownership of the media, to date there is a lack of legislation covering very critical issues such as cross-participation, cross-concentration and ownership transparency.

These new tendencies are putting into question Portuguese media transparency, independence and pluralism as pivotal elements for the good health of the democratic regime. Within this framework, the chapter debates how all this interplays with the Portuguese maturing democracy, and the impact it may have in the political process, more specifically how the economic crisis is raising once more tensions about how to balance the capitalist logic of the media with the public interest and democracy. Even though it is a peculiar case, it can help to enlighten what happens to the media when a severe financial crisis hits the companies operating in the sector. In fact, Portugal was one of the countries most affected by the crisis of sovereign debt that hit Europe after the international financial crisis of 2008 that emerged following the collapse of Lehman Brothers. While media companies are facing significant challenges in countries where the total advertising market has been stable in the last years, one must expect the media to be facing even bigger challenges in markets where total advertising has been declining, which has been the case of Portugal. Therefore, analyzing the disruption of the

Portuguese media market and the trends that have emerged following the 2008 crisis will allow us to understand how journalism is today being challenged in a country where the media faced several simultaneous crises: national crisis with a strong decline in GDP, crisis of the press that is now dealing with more competition and civic crisis which concerns the role of journalism.

The research presented is grounded on the intersection between political economy of the media and media democracy studies. Considering that the news and also media companies simultaneously reflect and promote a particular political culture, it seems highly relevant to generate knowledge on the new forms of media ownership that are emerging which might lead to changes in how we perceive journalism in Western countries. If we are to discuss the civic importance of journalism and its role in the promotion of democracy, it seems crucial to understand which new forms of ownership are emerging and how they might affect how journalism operates. The data presented were collected through official entities and also from the websites of the companies that will be analyzed. Additionally, we also resorted to news media that reported on the transformations taking place in ownership structure.

MEDIA DEMOCRACY

Born out of the eighteenth-century historical construction that shaped the identity of the media as one of the fundamental bodies in guaranteeing the Western newly democratic regimes, media democracy was built on the ideas of market freedom and freedom of expression and on values such as quality, diversity and plurality, which became cornerstone concepts of the principle of press freedom (Cornu, 1999; Garnham, 2000; Habermas, 1984; Keane, 2002; McNair, 2003).

Since then, this understanding has put great expectations around media democratic performance across Western countries as this meant that the media ought to fulfill the role of serving the public interest while producing profit in order to guarantee their editorial independence. Hence, it comes as no surprise that the enduring tension between business and public service has been continually latent within Western democratic societies and a continuous topic of debate among media scholars and journalists, and from time to time also in society at large.

The question of media's social responsibility started to be raised in the 1940s by the North-American Commission on Freedom of the Press, also known as the Hutchins Commission. The perception of the uneven balance between market freedom and freedom of expression led to public suspicion about media owners' motivations, considered to be more about interests in accumulating power and in commercial profit than in serving the public interest—i.e., the responsibility to inform, to explain and to promote debate on public issues by bringing awareness to society in order to engage citizens with the political process, along with media's role of scrutinizing the abuses of power (Norris, 2000, pp. 22–35). After deliberating for four years, in 1947 the Commission report reclaimed the eighteenth-century media matrix by reaffirming that the press was free for the purpose of both serving democracy and elevating society's standards (Siebert, Peterson, & Schramm, 1956).

Notwithstanding, in the 1980s this debate gained new light as changes in the discursive public culture (both market and entertainment-driven) had become more salient and the decline of people's awareness, interest and involvement in public affairs had risen. Therefore, and once more, the media's contribution to democratic disengagement—and ultimately its democratic role as a 'political sentinel' (Norris, 2010a, 2010b)—started to be examined (e.g., Bernstein, 1992; Gurevitch & Blumler, 1991; Postman, 1985). Within the debate of the media contribution to democratic disengagement, Neil Postman stood out with his very much debated book, *Amusing Ourselves to Death*, published in 1985. Postman argued about what he called the corrosive effects of television, entertainment and infotainment, which were, according to him, leading consumers to exchange their civic rights for entertainment. Consumers were becoming more interested in watching entertainment shows, knowing about celebrities and following entertainment news than in learning about hard politics and engaging in public affairs. According to Neil Postman, but also to other authors such as Cappella and Jamieson (1997) and Patterson (2003), the corrosive effects of entertainment and infotainment were leading society to a de-democratization process. Moreover, Carl Bernstein (1992) criticized the institutionalization of infotainment as the dominant way of practicing journalism. In his view, journalism's prerogatives of challenging citizens were losing terrain to the commercial imperative of amusing them. In addition, infotainment was leading to the erosion of the modern notion of public culture built on rationality, reflexivity and critical spirit (Habermas, 1984), and to the emergence of an "idiot culture," which, in his perspective, was becoming a new cultural norm in the late 20th century.

The critics highlighted the media's decreasing vigilance of government and the increased exposing of its excesses, which was leading to media watchdogs' losing terrain to media attack dogs. The aggressive reporting on politics began to stress strategy, wrongdoings and attacks among political counterparts, and to dramatize controversy (Patterson, 2003) while the context and content of public affairs were being devalued.

If the democratic role of the media was built around the idea that what was important to society was important to the media, the commercial ambitions of shareholders led to a distortion of this principle. What was good for the media business seemed not to be good for society, compromising, thus, media democratic performance by putting into evidence what Gurevitch and Blumler (1991) coined as the "civic communication decline".

The authors related the civic decadence of the media with the lack of media accountability, a topic elaborated by McQuail: "Accountable communication exists where authors...take responsibility for the quality and consequences of the publication, orient themselves to audiences and others affected, and respond to their expectations and those of the wider society" (2003, p. 19). Building on the ideas of Hodges (1986) and Christians (1988), McQuail stressed that globalization, commercialization, the increased scale and abundance of media, and their increasing concentration were leading, once more, to the conclusion that the media were institutions beyond control (McQuail, 2003).

Continuing the debate, John Keane (2002) questioned the strengths and weaknesses of the Western media cornerstone idea of freedom of expression. "Are there situations where freedom of the press may compromise the freedom of the press?" (p. 183). By answering affirmatively, Keane stated that media markets were self-paralyzing in the sense that their freedom without limits did not assure freedom *for* the press. It instead created censorship (Keane, 2002, 2013). In his view, markets generate structural contradictions and endemic dilemmas that deny their claims of openness and free access by favoring high levels of media concentration and accumulation of power without responsibility. In the highly competitive market of the present time where only media conglomerates seem to be able to operate and survive, it is not possible to say that market freedom guarantees media freedom and plurality.

Notwithstanding, the economic argument gained new layers as media companies entered into crisis in the 2000s. As the space for news in the digital age expanded, it has also brought retraction, as the business model for commercial news fell apart. The perception of the internet as a free-of-charge medium, the decreased value of news and the growing relevance of social media—harnessed by smartphones and by tablets—as alternative examples of information production and dissemination, have all contributed to the bankruptcy of the journalism business model, which had existed since its industrialization in the second half of the nineteenth century.

Moreover, the precarious conditions of the media sector increased significantly after the collapse of Lehman Brothers in 2008. In the last years, many media companies, particularly those operating in the press business, have entered into crisis, leading to newspaper closures, reduction of pages per edition and newsroom downsizing. This has led several publications to lose not only journalists but also resources that are important so that investigative work can be conducted.

As the media do not escape a range of responsibilities to society arising from their history and the position they occupy in society (McQuail, 2003, p. 17), on top of the financial constraints that have been imposed on the media, journalism seems to be facing, once more, what Jay Blumler (2012, p. xv) has described as a crisis of "civic adequacy, impoverishing the contributions of journalism to citizenship and democracy" due to its focus on soft news which can be seen as a consequence of the need to catch the attention of a fragmented audience that today has many choices and has lost the routine of reading the daily paper or watching the evening news (Patterson, 2010). In fact, journalists are not only committed to reporting the news but also to ensuring that the stories that do get told on the news are interesting to the audience and call their attention to political news that is not the motivation behind the consumption of newspapers, television or digital platforms (Schudson, 2008). A different perspective is furnished by McChesney and Nichols who consider that, even though the internet was "a central factor in the collapse of the commercial news media" (2010, p. 3), the roots of the journalism crisis are to be found in ownership concentration and in the fact that media companies in the last decades have valued much more the delivery of revenue to their shareholders than the fulfillment of their democratic functions. Even though these have been widely discussed (e.g., Norris, 2000; Schudson, 2008) their fulfillment is dependent on a series of values such as quality of information, diversity of perspectives and plurality of opinion (Keane, 2002) that have not always been considered as a priority for those operating in the sector. As pointed out by McChesney and Nichols (2010, p. 3), media owners have made "the commercial and entertainment values of the market drastically higher priorities than the civic and democratic values that are essential to good journalism and a good society" (McChesney & Nichols, 2010, p. 3).

The implications of the disruption of the traditional business model became once again a central topic of discussion in communication studies (Berte & De Bens, 2009; Curran, 2012; Franklin, 2012; Picard, 2009), with Leonard Downie and Michael Schudson (2009), following others, such as John B. Thompson (1995), suggesting the adoption of subsidy systems that would enable the press to perform its democratic role. In Downie and Schudson's own words, society "must take some collective responsibility for supporting independent news reporting in this new environment…through varying combinations of philanthropy, subsidy, and government policy" (2009).

Despite the way we approach the reality that journalism is living today, it seems clear that media companies are facing a financial crisis and a civic crisis. This will be at the center of the next section where we will analyze how the Portuguese media system has been reconfigured with regard to its forms of ownership and also its ability to perform its democratic role.

THE PORTUGUESE CRISES AND CHANGES IN THE MEDIA SECTOR

The value of news has changed quite significantly in the last decade and, even though the decline of the press can be traced back to the mid-1900s (Hardy, 2008), after the international crisis that became paramount after the collapse of Lehman Brothers, in 2009 the European Union entered into recession and some countries from the Eurozone became unable to refinance government debt (Shambaugh, 2012). In the case of Portugal, after Moody's Investors Service cut the country's sovereign bond rating, which took place in summer of 2010,[2] the government was put under pressure, which culminated in May 2011 with the request for a bailout package from the International Monetary Fund, the European Central Bank and the European Commission. In exchange for the loan that was given to Portugal, the foreign entities demanded a stabilization of public finances. This led to severe cuts in public spending, to a significant increase in the unemployment rate that peaked at 17.8% in April 2013[3] and also to the selling of strategic public sector companies, such as the national electricity company *EDP* and the Portuguese airport management company, *ANA*, both sold in 2012. Simultaneously, the most significant private companies, including those operating in the media business, started looking for international investors since they also had to face huge financial problems related to the economic recession that brought along a significant decrease in advertising expenditure. Between 2007 and 2013 the Portuguese advertising market decreased -43% with newspapers and magazines suffering the biggest losses (-64.2% and -62.7% respectively), followed by outdoor advertising (-51.3%) and television (-41.8%).[4] According to the media agency *Nova Expressão*,[5] between 2007 and 2013 the Portuguese advertisement market lost more than 330 million euros of its total value. In fact, during this period of six years the only segment that increased its revenue was internet advertising, that grew 244.6%, which allowed some companies with better digital strategies to slightly compensate some of the bigger losses in traditional media advertising.

Rupert Murdoch's announcement, in 2009, that he would charge for content on his websites (McChesney & Nichols, 2010) clearly marked a turning point in the discussion on the future of newspapers and journalism. Many other media companies have followed Murdoch's example, making content only available behind closed doors either through websites or mobile apps. This new business model together with the increasing advertisement investment in the internet helps to explain the creation in 2014 of two new exclusively digital projects, *Expresso Diário* and *Observador*, in a recessive media market such as the Portuguese one. The first is a byproduct of the strong weekly Portuguese newspaper *Expresso*, held by Impresa, one of the biggest Portuguese media companies. However, the creation of this online daily edition was a reaction to the announcement that *Observador* was going to be launched. The online daily was created by a Portuguese right-wing elite faction that since the 1980s has a tradition of creating weekly newspapers as a response to the professionalization of journalism (Figueiras, 2005, 2009). Considering that its ideological frame is under-represented in the Portuguese media, when *Expresso* affirmed itself as an independent journalistic project in the beginning of the 1980s, a small elite, wealthy, well-educated and politically active, founded the weekly *Semanário* in 1983. This paper turned out to be not financially viable and was not able to dispute the mainstream market with *Expresso*, and in 1988 its founders supported, both financially and politically, the creation of *O Independente*, which lasted until 1998. In 2006, some of the same investors were involved in the launch of *Sol* and more recently, in 2014, they invested in the online journalism project *Observador*.

The two new titles combine elements of innovation and tradition in business models. Following new trends in other markets, the ownership of *Observador* includes journalists and pundits, bringing back to memory an eighteenth-century tradition in the newspaper business before the separation between property and the newsroom (Albert & Terrou, 1979). This newspaper charges for content and despite its technological affordances, it only updates its news twice a day. Following individuals' news consumption practices, which indicate that the majority of people search for news in the evening, *Expresso Diário* comes out only once a day at six in the afternoon. This news cycle resembles the one in which evening newspapers used to work, although it is a business model that withdrew a long time ago from the Western mainstream media market.

While these new projects came online in 2014, in the last few years traditional media companies operating in the Portuguese market have encountered financial difficulties during the country's economic crisis,[6] which created an opportunity for new investors to enter the scene. In this regard, Angolan companies have become among the most active in acquiring significant positions in several sectors of the economy, namely in media and telecom.

After it gained independence, Angola[7] adopted a presidential system and since then it has been ruled by the MPLA. The incumbent President, José Eduardo dos Santos, has been in power since 1979, making him one of the two African presidents with the longest terms in office, along with Guinea's Teodoro Nguem. In the last decade, and after the end of the civil war, despite the socialist background of the MPLA, the country embraced capitalism and has become a fast-growing economy. GDP grew at an annual rate of 12.2% from 2004 to 2013[8] which is mostly driven by the exploration of national resources.[9]

While the economy has been growing significantly in the last decade, the wealth that is being generated has not reached most of the Angolan people, 37% of whom live below the poverty line, according to World Bank figures.[10] Many do not have access to potable water, electricity and transport. Even though several sectors of the Angolan economy have been opened up to private enterprise in the last few years, the economic resources are far from being evenly distributed, since the main businesses are oriented toward maximizing the gains of the ruling elite that controls the oil-diamond sectors and related businesses.

Politically dominated by the MPLA and led by a powerful president who now has been in office for 35 consecutive years, Angola has the characteristics of a semi-authoritarian regime (Hadland, 2012), which also translates into illiberal views on the role of the media. There is significant evidence of a lack of pluralism and press freedom restrictions imposed by the political power are quite visible even though the majority of the media are either controlled directly by the State or by businessmen with close connections to the ruling elite. The different types of control exercised over news reporting have been systematically denounced by a few Angolan journalists and also by the Reporters without Frontiers.[11]

Taking into account the circumstances under which the media operate in Angola and how they tend to be controlled by the political sphere, it is crucial to analyze how businessmen, coming from a semi-autocratic environment, have been expanding their investments in Portuguese media and telecommunication companies. In this regard, the three most significant investors are Isabel dos Santos, *Newshold* and António Mosquito, all belonging to or having close relations with the Angolan ruling elite. While the former has become one of the major investors in the Portuguese economy, the latter two have acquired significant stakes in media companies.

ANGOLAN INVESTORS ENTER THE SCENE

Isabel dos Santos is the eldest daughter of the Angolan president, José Eduardo dos Santos, considered by *Forbes* magazine the richest woman in Angola and the first and only woman billionaire in Africa. She owns some of the biggest and most powerful multi-sector business companies in her home country, with interests in strategic sectors such as oil, energy, banking, diamonds, communications and others. The evolution, growth and diversification of her businesses reflect the privatization and liberalization strategy followed by the government headed by her father in the last years as the Angolan economy departed from a communist to a capitalist economy (Figueiras & Ribeiro, 2013).

The president's daughter entered the business world in 1997 when she established Miami Beach Club, one of the first night clubs and beach restaurants in Angola's capital.[12] In this same year she also set up, along with her mother, the company TAIS (Trans Africa Investment Services). Two years later it became a major player in the diamond sector. In 1999, when Isabel dos Santos was then aged 26, the Angolan government, headed by her father, announced an agreement with TAIS, the Goldberg Group and Leviev Wellox to establish a diamond trading joint-venture, Angola Selling Corporation (Ascorp). The country is the world's fourth largest producer and Isabel dos Santos was then controlling 24.5% of the business that, according to *Forbes* magazine, yields "millions of dollars in dividends per month".[13] In the mid-2000s, when "blood-diamonds" started to garner international attention, she transferred the control of the company entirely to her mother.

This is not the only case in which the daughter of José Eduardo dos Santos has acquired stakes in important businesses that were opened up to private initiative by the government. Also in 1999 the Angolan government decided to grant a new telecom licensing without a public bid, allowing Unitel to become the first private mobile telephone operator in the country. Two of the shareholders were the state-owned oil company Sonangol and Isabel dos Santos with a 25% stake each. This meant that despite the supposed liberalization of the sector, it continued to be under the control of the country's ruling elite, illustrating the clientelistic practices that are taking place between the political and economic spheres in Angola. Another example of this is Urbana 2000, a company founded by Isabel dos Santos, that won the contract for cleaning-up and disinfecting Luanda and other Angolan cities.

In the last years her investments expanded and diversified into other areas, such as oil, tourism, real estate, cement, construction and banking. Furthermore, she has become a strategic partner in the major investments made by Portuguese companies in Angola, meaning that she serves as strategic gatekeeper for Portuguese investments in the country. This seems, in fact, to have become a common practice, since *Forbes* has also denounced the fact that Isabel dos Santos's financial empire has been built through clientelistic practices and from taking a chunk of the companies that intend to do business in the country.[14]

In banking, she has significant investments in Banco Espírito Santo Angola (BESA), and in 2011 she signed a partnership with the Portuguese Sonae group for the development and operation of a retail trading company in Angola. Sonae is one of the largest Portuguese companies and the largest private employer in Portugal. It is the leading company in the retail sector, whose president and main shareholder is Belmiro de Azevedo, one of the most influential Portuguese businessmen and a *Forbes* fortune figure. The start-up of the Portuguese group in Angola is expected to occur in 2014 or 2015 with the opening of its first supermarket.[15]

The involvement of Isabel dos Santos with the Sonae group dates back to the early days of her first investments in Portugal that started in 2008 when she took significant stakes in retail, finance, energy and telecommunication. In the case of the latter, besides stakes in the market leader PT, she invested in Zon Multimédia that operates in cable television (a sector in which it is market leader), broadband internet access, landline, virtual mobile, television broadcasting, film distribution, and movie theaters. Since 2012 the company was involved in the preparation of a merger with Optimus (owned by the Sonae group), one of the three mobile phone operators in Portugal, that took place in 2013 and led to the company's renaming as Nos in June 2014. This operation created the second largest telecommunication company in Portugal, in which Isabel dos Santos has a 50.01% stake, while Sonae is the second largest stakeholder.

In the banking sector, she has invested in the largest Portuguese bank, the state-owned Caixa Geral de Depósitos, and also in private banks, holding 25% of the Portuguese operation of the Angolan bank BIC Português, where she is a member of the board. She also owns 19.5% of Banco Português de Investimento (BPI), and is a major shareholder of Banco Português de Negócios (BPN), after this bank was acquired by Banco BIC in 2011. She has other major stakes together with the Angolan state oil company Sonangol (which is also the main shareholder of BCP, the largest private bank in Portugal). The most important of these is in the Portuguese oil company, Galp Energia. Furthermore, she controls 45% of Amorim Energia, a subsidiary holding of the Amorim Group (one of the largest Portuguese multinational companies, the world leader in cork production). This company, just like Isabel dos Santos, holds 25% of BIC Portugal, which is the major shareholder of Galp Energia.

Even though Isabel dos Santos has not yet invested directly in the companies involved in media production, as we have previously mentioned, she is now the major stakeholder of the second largest Portuguese telecom, Nos, leader in the distribution of cable and satellite television. The company does business with all the main Portuguese media groups, namely with the major private television producers, Media Capital and Impresa, that in the last few years have increased the number of channels available through cable, some of which are distributed exclusively by Nos. In 2012 the press reported that the daughter of the Angolan president was interested in extending her business to television production and that she would vie for the public bid that the government announced would take place in 2013 for the privatization of the main public service broadcasting television channel, RTP1. Ultimately this did not take place, since divergences in the governmental coalition led the state not to go ahead with the sale.

Even though Isabel dos Santos has been the Angolan business person who most invested in Portugal during the years of the crisis, as far as the media sector is concerned, the major stakes have been acquired by Newshold, a company held by Pineview Overseas, an offshore entity with headquarters in Panama, and more recently António Mosquito, also known for his major business activities in Angola. The former was the first to enter the scene back in 2009 with the acquisition of the weekly newspaper *Sol*, when the paper was struggling with financial difficulties. *Sol* is one of the two weekly newspapers published in Portugal and second in circulation. Following its acquisition by Newshold, the paper started to also produce Angolan and Mozambican editions.

Since 2009 Newshold has expanded its investments. In the media sector it became a stakeholder of two of the most important Portuguese private media groups: Impresa (1.05%) and Cofina. In the case of the latter, the first investment by the Angolan company was made in October 2011 when it acquired a stake of 6.16%. In the following months it increased its stake to 15.08% but in November 2013, a few days after it reinforced its investment in Impresa, it reduced its position in Cofina to 12.21%.[16] Curiously, it was also in this same month that another Portuguese media group, Controlinveste, was partially acquired by another Angolan businessman, António Mosquito: an acquisition that will be detailed below.

In the last few years Newshold has also made investments in other sectors besides media and communication, namely in the Sporting football club, where it holds a 25% stake, and Cofaco, a company operating in the fish canning industry, where it now owns 80%. Despite these businesses, the Angolan company is mostly known for its involvement in the media sector since, as mentioned above, both Impresa and Cofina are two of the three major media companies operating in the Portuguese market. Impresa is, in fact, the largest private media company, with interests extending from newspaper and magazine publishing to television, both free to air and cable television, and also digital media. The group was founded in the 1970s by former prime minister Francisco Pinto Balsemão and although he started the business with the publication of a weekly newspaper, the group expanded mostly in the 1990s when it was one of the two companies to win the public bid for the creation of private free to air television channels, putting an end to State-owned television monopoly (Correia, 1997). Today it also operates several cable channels, one of which, SIC Caras, has an agreement for exclusive distribution with *Nos*, the company controlled by Isabel dos Santos. In 2011, Impresa attempted to expand its business to Angola with the launch of a weekly economic magazine entitled *Rumo*, 30% of which was owned by Impresa and 70% by the Angolan holding, Finicapital.[17] It was, nevertheless, a failure and the magazine closed in December 2012.

The other media company in which Newshold has a significant stake (12.21%), Cofina, is the largest in the newspaper and magazine businesses. Its daily popular tabloid, *Correio da Manhã*, published since 1979, is the most read in the country, while its daily sports (*Record*) and business (*Jornal de Negócios*) newspapers occupy the #2 spots in the rankings of their market segments. Furthermore, after acquiring *Metro* in 2009, it also owns the only two free daily newspapers published in Portugal and in 2013 it expanded its business into the television sector with the launch of a news channel, Correio da Manhã TV, that follows the editorial line of its tabloid paper of the same name.

Even though Newshold has been operating in Portugal since 2009, the ownership of the company was maintained in secrecy until 2012. The public disclosure of the names of owners only took place after the company announced its interest in participating in the bid that the government intended to launch in order to privatize one of the public service television channels. Even though the State did not go ahead with this plan, the possible participation in the bid made the disclosure of the company's ownership structure inevitable. It was then revealed that it belonged to the Madaleno family which has close ties with the Angolan political elite.[18] One of the five proprietors and CEO of the company is Álvaro Madaleno who is also an investor (5%) in BESA, a bank where Isabel dos Santos also owns a major stake.

From the point of view of the democratic role of the media, what this case reveals is quite disturbing. In fact, it was possible for a company operating in the media sector to maintain an opacity regarding its owners, which clearly represents a serious threat to the ideal of media ownership transparency, essential for the existence of media pluralism. Despite the fact that the country's constitution states that an independent administrative entity shall guarantee the non-concentration of ownership of the media, to date there is a lack of legislation covering very critical issues such as cross-participation, cross-concentration and ownership transparency. These issues have been on the political agenda since 2009 but the network of clientelistic interests involved has made it impossible for political entities to legislate on these matters. These kinds of practices have been identified by Hallin & Mancini (2004) in what they proposed as the pluralist polarized model that is said to be characteristic of Southern European countries.

The last of the three Angolan investors to enter the telecom and media sectors was António Mosquito, who is known for not being directly involved in politics in his home country. Nevertheless, his businesses have grown with the support of president José Eduardo dos Santos, and they extend from diamonds to banking and car importation.[19] After a long period of negotiations, in 2014 he acquired 27.5% of Controlinveste, meaning that he invested 10 million euros in the company,[20] while 15% is controlled by BCP bank whose major stakeholder is Sonangol (19.44%),[21] the largest state-owned Angolan company. Controlinveste is at present one of the four largest private Portuguese media companies, owner of *Diário de Notícias* (the oldest daily newspaper in circulation founded in 1864), *Jornal de Notícias* (ranked #2 of the daily tabloid press), *O Jogo* (sports daily paper), *Dinheiro Vivo* (digital paper specializing in economic issues) and TSF (the only Portuguese news radio).

After the entrance of the new management, Controlinveste announced that it would enter into internal restructuring which would be done through the dismissal of 160 employees,[22] including 65 journalists, a figure which, as in the case of the *New York Times*, raised the question of how the newsroom would guarantee the quality of its investigative research if most of the senior journalists will be gone.

Besides its economic restructure, the group has admitted that what will follow in 2015 is an editorial change in the most symbolic assets of the group: *Diário de Notícias* and TSF, which will also include alterations in the editors-in-chief. Other media have stressed the sensitivity of this subject considering, on the one hand, the media cultural ethos of the new owner of the company, and, on the other hand, the fact that in the next year general elections will happen in the country.[23]

Along with these investments in the media sector, António Mosquito has also acquired 66.7% of the construction company Soares da Costa for 70 million euros, one of the largest Portuguese companies operating in Africa, namely Angola and Mozambique, and also aiming to expand to Brazil. With this acquisition the decision center of the company moved from Porto to Luanda, because of its main owner, António Mosquito, but also because four CEOs of the company also live in Luanda. Mosquito also owns 50% of the business of Novabase (a Portuguese-based company) in Angola.

CONCLUSION

The relationship between the media and democracy must not be taken for granted, in the sense that in order for that alliance to work certain requisites must be guaranteed, namely both market freedom and freedom of expression. In the nineteenth century, building on the ideas of John Locke or Baron de Montesquieu, the founding fathers of the fourth estate model of the press considered markets to be an essential source of revenue for newspapers that would allow them to become independent from political interference. However, the last century has shown that markets do not have a democratic core and therefore, if journalism can contribute to democratizing societies, it may also be a powerful force in processes of "de-democratization" (Fenton, 2010, p. 43).

In the Portuguese case, the entrance of Angolan investors in the economy, particularly in the media sector, became paramount during the economic crisis that led to a significant decrease in advertisement spending which is private media's main revenue source. Although in the last years some Portuguese media groups have started to charge for some of their content available on the internet and mobile apps, the revenues generated by subscriptions are still very small when compared to what media earn from advertising. Therefore, when the Portuguese media companies entered into financial difficulties a need to attract new investors became evident. This allowed for Angolan companies to enter the scene, meaning that the changes of ownership that have been taking place in the last few years in the Portuguese market have much to do with the disruption of the traditional business models that have been affected by the financial crisis and also by the new challenges brought by the digital environment.

The impact of ownership changes in the media sector should be assessed, bearing in mind journalism's civic role and its importance for the democratic process. Therefore, in this article we have described the background from which the new Angolan investors are emerging. While in their home country the media are subject to close scrutiny and to severe limitations in regard to freedom of reporting, it is necessary to monitor how this cultural background will affect how these new owners foresee the role of the media in the Portuguese context. In fact, while in Western democracies the press is given the role of contributing to the democratic process, which requires the public scrutiny of both political and economic decisions, in autocratic regimes the media are mostly perceived as tools used to perpetuate the elite in power (Hadland, 2012). Therefore, the changes taking place in the Portuguese media sector represent a challenge for the institutions that have the responsibility to assure that pluralism and diversity of information are available to citizens. This is particularly crucial, bearing in mind that Portugal inaugurated what would later be classified as the third wave of democratization (Huntington, 1991), meaning that it has a young democratic regime that certainly needs a free press to perform its civic duties well. This requires not only the transmission of relevant political news but also the production of investigative journalism that might be at risk if the new owners bring along an autocratic approach to the media in which journalism is not expected to act as a watchdog but is instead perceived as a weapon to promote and contribute to the success of the political and economic elites. Within this context, there are two strong trends that seem to be emerging in the news media in Portugal. While, on the one hand, there is an increasing presence of news related to Angola, mostly presented with a positive frame (namely by covering successful businesses in the country and by promoting Angolan businessmen and companies), on the other hand, there is also an increasing absence of news that could compromise the Angolan political and economic elite (namely news about how the regime has been dealing with human rights and citizens' protests against the government). Hence, the economic crisis is raising once more tensions about how to balance the capitalist logic of the media with its role as a safeguard of the public interest and democracy.

REFERENCES

Albert, P., & Terrou, F. (1979). *Histoire de la presse.* Paris: PUF.

Bernstein, C. (1992). The idiot culture. *The New Republic*, 22–28.

Berte, K., & De Bens, E. (2009). Newspapers go for advertising! Challenges and opportunities in a changing media environment. In B. Franklin (Ed.), *The future of newspapers.* London, UK: Routledge.

Blumler, J. G. (2012). Foreword: The two-legged crisis of journalism. In B. Franklin (Ed.), *The future of journalism* (pp. xv–xvii). London, UK: Routledge.

Cappella, J. N., & Jamieson, K. H. (1997). *Spiral of cynicism: The press and the public good.* New York, NY: Oxford University Press.

Christians, C. (1988). Can the public be held accountable? *Journal of Mass Media Ethics, 1*, 50–58.

Cornu, D. (1999). *Jornalismo e verdade. Para uma ética da informação.* Lisboa, Portugal: Instituto Piaget.

Correia, F. (1997). *Os jornalistas e as notícias.* Porto, Portugal: Caminho.

Curran, J. (2012). The future of journalism. In B. Franklin (Ed.), *The future of journalism* (pp. 23–35). London, UK: Routledge.

Downie, L., & Schudson, M. (2009). The reconstruction of American journalism. Retrieved from www.cjr.org/reconstruction/the_reconstruction_of_american.php?page=all

Fenton, N. (2010). New media, journalism and democracy: Figments of a neo-liberal imagination? *Media & Jornalismo*, 17 (9/2), 41–52.

Ferreira, J. M. (1994). Portugal em transe. In J. Mattoso (Org.), *História de Portugal* (vol. 8). Lisboa, Portugal: Editorial Estampa.

Figueiras, R. (2005). *Os Comentadores e os media*. Lisboa, Portugal: Livros Horizonte.

Figueiras, R. (2009). *O comentário político e a política do comentário*. Lisboa, Portugal: Paulus.

Figueiras, R., & Ribeiro, N. (2013). New global flows of capital in media industries after the 2008 financial crisis: The Angola–Portugal relationship. *International Journal of Press/Politics, 18*(4), 508–524.

Franklin, B. (2012). Introduction. In B. Franklin (Ed.), *The future of newspapers*. London, UK: Routledge.

Garnham, N. (2000). *Emancipation, the media and modernity*. Oxford, UK: Oxford University Press.

Gurevitch, M., & Blumler, J. (1991). Political communication system and democracy. In J. Lichtenberg, *Democracy and the mass media* (pp. 269–289). Cambridge , UK: Cambridge University Press.

Habermas, J. (1984). *Mudança estrutural da esfera pública*. Rio de Janeiro, Brazil: Tempo Brasileiro.

Hadland, A. (2012). Africanizing three models of media and politics: The South African experience. In D. Hallin & P. Mancini (Eds.), *Comparing media systems beyond the Western world* (pp. 96–118). Cambridge, UK: Cambridge University Press.

Hallin, D., & Mancini, P. (2004). Comparing media systems. Cambridge, UK: Cambridge University Press.

Hardy, J. (2008). *Western media systems*. London, UK: Routledge.

Hodges, L. W. (1986). Defining press accountability: A functional approach. In D. Elliot (Ed.) *Responsible Journalism* (pp. 13–31). Beverly Hills, CA: Sage.

Huntington, S. P. (1991). *The third wave: Democratization in the late 20th century*. Norman, OK: University of Oklahoma Press.

Keane, J. (2002). *Os media e a democracia*. Lisboa, Portugal: Temas & Debates.

Keane, J. (2013). *Democracy and media decadence*. Cambridge, UK: Cambridge University Press.

McChesney, R., & Nichols, J. (2010). *The death and life of American journalism: The media revolution that will begin the world again*. Philadelphia, PA: Nation Books.

McNair, B. (2003). *An introduction to political communication*. London, UK: Routledge.

McQuail, D. (2003). *Teoria da comunicação de massas*. Lisboa, Portugal: Fundação Calouste Gulbenkian.

Norris, P. (2000). *A virtuous circle: Political communications in postindustrial societies*. Cambridge, UK: Cambridge University Press.

Norris, P. (2010a). *Democratic deficit: Critical citizens revisited*. Cambridge, UK: Cambridge University Press.

Norris, P. (2010b). *Public sentinel: News media & governance reform*. Washington, DC: World Bank.

Patterson, T. (2003). Tendências do jornalismo contemporâneo. *Media & Jornalismo, 2*, 19–47.

Patterson, T. (2010). Media abundance and democracy. *Media & Jornalismo*, 17 (9/2), 13–29.

Picard, R. (2009). Shifts in newspaper advertising expenditures and their implications for the future of newspapers. In B. Franklin (Ed.), *The future of newspapers*. London, UK: Routledge.

Postman, N. (1985). *Amusing ourselves to death: Public discourse in the age of show business.* New York, NY: Viking.

Schudson, M. (2008). *Why democracies need an unlovable press.* Cambridge, UK: Polity Press.

Shambaugh, J. C. (2012). The euro's three crises. *Brookings Papers on Economic Activity,* Spring, 157–211. Retrieved from http://www.brookings.edu/~/media/Projects/BPEA/Spring%202012/2012a_Shambaugh.pdf

Siebert, F. S., Peterson, T., & Schramm, W. (1956). *Four theories of the press.* Urbana, IL: University of Illinois Press.

Thompson, J. B. (1995). *The media and modernity: a social theory of the media.* Stanford, CA: Stanford University Press.

NOTES

1. Michael Calderone, "New York Times Buyouts Push Veteran Journalists to the Exits." *Huffington Post.* January 24, 2013. Retrieved May 30, 2014 from http://www.huffingtonpost.com/2013/01/24/new-york-times-buyouts-veteran-editors-leave_n_2544574.html
2. BBC News, "Moody's Downgrades Portugal Debt." July 13, 2010. Retrieved August 3, 2013 from http://www.bbc.co.uk/news/10610673
3. Pedro Crisóstomo, "Taxa de Desemprego Atinge Novo Máximo de 17,8%." *Público.* May 31, 2013. Retrieved May 31, 2013 from http://www.publico.pt/economia/noticia/taxa-de-desemprego-sobe-para-178–1596045
4. *Público,* "Mercado Publicitário Digital Foi o Único a Crescer em Quota e Valor nos Últimos Anos." January 26, 2014. Retrieved January 31, 2014 from http://www.publico.pt/economia/noticia/mercado-publicitario-digital-foi-o-unico-a-crescer-em-quota-e-valor-nos-ultimos-anos-1621177
5. Adriano Nobre, "Publicidade Volta a Crescer Cinco Anos Depois." *Expresso.* May 10, 2014. Retrieved June 15, 2014 from http://expresso.sapo.pt/publicidade-volta-a-crescer-cinco-anos-depois=f869344
6. The same trend has been witnessed in other European markets such as Spain. See "Investimento Publicitário Crescerá 1% em Espanha em 2014." *Notícias Ao Minuto.* November 25, 2013. Retrieved June 29, 2014 from http://www.noticiasaominuto.com/economia/136297/investimento-publicitario-crescera-1-em-espanha-em-2014
7. Angola's relations with Portugal date back to the 16th century when the Portuguese settled in several territories in Africa during the period of the maritime discoveries. It would remain as a Portuguese colony until 1975 when, following the overthrow of the Lisbon dictatorship, independence was finally given to the African territories. Following independence, the history of Angola is mostly marked by the civil war that took place between 1975 and 2002 even though during these 27 years of military conflict there were some peace periods. The war was between two of the liberation movements that had fought Portugal's colonial rule: the MPLA (People's Movement for the Liberation of Angola), with close connections to the Soviet Union; and the UNITA (National Union for the Total Independence of Angola), that also positioned itself as a socialist party but with closer connections with the West. During the Cold War, both parties had international support from different countries, namely the US, Soviet Union and Cuba (Ferreira, 1994).
8. Tradingeconomics.com; http://www.tradingeconomics.com/angola/gdp-growth

9. Angola became a member of OPEC (Organization of the Petroleum Exporting Countries) in 2006. It is currently Africa's second largest oil producer, behind Nigeria, with a production of 1.70 million barrels a day, representing around 45% of its GDP and 95% of its exports. Diamond exploration is another flourishing sector that currently represents only 1% of the country's GDP but that is also expected to grow; in Muzima, J., & Mazivila, D. (2014). *Angola 2014*. Retrieved May 19, 2014 from http://www.africaneconomicoutlook.org/fileadmin/uploads/aeo/2014/PDF/CN_Long_EN/Angola_ENG.pdf
10. http://data.worldbank.org/country/angola. Retrieved May 29, 2014.
11. In 2013 Angola ranked number 130 among 179 countries analyzed on the Press Freedom Index. Retrieved May 29, 2014 from http://en.rsf.org/press-freedom-index-2011-2012,1043.htm
12. "Daddy's Girl: How an African 'Princess' Banked $3 Billion in a Country Living on $2 a Day." *Forbes*. August 14, 2014. Retrieved May 19, 2014 from http://www.forbes.com/sites/kerryadolan/2013/08/14/how-isabel-dos-santos-took-the-short-route-to-become-africas-richest-woman/2/
13. See note 12.
14. See note 12.
15. José Manuel Rocha and Rosa Soares, "Sonae não se Compromete com Datas para o Lançamento de Hipermercados em Angola." *Público*. March 19, 2014. Retrieved May 19, 2014 from http://www.publico.pt/economia/noticia/sonae-nao-se-compromete-com-datas-para-o-lancamento-de-hipermercados-em-angola-1628910
16. Ana Brito, "Angolana Newshold Reduz Posição na Cofina para 12,21% do Capital e Votos." *Público*. November 1, 2013. Retrieved January 13, 2014 from http://www.publico.pt/economia/noticia/angolana-newshold-reduz-posicao-na-cofina-para-1221-do-capital-e-votos-1611096
17. "Conheça a Nova Revista Rumo." *Visão*. December 7, 2011. Retrieved June 1, 2012 from http://visao.sapo.pt/conheca-a-nova-revista-rumo=f637719
18. Maria Lopes, "Empresa *offshore* Pineview Overseas, Dona da Newshold, é Toda da Família Madaleno." *Público*. December 28, 2012. Retrieved February 11, 2013 from http://www.publico.pt/portugal/noticia/empresa-offshore-pineview-overseas-dona-da-newshold-e-toda-da-familia-madaleno-1578871
19. Celso Filipe, "O ABC do Poder Angolano." *Jornal de Negócios*. October 15, 2013. Retrieved May 12, 2014 from http://www.jornaldenegocios.pt/economia/detalhe/2013_10_15_o_abc_do_poder_angolano.html
20. Luís Villalobos, "António Mosquito Pagou dez Milhões para Ficar com 27,5% da Controlinveste." *Público*. April 3, 2014. Retrieved May 30, 2014 from http://www.publico.pt/economia/noticia/antonio-mosquito-pagou-10-milhoes-para-ficar-com-275-da-controlinveste-1630758
21. Retrieved May 30, 2014 from http://ind.millenniumbcp.pt/pt/Institucional/investidores/Pages/EstruturaAcionista.aspx
22. Official note produced by Controlinveste Management, 11 June 2014. Retrieved June 28, 2014 from http://www.controlinveste.pt/Pt/Imprensa/NoticiaInterior.aspx?content_id=3965971
23. "Reestruturações de Mosquito Aceleram." *Expresso*. June 21, 2014.

CHAPTER TWELVE

Africa in Spanish Newspapers: From Indifference to Irrelevance

LUIS CONCEPCIÓN SEPÚLVEDA AND ALFONS MEDINA

INTRODUCTION: DISPERSION TO SPAIN

The 1990s marked the start of an unprecedented over-representation of Sub-Saharans in news stories related to immigration in the Spanish press (Bauböck, 2004; Concepción & Medina, 2011; Concepción, Rodrigo, & Medina, 2008). In 2005, Sub-Saharan Africans multiplied their attempts to cross the fences of Ceuta and Melilla, fences which separate two different worlds. Journalistic discourse about this type of migration was more concerned with impact and emotions than with the actual percentage of African immigrants compared to the total number of immigrants arriving in Spain. It appeared that the demise of the media value chain paradigm compelled the newspapers to modify their style of news coverage in their online versions in ways designed to attract more readers. In fact, Africans did not constitute the largest immigrant groups; however, images of Africans abounded in the media representation of the diaspora. We use the concept of "diaspora", as we believe it is a more appropriate term to describe the ongoing dispersion of certain migrating peoples around the world, such as the Jewish people, for whom exodus is practically a defining trait (Concepción & Medina, 2011). Increasingly detrimental forms of media representation were in evidence from then on, until the financial crisis eventually overshadowed immigration in the media and the issue became a secondary concern. According to the data of the Centre for Sociological

Research (CIS, www.cis.es), in April 2005, 25.9% of Spanish people considered immigration to be one of the three main problems facing the country; in September 2006, it had risen to 59.6%, and in October 2006, 49% of Spanish people thought the same. From 2012 to the present day, the percentage has fallen dramatically to approximately 5% or significantly lower (in February 2014, only 2.1% of the population considered immigration to be one of the three main problems in Spain).

Despite the importance of journalistic discourse in the social perception of Africa and Africans, there has been little study of the media approach to the subject. The present study is the result of a wish to gain first-hand knowledge of how the leading Spanish newspapers deal with Africa and to identify the predominant images of Africa on the Internet. The analysis focuses on the digital versions of two of the leading newspapers in the Spanish-speaking world: www.elmundo.es and www.elpais.com. In data published by the Oficina para la Justificación de la Difusión (Spanish Audit Bureau of Circulation), OJD Interactiva, in September 2013, www.elmundo.es was ranked in second place, with over 92 million visits per month. According to the website Alexa.com, *El Mundo* is the tenth most visited Spanish website, and ranked number 410 worldwide. The print edition of *El País* is the most widely read newspaper in Spain, with an average circulation of 377,603 copies in January 2014, far more than the sports press (Marca and As) and *El Mundo* (267,151 copies). Its website is, according to Alexa.com, the thirteenth most visited Spanish site.

However, we did not want the scope of this chapter to be limited to a typical content analysis. Our aim was to devise a theoretical framework and a methodology which would allow us to deviate from the work already undertaken in other studies. We were searching for a change of direction which would enable us to go beyond mere description of the media image of Africa.

We also aimed to broaden the scope of the research in order to understand how the journalist engages communicatively with the reader through news stories. Some of the attitude and the interest invested in the way Africa-related news is transmitted may be explored by redefining the role played by the news report and by semantics in the content analysis. By doing so, keys to interpretation and results which differ from those found in the conventional approach to discourse can be provided.

The starting point

Our theoretical framework takes as its starting point the rupture with the concept of reason focused on an individual cognitive subject. The philosophy of the subject links the thought systems of most of the great philosophers up to the present day. This tradition has dominated thought for centuries, and its most common form of expression, individualism, is gradually becoming the source of normative guidance in people's everyday life (Habermas, 2008). Habermas's theory of knowledge is based on a lone individual who seeks out objects he wishes to know and manipulate. Subjectivity gives free rein to objectivity and the knowledge of objects becomes the only way of engaging with the world and understanding reason. This reduction of the possibilities of reason also encompasses language, which can only carry out a cognitive function. It represents only objects and facts, and is limited to pronouncing true statements (Habermas, 2008, p. 338).

However, with the emergence of the complex notion of *Lebenswelt* or "life-world" (a re-elaboration of the Husserlian concept of the life-world, corrected and broadened by Habermas and extended to a theory of communication), language became open to new dimensions of analysis:

-Social Dimension
-Subjective Dimension
-Objective Dimension.

By taking precisely this concept as a basis, the body of pre-reflective knowledge of community life, Jürgen Habermas assembled the pieces of a theoretical framework which would lead to the development of an interesting methodology for discourse analysis. He connected Austin's (1982) and Searle's (2001) speech acts from Anglo-Saxon language philosophy, Karl Bühler's functions of language and, from a more epistemological point of view, Karl Popper's three worlds of knowledge (Habermas, 2008). Under Habermasian analysis, language was no longer subject to only a representative or constative function, linked to a world of objects. There were now two new complementary dimensions: the subjective world of expressive function and the social world which regulates human relationships. The life-world forms the basis for processes such as cultural reproduction, social integration and cooperative action, but also for socialization of the individual. The communicative engineering of language, language defined in terms of communication, is the key to travelling through the different spheres, connected to each other by a fragile system of inter-dependence. Indeed, it is the communicative potential of language which makes it possible.

As mentioned above, employing a methodology with a major theoretical component is a clear indication that this study intends to take a different direction to traditional content analysis-based studies. We say major theoretical component because the introduction of the "life-world" or *Lebenswelt* into the area of Formal Pragmatics and into the Habermasian interpretation of speech acts helps situate language outside the instrumental conception of neo-positivism and the philosophy of the subject.

In this way, communication takes centre stage, resulting in language going beyond a linguistic framework to be studied from other perspectives, from sociology to the aesthetics of the subjective world. In a news report, the individual, social and cultural worlds are interwoven in a way that has rarely been explored previously.

A THREE-TIER METHODOLOGY

For the analysis, twenty news stories (40 in total) were selected from the digital editions of *El Mundo* and *El País* in March and April of 2012. The selection was made by using "Africa" as the keyword in a search of their respective digital archives. When designing a viable analysis tool, it is necessary to attempt to overcome recurring bipolarities which often appear in content analysis studies. Positioning the methodology at an intermediate point, avoiding extremes, should be a categorical imperative. In this way, more elaborate interpretations may be achieved, such as those which interlink text and extra-textual reality.

This methodological proposal attempts to depart from some of the conventions of content analysis:

- A freer relationship with the text:

The formal pragmatics of Habermas allows the news story to be understood at a level beyond the text itself. It provides the basis for a freer relationship with the text, which goes beyond excessively linguistic interpretations while avoiding overly sociological interpretations. Two extremes are thus avoided; at one extreme, those analyses which deal with language as a substitute for social reality, expressing no more than its literal meaning; at the other, those which neglect to connect the text with the social reality to which it belongs. A good snapshot of Africa should place the contextual conditions (social, historical, media-related) present in the text and the role which language plays in the production of social practices and processes on the same level (Alonso & Callejo, 1999, p. 67).

- Overcoming the limited conception of meaning:

Traditionally, content analysis of news stories has been confined to studying the intentions of the journalist through the meaning of the text. However, semantics should be placed on the interpersonal level of the media product. Meaning is "conventionally regulated", since the reader or listener should recognize and understand it (Muñoz, 2013, p. 112). Meaning cannot therefore be attributed solely to the transmitter or the text; rather, it is an unfinished product which does not depend on the journalist alone. Ultimately, semantics builds bridges between the transmitter and the receiver and, although the latter cannot be invoked in the analysis, it is possible to carry out approximations through the text.

- Going beyond the representative function of language:

This means deviating from the path established by philosophy of the subject, from a model of knowledge based solely on the cognitive aspect and on an objective world.

- An interpretative analysis:

The theoretical framework of this methodology allows us to depart from a descriptive level of analysis, which does not usually enable more complex interpretations to be generated.

- Combining global and local perspectives:

Most content analysis studies are based on a global view of the text and summarize the major narrative lines of the media representation of the object of study. However, while the more general ideas expressed in the headline have the power of first impressions on the reader, the local aspects of the text contain a symbolic component, underestimated in numerous studies and yet as important as the global analysis of the news piece. Because of their subtlety, the latent contents interact and negotiate their meanings with the receiver from a position of superiority, as they operate at a "subliminal" level.

Our model of analysis is three-pronged, consisting of journalistic analysis, semantic analysis and formal pragmatic analysis.

JOURNALISTIC ANALYSIS:

The quality of the information and the type of coverage undertaken by the journalist is evaluated. The evaluation criteria are based on those proposed by María del Mar Blanco Leal in her book, *Modelos de Análisis para el Estudio Crítico de la Prensa* (2008):

a) Content and placement of the news story:
   - Topic of the news story
   - Section in which it appears
   - Type of story
   - Information: complete / incomplete
   - Sources

- Source types
- Journalistic genre

b) Way of presenting the information:
- Is it restricted to the superficial aspect of events, or does it go into detail?
- Are both positive and negative aspects assessed?
- Are human values which help build community and promote mankind transmitted?
- Does it attempt to develop cultural and moral sensitivity in the readership, promoting open dialogue and critical sense?

SEMANTIC ANALYSIS OF THE TEXT

According to the Jensen and Jankowski model (1993), textual semantics studies the significance of news articles on two levels: global semantics and local semantics. In the former, on the one hand, emphasis is placed on the study of the more general semantics, on the more abstract ideas of the piece, which are often embedded in the headline. This occupies the most hierarchical position within the thematic structure of the text. On the other hand, local semantics is broken down into major categories to allow for a more detailed analysis of the news story. In this way, important elements such as local coherence (or links between sentences), style and rhetoric are taken into account.

FORMAL PRAGMATIC ANALYSIS

Thanks to formal pragmatics, it is possible to go beyond the text of the news story and identify the type of communication established between the journalist and the reader. Traditionally, linguists and philosophers had focused on the semantic, syntactic and phonetic aspects of the linguistic structures of language, without examining the pragmatic aspects of speech, related to extra-linguistic elements, such as the use and linguistic execution of effective speech (Muñoz, 2013). Thus, with the Speech Acts Theory of Austin (1982) and Searle (2001), linguistics began to move in another direction. Rather than being restricted to the text, meaning can be considered within the framework of an interpersonal relationship or a speech act.

Habermas re-visited Speech Acts in his ambitious *Theory of Communicative Action* (1999a, 1999b), pointing out that forms of speech or uses of language are social actions with a dynamic role in the major spheres of human life: society, personality and culture. Each one of these is related to one of the three worlds of Karl Popper—the objective world, the social world and the subjective world—and serves communicative and social functions. Our analysis of the news stories has been informed by the following classification, which shows the most frequent types of speech.

– Constative Speech:

- A form of cognitive communication. It is related to knowledge.
- The transmitter refers to an external, objective reality; an objective world.
- Convictions are expressed.
- It has an objectifying attitude.
- The communicative function of language is the presentation of a state of affairs.
- The first social function of language is to generate understanding; the second, to activate transmission of cultural knowledge. Consequently, the most obvious propositional component is the representation of knowledge.
- The validity claim of the text or speech act is a claim to truth.
- The authority of the text is derived from the objectivity of the experience of the journalist or speaker.

Source: Designed by the authors based on Habermas (1999b, pp. 93, 94, 105).

– Regulative Speech:

- This is an interactive form of communication, as there is a close relationship between speech and action.
- The transmitter of the message refers to something in the common social world, in the sense of establishing an interpersonal relationship which is recognized as legitimate.
- The journalist displays an attitude which conforms to social norms.
- It is the most social of these forms of language and is linked to action. Its pre-linguistic origin must be taken into account, based on the Durkheimian concept of ritual solidarity which derives from religious faith. The communicative function of the language is appellative. In the first instance, it coordinates action; in the second, it triggers behaviours which conform to norms and traditions, and contributes to the social integration of the individual.
- The speaker's validity claim is normative, based on the habits and customs of a certain community.
- The authority of the text is moral truth but in the shape of normative validity; impersonal and abstract in nature and removed from time. It is the result of an idealized agreement and is the use of language most strongly influenced by Habermasian inter-subjectivity.
- It is the use of language which most greatly motivates the reader or Internet user to accept the offer of the speech act.

Source: Designed by the authors based on Habermas (1999a, p. 416; 1999b, pp. 93, 94, 100, 105, 110).

– Expressive Speech:

- It is an expressive form of communication.
- The speaker refers to something belonging to his subjective world, in the sense of disclosing a personal experience.
- The function of the language is expressive, as the speaker is in some way representing himself.
- The validity claim is subjective.

Source: Designed by the authors based on Habermas (1999a, p. 418).

COMPARATIVE ANALYSIS OF AFRICA AT ELMUNDO.COM AND ELPAIS.COM

El Mundo, a sterile approach

In the articles selected from *El Mundo*, the range of subjects which bear some relation to Africa is wider than those from *El País*. However, what might at first suggest a more multi-faceted view of a vast continent ends up being an illusion. The assorted contexts in which it features make up a miscellany of news stories which have little to do with Africa.

The irrelevance of Africa becomes clearer each time a "distant story" is found. We are not talking here about the distance necessary to gain impartiality or perspective concerning what is happening in the major focal point of the news—the Mali crisis—but rather the result of lack of interest. For *El Mundo*, the armed conflict between the leaders of the military coup and the different Tuareg rebel factions is merely a "popular and military protest", with negative connotations, typical of the African continent:

"Los golpistas de Malí prometen juzgar al presidente derrocado" (3-4-2012).
(The Mali coup leaders promise to judge the ousted President)

"Los rebeldes tuaregs ganan terreno en Malí y entran en la estratégica ciudad de Gao" (31-3-2012).
(Tuareg rebels gain ground in Mali and enter the strategic city of Gao)

"Los países vecinos de Malí declaran un embargo contra la Junta Militar y enviarán tropas" (2-4-2012).
(Mali's neighbouring countries declare an embargo against the Military Junta and will send troops)

Africa is, in short, a place far removed from Spanish reality, and located outside the centres of world power. The few resources that *El Mundo* devotes to Mali are proportional to the lack of importance it attributes to the conflict; as a result, its journalists are unable to form a solid opinion and the newspaper does not take a clear stance. This explains why the newspaper does not take sides in such a relevant conflict, and why it does not send any correspondents or special envoys to cover the events at first-hand. Given this situation, the story is cloaked in sterile reporting of a markedly descriptive nature, such as the news stories which merely reproduce the statements of Captain Amadou Haya Sanogo which appear in Agence France-Presse (AFP):

> **"El jefe de la Junta Militar de Malí restablece la Constitución"** (2-4-2012).
> *(The head of the Military Junta in Mali restores the constitution)*
>
> **"Los países vecinos de Malí declaran un embargo contra la Junta Militar y enviarán tropas"** (2-4-2012).
> *(Mali's neighbouring countries declare an embargo against the Military Junta and will send troops)*

The fact that *El Mundo* does not manage to construct its own interpretations of the Mali crisis also responds to the architecture of the story. As no journalists have been assigned to the region, the newspaper is obliged to become part of a rigid production line of information, which affords it little room for manoeuvre to provide added value by publishing less news from official sources. News agencies—primarily EFE, followed by Reuters and France-Presse—gather the information on-site through press conferences and official press releases offered by the military junta, now holding political power and able to articulate its own discourse. The newspaper has no option but to report on the conflict through the most economical and conventional genre, the news report, as it has no sources other than the apparatus of the institutional actors, which provide prefabricated communication. As a result, *El Mundo* reduces the number of actors involved in the story and diminishes the complexity of the events.

While it is true that a negative image hovers over practically all of the news, the text strategies employed by the journalists to transfer their preconceptions to society are usually subtle rather than obvious. The journalist's reluctance to make what tends to be a latent mental representation of Africa too explicit manifests itself at deeper, more local levels of the text and in the relationship with the reader. It also manifests itself in what is *not* said.

At no time does the newspaper do anything other than present the state of affairs from a constative perspective, where the power of the facts is presented as an objective truth. The validity claim of the information is left to the news agency, and the newspaper merely makes itself available as a medium for transferring pre-selected and prioritized news to its readership.

SCIENCE IN *EL MUNDO*

The second thematic area which dominates the African panorama is science. The continent is fertile ground for archaeological discoveries. Three of the twenty news items selected are about the prehistoric past of a continent which arouses the curiosity of researchers:

"Los restos de la hoguera más antigua" (03-4-2012).
(The remains of the oldest bonfire)

"'Águila Roja' premiada en el World Media Festival de Hamburgo 2012" (29-3-2012).
('Águila Roja' *receives an award at the World Media Festival in Hamburg 2012*)—The same story mentions a Spanish-made documentary that also received an award at the festival.

"El homínido 'torpe' de hace 3,4 millones de años" (29-3-2012).
(The "clumsy" hominid from 3.4 million years ago)

Here we find documentary narratives which perpetuate the traditional way of dealing with the enigmas of a continent which is not only an inexhaustible source of fauna and flora for western countries, but which is also the cradle of mankind.

From a journalistic point of view, this type of news item diverges from the negative image of Africa which predominates in practically all news coverage. Firstly, because of the fact that scientific discoveries and the aforementioned documentaries are accompanied by a significant amount of contextualization, with a variety of expert sources in the subject matter, unlike in the other news items. Furthermore, these news stories transmit "human values which contribute to the construction of community and the promotion of mankind" and "attempt to develop the cultural sensitivity of the audience" (Blanco Leal, 2008), as Africa is considered the birthplace of human evolution.

These constative speech acts make up a form of cognitive communication in which the journalist refers to an objective world of scientific discoveries. Here, the values of a social world tacitly negotiated between journalists and readers do not come into play, so the function of communication is that of a transfer of knowledge. As a result, the news item is not classified as part of a process of social coordination (Habermas, 1999a), because the ultimate aim is not to persuade the reader to adopt a position or initiate an action. In the events recounted, there is an internal connection between meaning and validity, with the validity claim residing in scientific truths. The thematic centre of gravity lies more specifically in the scientific advances in the field of palaeontology themselves.

HEALTH IN AFRICA, UP FOR DEBATE

In terms of number of appearances, two stories related to health in Africa are ranked in third place.

"Oftalmólogos en peligro de extinción" (2-4-2012).
(Eye doctors: an endangered species)

"El tratamiento preventivo de la malaria es eficaz fuera de África" (29-3-2012).
(Preventative treatment of malaria is effective outside Africa)

These constitute a type of news story which offers greater quality of information and which shares certain technical parallels with the archaeological section. These pieces contain information which is more thorough and wider-ranging than usual, and negative rather than positive aspects are more apparent. Madrid-based *El Mundo* journalists write interpretative articles to which resources have been allocated so as not to depend solely on the news agencies; they cite expert opinions, leading scientific journals and researchers, providing the information with added value. Once again, Africa occupies a collateral position in news stories which report the results of international studies about the lack of ophthalmic opticians in the world and about treatment to prevent malaria outside the African continent. Despite the variety of sources used in the narration, they are published as news stories rather than as investigative journalism or other types of article. These texts are not lacking in depth, however, and a certain formality or neutrality of language is employed, which does not directly attack the image of Africa.

From a Formal Pragmatics perspective, the news stories in the health section are future-oriented communicative acts, since they always warn of situations which will worsen with time. As a result of the human drama dimension, they are regulative texts which seek to involve the reader by appealing to a social world with shared values. This socio-cultural element is seated in the historical experience of a welfare society which, over time, has constructed a free, universal public health service in Spain. The appeal to the reader is an important element in re-activating the role played by *El Mundo* in the public space.

EL PAÍS FORGETS THE READER

Although Africa is presented from fewer angles in *El País*, it is approached in a more impartial way, closer to reality, with a greater number of sources consulted. In the predominant news story, the military crisis in Mali, the story is told in a more complex and multi-faceted way, as a greater number of actors, settings and versions of the event are involved. In essence, the dialogue between stakeholders is broader in scope.

El País covers the Mali conflict in two different scenarios: in Mali itself, and in the diplomatic circles of the UN headquarters in New York. The first scenario is covered by a journalist assigned to the region, Fátima Valcárcel; as a result, media coverage of events is bound to improve as, in some cases, the sources will be studied more closely in the field:

"Los tuaregs toman por primera vez una capital de región" (31-3-2012).
(Tuaregs take a regional capital for the first time)

"Los independentistas tuareg toman las grandes ciudades del norte" (1-4-2012).
(Tuareg pro-independence forces take the great northern cities)

At this early stage, the news story is the most common genre used to report the Tuareg advance after the coup in Mali.

In general, there is no clear intention to strengthen ties with the reader by exploring a mutual ideology. There is no obvious attempt to seek complicity on the basis of shared social norms. As the news story does not try to compromise the reader's response explicitly, it is unlikely to draw attention or provoke opinions, attitudes and actions with the same intensity. Thus, there is no internal connection between receiving the news and action (reader response). These are constative texts in which language presents a state of affairs in a cognitive form of communication, and bears little relation to the social world of Spanish culture to which journalists and readers belong.

Yet *El País* appears to be more interested in emphasizing authorship and the presence of the journalists in the narration. This means that the subjective aspect of the media professionals, and also of the African characters from international institutions, is noteworthy in the Mali coverage. As a result, from the formal pragmatics perspective, more expressive elements are in evidence. This is true of the interview with the head of the African unit of UNESCO, Lazare Eloundou:

"Hay que salvar el patrimonio de Tombuctú" (3-4-2012).
(Timbuktu heritage must be saved)

An analysis of the global semantics of the news story reveals the prevalence of the Tuaregs in the grammatical structure in practically half of the headlines. The newspaper has sought to bridge the gap between Tuareg groups and, at certain moments, has integrated them as a source of information and as protagonists of the story. Their position as subjects of the sentence in the ultimate expression of the news story, the headline, gives them a leading role in the body of the text.

However, their presence in the headlines receives imbalanced treatment, as here they are characterized only by the actions they take in the conquest of the principal cities in the north, and never by what they say:

> **"Los independentistas tuareg toman las grandes ciudades del norte" (1-4-2012).**
> *(Tuareg pro-independence forces take the great northern cities)*

It is almost as if the spoken word is reserved for other actors in this sequenced story, such as France and those who occupy prominent positions in international bodies, such as the aforementioned Lazare Eloundou at UNESCO:

> **"Francia reclama en la ONU la máxima dureza contra los golpistas de Malí" (3-4-2012).**
> *(France demands strong action against Mali coup leaders at the UN)*
>
> **"Hay que salvar el patrimonio de Tombuctú" (3-4-2012).**
> *(Timbuktu heritage must be saved)*

However, the Tuaregs are also the object of an ambiguous language which recognizes the legitimacy of their demands while putting forward the hypothesis of a dangerous synergy between the nomad rebels and Islamic Jihad groups. The sinister shadow of Al Qaeda always seems to be present in the news.

> **"Los independentistas tuareg toman las grandes ciudades del norte de Malí" (1-4-2012).**
> *(Tuareg pro-independence forces take the great northern cities)*
>
> **"Malí sí importa" (29-3-2012).**
> *(Mali does matter)*

IRREGULAR IMMIGRATION

A report presented to the Council of Europe by Tineke Strip, Dutch senator for the Green Party, showed that NATO did not heed the cries for help of Sub-Saharan castaways, who were fleeing the war against Gaddafi the year before. *El País* follows the trail of one of the few survivors of the shipwreck, who arrived in Holland after an arduous journey through different countries. The newspaper condemns, firstly by means of a translated article from *The Guardian*, the irresponsibility of the NATO countries in not coming to the aid of the people on the perilous boat journey, when that zone of the Mediterranean was full of warships and aeroplanes.

"Los responsables de la tragedia" (29-3-2012).
(The Culprits of the Tragedy)

There is no ambiguity in the newspaper's stance in a second news story, where it criticises the Dutch government's intention to deport the shipwreck survivor, Ethiopian citizen, Abu Kurke Kebato. This becomes even clearer when the newspaper publishes an editorial in which it states its position in this case, in which basic human rights to political asylum are violated, in an even more explicit and open way.

"Holanda ordena detener y expulsar a uno de los náufragos que ignoró la OTAN" (30-3-2012).
(Holland orders the detention and deportation of one of the castaways ignored by NATO)

"La obligación de rescatar" (editorial), (1-4-2012).
(The Obligation to Rescue), **editorial**

El País publishes articles with a strong opinion component, based on Tineke Strip's report. In terms of journalistic quality criteria, these articles go into detail about the event narrated, from the history of the drifting boat with 72 Sub-Saharans on board, to the description of the personal story of Abu Kurke Kebato in Holland. Furthermore, in the different news pieces human values which contribute to the construction of community are transmitted, and they help develop moral sensitivity in the readership. However, the ability to reflect different points of view about the same issue, such as in the case of the Mali conflict, is not demonstrated here in the shape of an open, thoughtful dialogue which allows conflicting voices to be heard. While it is fundamental to clearly state who is the victim and who is the culprit, if there is sufficient evidence to do so, it is also fundamental to generate pluralistic discourse. *El País* only includes Strip's report, and the statements of Abu Kurke Kebato's lawyer, Marq Wijngaarden, and Amnesty International. These all agree that NATO authorities ignored the cries and messages for help and that the Dutch government was wrong to expel the shipwrecked man, a decision which the newspaper attributes to the influence of the extreme right in the Netherlands.

It is the sheer scale of the tragedy, with 73 Sub-Saharans—most of whom would perish—adrift on a small boat, and the cruelty shown by a European government in deporting one of the survivors, who had also endured a long, difficult journey through different countries, which forces *El País* to take a stand. Therefore, it produces regulative texts which attempt to reduce the distance and increase complicity between the journalist, the reader and the international community. First of all, it calls for clarification of what happened to the Sub-Saharans on the drifting boat, invoking the obligation to protect both the victims of armed conflict and those attempting to escape the horrors of war. The news story is set against a background of socially accepted values in interpersonal relationships (Habermas, 1999a, pp. 415, 416), through an expression of outrage. This can be read between the lines by means of short, forceful phrases: "He didn't make it"; "They were not rescued". The different episodes of the ill-fated adventure are also contextualized: "The journey of Kurke, a 23-year-old Ethiopian who left his home to escape the violence, has floundered again"; "Just as in Libya, the current sends Kurke back against his will." There is an internal relationship between what is said and a consensus, a tacit agreement, which connects the journalist with the reader in a common framework of interpretation which is drawn from culture and is set in motion thanks to socialization.

"Holanda ordena detener y expulsar a uno de los náufragos que ignoró la OTAN" (30-3-2012).
(Holland orders the detention and deportation of one of the castaways ignored by NATO)

On analyzing how meaning is developed on a local scale in the text, what immediately stands out is the victimization of the Sub-Saharan castaways. It should also be pointed out that the newspaper comes to the defence of the victims at every moment, and supports the Dutch senator's version of events. It also eschews the typical anonymity of Africans in the media, applying an unprecedented personalization process to the Ethiopian Abu Kurke Kebato. As well as giving his name, surnames, age and nationality, the newspaper also explains the reason why he is leaving his home behind—namely, violence. In this way, the newspaper also moves away from the stereotype of the African who emigrates out of financial necessity. At the same time, the sea voyage and his determination to survive are recounted. However, the news discourse concedes these individual identities on very few occasions, when Africans are victims of tragedies of a different nature.

HEALTH

There are two feature articles which, despite not belonging to the most common topic areas in this sample, are worth mentioning because of their semantic density. They deal with very sensitive issues, all related to disease and famine, all related in some way to health and child mortality. They also provoke the greatest reaction on the Internet of all the news stories analyzed. In all likelihood, this is due to the fact that these articles accentuate the human side of the characters, and the actors themselves are the centre of gravity of the subject matter.

The first report focuses on one of the least-known diseases which ravage Africa, an epidemic which preys on the most vulnerable—children. It provokes a huge response from readers on social networks.

"El síndrome que solo mata niños" (25-3-2012). *(The syndrome which only kills children)*

An interview with US doctor and missionary Warren Cooper serves to introduce the reader to specific cases of nodding syndrome, a disease which has been decimating the child population in pockets of East Africa, such as South Sudan, northern Uganda and southern Tanzania, for many years. The report uses Cooper's experience to try to pinpoint the mysterious origins of the rare disease. The child mortality caused by the disease is a major argument for the direct involvement of the journalist in the story. It also appeals to the digital reader to become involved, as there are few subjects in the news able to mobilize both journalists and readers to such an extent.

The second feature reports on the severe food crisis which looks likely to affect Chad; this also had a big impact on social networks. As with the previous report, there is no degree of dependence on news agencies and international bodies and institutions, because what matters here is the first person account of the journalist.

"La vida al borde del hambre" (24-3-2012). *(Life on the verge of famine)*

At the highest, most general semantic level, the grammatical subject of the headline is life, which alerts the reader that the focus of the piece will be the human aspect. Malnutrition is ravaging the population of Chad, but many families are unable to identify the symptoms and try to treat it with traditional healing methods. In addition to the tragic lack of information, the situation is compounded by the return of some 90,000 Chadians from Libya, to find a homeland beset by poverty. The local meaning deployed in the words, phrases and the journalistic style of the two articles has some important connecting factors. In both articles, there is a process of individualization of the characters; the discourse revolves around them, and they are the focus of the journalists' viewpoint. They endure inhumane situations and bring individual personal accounts to human dramas which are often told from a macro-social perspective. Alongside the subjectivity of the actors, the report shows recalcitrant images of the African world. In this genre, journalists lower their guard in terms of self-censorship, giving free rein to the most spontaneous, free representations of the African world; as a result, their own definitions of Africa are more in evidence. The abandoning of formal conventions, of the strict style guidelines of the news piece, gives the journalist licence to be more subjective, more human, and to recount personal experience. This makes it more likely that common spaces and the most long-held western views of the most atavistic Africa will come into play. While the report raises awareness of and humanizes the numbers of these tragedies by transmitting human values, it also reveals the subjective world (or life-world) of the media professional. Prejudices or stereotypical images can slip into these expressive texts because, in some way, the "objectivity or impartiality" of the news story is broken. In this context, there is a recurring dialectic: the tribal, pre-scientific landscape of Africa clashes with the scientific West. Tribal witchdoctors, the supernatural theories behind the advice of village elders, and African cultural issues all clash with western medical practice.

A few examples from the article "La vida al borde del hambre" (*Life on the verge of famine*):[1]

"Nobody in the villages has any explanation for what is wrong with the children. The oldest villagers have told researchers the strangest theories. The Dinkas, the largest tribe in South Sudan, blamed the illness on the practice of eating monkey meat in some tribes. Superstition also pointed the finger of blame at western vaccines, chemical weapons used in the conflicts, marriages between tribespeople and people displaced by war, a plague of flies, and other supernatural causes, according to what a group of Sudanese experts were told in 2011 in Witto Payam, to the west of South Sudan. (Investigation into Nodding Syndrome in Witto Payam, Western Equatorial State, 2010, Southern Sudan Medical Journal)".

"Doctor Cooper tried to carry out a cerebral biopsy on a child who had died. 'I couldn't persuade them to let me do it, probably for cultural reasons.'"

"Neither did it work when little Koubra, three months old, was burned with a hot iron and a cotton tip on the chest when he started having trouble breathing. Many other parents in remote areas of Chad turn to traditional remedies to cure problems they are not always able to diagnose."

"A medieval market must have looked very much like the one in Mao, where flies and pack mules move around the narrow streets, packed with people and stalls selling dried tomatoes, carrots and cereals, and the occasional stall selling soap and Chinese cosmetics."

CONCLUSIONS

Not wishing to reduce the analysis to the purely linguistic, we sought a change in the dialogue between researcher and news story. The triple perspective of this analysis allows us to approach discourse in a more open, global way. The journalistic aspect helps us to re-think the news story as a media product which responds to productive routines and quality criteria; meanwhile, Habermas's formal pragmatics enable us to frame it within the communicative situation between journalist and readers. Semantics, communicology and formal pragmatics work together to question the news story beyond the news story itself, in other scenarios where it operates and may be understood.

Thus, from the perspective of semantics we see that the media representation of Africa in the digital versions of the two leading Spanish newspapers, *El País* and *El Mundo*, is conditioned by a previous stage. Africa remains imprisoned behind the bars of an individual and collective imagery which confines it to a semantic place and a residual space in the mental geography of the journalist. The negative construction of the image of Africa is symbolic rather than textual, social rather than journalistic. It manifests itself most frequently in local and underlying aspects of the text, but also in what is omitted by the journalist and in the way in which the actors are characterized. The case of the Tuaregs in the Mali conflict is a flagrant example: they are defined by their actions and not by their words, in contrast to what occurs with foreign powers.

According to the journalistic analysis model of María del Mar Blanco Leal, the lack of resources allocated to writing about Africa and an excessive reliance on secondary sources restrict these newspapers to the news story as the most economical genre. Reportage and features, in contrast, demand more resources and more comprehensive coverage. In the case of *El Mundo*, news agencies dictate the filter and the architecture of the narration, while at *El País* it is rather the Mali state media. Stylistic conventions, the apparent formality of the language and the rigid narrative structure of the news story help conceal the most recalcitrant images of the African world.

In addition, this indifferent approach invalidates any possibility of selecting other newsworthy subjects and of constructing a good situational map of events. An insurmountable gap emerges between the journalist and the narrated reality, a distance which ends up dominating the journalistic viewpoint itself. With their distant stance, both newspapers neglect to construct a well-crafted discourse, and also neglect their role as information specialists in an advanced society. The principle of least effort also explains how the interpretations of the agencies and the state media in Mali are accepted, as long as they coincide with the journalists' common places. This lack of structural definition in the position they adopt results in contradictions, ambiguity in the treatment of the actors, and voices which are silenced. In the end, the Mali conflict falls outside the framework of socio-cultural interpretation of the most widely read and influential newspapers of the Spanish-speaking world.

In terms of Habermas's formal pragmatics, the journalists have been unable to appeal to the reader, to involve him in the story, or to share the wealth of values which connect them through the news. In most cases, it is only possible to present a state of affairs of a faraway, insignificant reality. As a result, the power of the events (narrated by other agents) prevails as an objective truth. Furthermore, the sobriety of the objectivist language creates the effect of a false authenticity which covers the semantic basis of the information.

The fact that the stories are formulated as constative texts within news discourse can basically be explained by journalistic apathy. The conflict in Mali and the scientific discoveries are written from this perspective. Regulative texts which signal a change in attitude towards trying to capture the reader's attention are in the minority. *El Mundo* rouses from its indifference in the stories related to health and poverty, in which a traditional view of Africa can be observed; *El País*, meanwhile, shakes off its passive attitude when it takes the side of the Sub-Saharans fleeing armed conflict in Libya, in the section entitled "Irregular immigration". The newspapers only establish ways of bonding with the reader in certain human tragedies, which tie in with the adversity that has always been associated with the continent.

However, in the feature articles in *El País* about famine and disease, all rules of news discourse are broken. In these stories, style and "objectivity", partially constructed, keep at bay the more openly conservative prejudices of the journalist's subjective world and of the socio-cultural sphere in which he lives. Nevertheless, the expressive texts of the articles allow the writer's personal views and literary resources to intrude. In feature writing, there are fewer mechanisms to restrain or conceal prejudices and common places, and these are exposed. The starkest images of Africa are found in news stories which are highly emotionally charged and thus provoke a significant virtual response. Indeed, with respect to the online versions of *El País* and *El Mundo*, the breakdown of the media value chain resulted in a kind of news coverage that lacked the added value of an adequate interpretation of the communication medium in question. As a consequence, the media outlets in question forfeited their traditional role of managing and controlling their own discourse on account of their excessive dependence on news agencies and public news media.

BIBLIOGRAPHY

Alonso, L. E., & Callejo, J. (1999). El análisis del discurso: Del postmodernismo a las razones prácticas. *Reis, 88*, 37–73. Retrieved from http://www.reis.cis.es/REIS/PDF/REIS_088_04.pdf

Austin, J. L. (1982). *Cómo hacer cosas con palabras: Palabras y acciones*. Barcelona, Spain: Paidós.

Bauböck, R. (2004). Cómo transforma la inmigración a la ciudadanía: Perspectivas internacionales, multinacionales y transnacionales. In A. Aubarell & R. Zapata (Eds.), *Inmigración y procesos de cambio: Europa y el Mediterráneo en el contexto global* (pp. 177–214). Barcelona, Spain: Icaria.

Blanco Leal, M. Del Mar. (2008). *Modelos de análisis para el estudio crítico de la prensa*. Madrid, Spain: Ediciones Internacionales Universitarias.

Concepción, L. G., & Medina, A. (2011). Claves teóricas para una nueva visión de la recepción mediática desde la experiencia migratoria. *Correspondencias & Análisis, 1*, 369–384.

Concepción, L. G., Rodrigo, M., & Medina, P. (2008). Niveles semánticos de las representaciones sociales de la inmigración subsahariana: Los sucesos de Ceuta y Melilla según ABC. *Estudios sobre el Mensaje Periodístico, 14*, 129–148.

Habermas, J. (1999a). *Teoría de la acción comunicativa, I. Racionalidad de la acción y racionalización social.* Madrid, Spain: Santillana.

Habermas, J. (1999b). *Teoría de la acción comunicativa, II. Crítica a la razón funcionalista.* Madrid, Spain: Santillana.

Habermas, J. (2008). *El discurso filosófico de la modernidad.* Madrid, Spain: Katz Editores.

Jensen, K. B., & Jankowski, N. W. (1993). *Metodologías cualitativas de investigación en comunicación de masas.* Barcelona, Spain: Bosch.

Leung, L. (2008). *Etnicidad virtual: Raza, resistencia y World Wide Web.* Barcelona, Spain: Gedisa.

Muñoz, C. (2013). Jürgen Habermas y la teoría de los actos de habla. Retrieved from http://media.wix.com/ugd/6de50a_2431d5cfa4d776e6ef0a3cafa402642a.pdf?dn=lectura_modulo_etica_del_discurso.pdf

Searle, J. (2001). *Actos de habla.* Madrid, Spain: Cátedra.

NOTE

1. "Nadie en las aldeas tiene explicación para lo que les pasa a los niños. Los más viejos han contado a los investigadores las teorías más peregrinas. Los Dinka, la tribu mayoritaria en Sudán del Sur, culpaban del mal a la costumbre de algunas tribus de comer carne de mono. La superstición también sembró dudas sobre las vacunas occidentales, las armas químicas utilizadas durante los conflictos, los matrimonios entre los miembros de algunas tribus con desplazados de la guerra, el ataque de unas moscas y otras causas sobrenaturales, según relataron en 2011 a un grupo de expertos sudaneses en Witto Payam, al oeste de Sudán del Sur. (Investigation into the Nodding syndrome in Witto Payam, Western Equatorial State, 2010, Southern Sudan Medical Journal)".
   "El doctor Cooper, que intentó hacer una biopsia cerebral a un niño que había fallecido…'No conseguí que me dejaran, probablemente por razones culturales.'"
   "Tampoco funcionó que al pequeño Koubra, de tres meses, le quemaran con un hierro candente y una punta de algodón en el pecho cuando empezó a tener problemas para respirar. Muchos otros padres en las zonas remotas de Chad acuden a los remedios tradicionales para sanar algo que no siempre son capaces de identificar."
   "Un mercado medieval debía ser muy parecido al de Mao, donde las moscas y los burros de carga trasiegan en las callejuelas abarrotadas de gente y de puestos de tomates secos, zanahorias, cereales y alguno de jabón y cosméticos chinos."

Contributors

Ilona Biernacka-Ligieza is a professor of humanities and she works at the Faculty of Political Studies, Maria Curie-Skłodowska University. From September 2008 until October 2011 she has been the research fellow of the Institute of Media and Communication, University of Oslo. Her research interests include: local media; mass communication; new media; cross-cultural communication; journalism studies; local democracy; globalization; glocalization; media and politics; media and identity. Some of the research projects she has coordinated or participated in are: 1) *Local Media in Northern Europe—Society, Culture, Market and Politics;* 2) *Local Public Spheres Development in the Age of the ICT—The Case of Norway and Poland;* 3) *ICT—A Challenge for Local Political Communication and Local Democracy;* 4) *Local Media and Local Politics—Comparing Voting Campaigns in Poland and Norway;* 5) *The European Union Through Media: Truth or Lie;* 6) *Open Europe—Cultural Dialogue Across Borders.*

Nika Bogdanowska is Assistant Professor in the Department of Historical Poetics and Interpretation, the Institute of Polish Literature Studies, University of Silesia in Katowice. Her research interests are: text theory, discourse studies, and rhetoric. She is the author of the monograph *Komentarz* *i Komentowanie: Zagadnienia Konstrukcji Tekstu* (Wydawnictwo Uniwersytetu Śląskiego, 2003).

Ewa Bogdanowska-Jakubowska is Associate Professor of Linguistics. She is head of the Department of Pragmatics in the Institute of English at the University of Silesia, Katowice, Poland. Her work spans linguistic pragmatics, sociolinguistics, cross-cultural communication and the cognitive approach to metaphor. Her main research interests are (im)politeness, self-presentation and the concept of face. Her publications include *Cross-Cultural Dimensions of Politeness in the Case of Polish and English* (Wydawnictwo Uniwersytetu Śląskiego, 1999) and the monograph *Face: An Interdisciplinary Perspective* (Wydawnictwo Uniwersytetu Śląskiego, 2010).

Josep María Carbonell is currently the Dean of the Blanquerna School of Communication and International Relations at Ramon Llull University in Barcelona, where he has been teaching political science and media studies since 1996. In 2010, he was visiting scholar at the CSLS at Oxford University. From 1987 to 1995, he was deputy assistant to the President of the Country Council of Barcelona. From 1996 to 2005, he was a Member of the Parliament of Catalonia. From 2005 to 2009, he held the Presidency of the Catalan Audiovisual Council (CAC), and from 2007 to 2008, he acted as the President of the Mediterranean Network of Regulatory Bodies of Media (RIRM).

Araceli Castelló-Martínez holds a Doctorate in Communications, a Master's Degree in Global Communication, an Executive Master's in Community Management and a Degree in Advertising and Public Relations, with extraordinary degree award and second national award. Dr. Castelló currently teaches Advertising and Public Relations studies at the University of Alicante (Spain), where she is in charge of the Changing Communications Observatory, and she also works as a teacher in postgraduate studies at some prestigious Spanish universities. She has worked in several media (Carat, Initiative) and digital media (Ya.com, Vocento) agencies in Spain and Belgium, and published numerous publications and research work in the areas of digital communications and social media marketing.

Luis Concepción Sepúlveda holds a PhD in Communication and a BA in Journalism (Blanquerna School of Communication Studies). Researcher at CONinCOM Network (Conflict, Childhood and Communication) at the Blanquerna School of Communication Studies (Universitat Ramon Llull–Barcelona), he is the recipient of the Young Scholars Excellence Award 2013 Blanquerna (CICR, 2013) for the paper, "África, Rumbo a la Irrelevancia en los Diarios Digitales." He has authored *La Inmigración Subsahariana en la Retina de ABC: Los Sucesos de las Vallas de Ceuta y Melilla* (2012). He writes and publishes on communication and immigration, and the media representations of Africa.

Nelson Costa Ribeiro is an assistant professor and coordinator of communication studies at the Catholic University of Portugal. He holds a PhD from the University of Lincoln (UK) and has authored *BBC Broadcasts to Portugal During World War II: How Radio Was Used as a Weapon of War* (2011), along with two other books, several chapters, and journal articles dealing with media history, political economy of the media, and the history of media studies. He is a member of the board at the Research Center for Communication and Culture in Lisbon. He is also Vice-Chair of the Communication History Section at the European Communication Research and Education Association (ECREA).

Joan Cuenca is a public relations expert and he holds a PhD in Communication Studies, an MA in Social Communication, and a BA in Advertising and Public Relations from Ramon Llull University in Barcelona, Spain. He is a faculty member in the department of Advertising and Public Relations, and a member of the applied research group DIGILAB (Media, Strategy and Regulation) at the Blanquerna School of Communication and International Relations, where he teaches Advertising and Public Relations Strategy. He has been a visiting lecturer and researcher in the Department of Advertising, Public Relations and Media Design at the College of Media, Communication and Information (University of Colorado at Boulder). His most recent book publication is *Cómo hacer un plan estratégico de comunicación. Volumen III. La investigación preliminar* (2016). He has co-edited *Life Without Media* (2013), and jointly with Klaus Zilles coordinated the 6th, 7th, and 8th editions (2011, 2013, 2015) of the International Conference of Communication and Reality. He is a board member of the Spanish Association of Researchers in Public Relations (AIRP). Professionally, he works as a strategic consultant in communication.

Patrícia Dias is a researcher and teacher on communication and marketing for social and mobile media at the Catholic University of Portugal, in Lisbon, where she integrates the Research Center on Communication and Culture (CECC). She also coordinates the Post-graduate Course on Communication and Social Media [www.mediasociais.pt]. Specialized in the mediation and social impact of digital technologies, Patrícia Dias holds a PhD in Communication Sciences from the Catholic University of Portugal.

Author of "Living in the Digital Society" (2014) and "The Mobile Phone and Daily Life," her work includes several other scientific publications and presentations. More recently, she has been researching smartphone adoption in Portugal, best Portuguese cases of social media marketing and PR, and second screening. She is also one of the founding partners of Why Research [www. hyresearch.net], an organization specialized in qualitative studies and consulting.

Elisenda Estanyol is Lecturer at the Department of Information and Communication Sciences Department at the Universitat Oberta de Catalunya (UOC), Barcelona, Spain. She holds a PhD in Advertising and Public Relations from Universitat Autònoma de Barcelona (UAB) and a Master's Degree in Corporate Communication from Universitat Pompeu Fabra (UPF), Barcelona, Spain. Before joining the university, she worked for several years in public relations consultancies and in-house communication departments. She has also been an Associate Professor at the Department of Communication at the Universitat Pompeu Fabra and at the Istituto Europeo di Design. Her research interests are focused on public relations, creativity, social media and gamification.

Rita Figueiras is an assistant professor and coordinator of the PhD program in Communication Studies at the Catholic University of Portugal (UCP). She holds a PhD from UCP. She is a member of the Board at the Research Center for Communication and Culture in Lisbon. She is the coordinator of the research project, "South Atlantic Media Groups: Singularities of Lusophone Modernity," financed by the Portuguese Scientific Research Council–FCT. Her work focuses mainly on political communication, political economy of the media, and, more broadly, on the relationship between Media and Democracy. She has authored several books, book chapters, and journal articles.

Ferran Lalueza serves as director of the Information and Communication Sciences Department at the Universitat Oberta de Catalunya (UOC), Barcelona (Spain). He holds a BA in Communication Sciences from the Universitat Autònoma de Barcelona (UAB), an MA in Journalism Writing from the UAB and a PhD in Journalism from the Pompeu Fabra University (UPF), Barcelona, Spain. He also is adjunct Lecturer of the Communication Department at the UPF. His main research interests are focused on crisis communication, persuasive communication and ICT, public relations strategies, social media as a corporate communication tool and gamification. He has experience as a journalist and as a public relations consultant in multinational firms such as Burson-Marseteller.

Guillem Marca holds a PhD in Communication from the Rovira i Virgili University-RVU and a Master's in Communication Management from EAE-School of Business Administration. Dr. Marca is Professor at the University of Vic and at the Rovira i Virgili University. He is a founding member of the research group ESTISMA-Strategy and Issues Management in Public Relations and Corporate Communication in the Faculty of Communication of Ramon Llull University. He has published several book chapters and scientific articles in journals such as *Public Relations Review, FISEC-Estrategias*, and *BMC Health Services Research*, among others. He is Manager at *AlaOeste* Communication Agency.

Kathy Matilla holds a PhD in Communication and a Master's in Social Communication from Ramon Llull University-RLU. She holds a Master's in Marketing from ESADE-RLU and is Professor at the Faculty of Communication at RLU. Dr. Matilla is a founding member and Coordinator of the research group ESTISMA-Strategy and Issues Management in Public Relations and Corporate Communication in the Faculty of Communication of Ramon Llull University. She is the author of several books, book chapters, and scientific articles in academic journals such as *Public Relations Review, Razón y Palabra, Hologramática, AdResearch, FISEC-Estrategias, and Revista Internacional de RP*, among others. She is a Consultant on Public Relations, Corporate Communication and Management.

Alfons Medina is professor at the Blanquerna School of Communication Studies and International Relations at Ramon Llull University in Barcelona, Spain. He holds a PhD in Sociology from the Universitat de Barcelona, a BA in Sociology and Political Sciences from the Universitat Autonoma de Barcelona, and a BA in Geography and History from Universitat de Barcelona. He is a researcher at CONinCOM Research Network (Conflict, Childhood and Communication) and Head of Quality Unit at the School. He has co-authored "La Recerca en Comunicació" (2006) with Jordi Busquet and Josep Sort, and "Sociologia de la Comunicació" (2013) with J. Busquet. He co-edited with Josep Rom and Francesc Canosa, *Metamorphosis of the Media Space* (2009). Alfons Medina also coordinated the 5th (2009) International Conference of Communication and Reality. Alfons Medina writes and publishes on sociology of communication, ICT, communication competence, immigration and deliberative democracy.

Juan Monserrat-Gauchi is an organizational communication expert and holds a PhD in Information Science from the Cardenal Herrera University-CEU, Valencia, (Spain). He has a Degree in Information Science: Advertising and Public Relations, from the Polytechnic University of Valencia. Professionally, he has worked as a consultant in communication (1995–2002). In the academic field, he has been a member of the faculty teaching staff of the Department of Communication and Social Psychology in the Faculty of Economics and Business Sciences at the University of Alicante, (Spain) since 2002. He teaches the core subjects, Systems and Processes in Advertising and Public Relations, for the degree in Advertising and Public Relations. He also teaches courses within the Communication and Creative Industries Master, and in the Sports Management Master at the Polytechnic University of Valencia. He has been visiting professor at Playa Ancha University of Educational Sciences, Valparaíso, Chile; National School of Public Relations, Chile; The California State University (Sonoma), California, USA; and Universidad Nacional Autónoma de México (Mexico).

He has published several articles in specialized magazines and web portals, and collaborated in different specialized publications. Dr. Monserrat-Gauchi has participated as a lecturer in different courses and forums about organizational communication. His most recent publication is *Cómo Hacer un Plan Estratégico de Comunicación*, 2014 (How to Write a Strategic Communications Plan).

He is a member of the research group COMPUBES (Communication and Specific Targets) at the University of Alicante. He is also a member of *Observatorio de Revistas Científicas de Ciencias Sociales* (Scientific Social Journals Observatory). He is a member of FISEC (Latin-American Forum of Communication Strategies). He has recently been awarded at the International Franchising Fair and Spanish Franchisors Association with the first National Award for the best Research in Franchising.

Mireia Montaña is a media planning expert and she holds a Ph.D. in CommunicationStudies from Universitat Pompeu Fabra, Barcelona, Spain, as well as a Master's Degreein Social Communication from Universitat Ramon Llull, Barcelona, Spain. After several years working in multinational advertising agencies she is now a lecturer at the Department of Information and Communication and Sciences Department, Universitat Oberta deCatalunya (UOC), Barcelona, Spain. She has also held a position as Associate Professor atthe Department of Communication, Universitat Pompeu Fabra, Barcelona and at theEnterprise and Communication Department at the

Universitat de Vic, Barcelona. Sheis the Academic Director of the Postgraduate Course "Advertising on theInternet and other digital media" at the Universitat Oberta de Catalunya, Barcelona, Spain. Her research interests are communication 3.0, advertising, strategy, media planning, gamification, consumption and youth.

Andréa Oliveira holds a PhD in Communication from the Rovira i Virgili University-RVU, a Master's in Communication Management from EAE-School of Business Administration, and a Postgraduate in Crisis Communication from the Faculty of Communication at RLU. Dr. Oliveira is a professor at the University of Girona and at the Rovira i Virgili University. Dr. Oliveira is also a founding member of the research group ESTISMA-Strategy and Issues Management in Public Relations and Corporate Communication in the Faculty of Communication at Ramon Llull University. Dr. Oliveira has published several book chapters and scientific articles in journals such as *El Profesional de la Información*, and *FISEC-Estrategias*, among others., and is a Consultant on Public Relations and Corporate Communication.

Boris Ružić is a teaching assistant in the Department of Cultural Studies, Faculty of Humanities and Social Sciences, University of Rijeka, Croatia. He is a PhD student of "Interdisciplinary Humanities," researching the dialectics of the "filmic" image with the thesis, "The Gaze Behind the Screen: Perception of Images in Media Texts." He holds four seminar courses at the Department of Cultural Studies. He is an editor of "The Window Into the Digital" on the Croatian radio, a programme dealing with topics such as technology, media, visuality, and philosophy in contemporary society. He is a member of the editorial board for the international project funded by the EU (ERSTE Stiftung), *The Cultural Policy and Management Platform.* He is a coauthor of one book in Croatian (*The Fragments of the Image of the World: Critical Analysis of Contemporary Film and Media Production*), as well as several scientific articles in English and Croatian. His publications deal with the comparative dialectics of analogue and digital media and film. His scientific interests lie in the liminal zone of visual images, analogue and digital film image, and the semiotics of the virtual filmic state.

Felip Vidal received his PhD in Communication Studies from Complutense University of Madrid, Spain, with a dissertation entitled, "The Value of Experience in Signification Advertising." He graduated in Law from Girona University and in Philosophy from UNED. He has an MA in History of Philosophy, Aesthetics and Culture Theory, from Barcelona University. His research interests include advertising theory, branding, semiotics, and cultural theory. He has published several articles on the new forms of advertising and media culture. He is a member of the research group ARPA (Analysis of Audiovisuals Screens Reception) at Girona University, and he is also on the Editorial Board of *Communication Papers: Media Literacy & Gender Studies*.

Klaus Zilles is an associate professor at the Blanquerna School of Communication Studies and International Relations at Ramon Llull University in Barcelona, Spain. He holds a PhD in English and German Philology from the University of Heidelberg. He has authored *Rolando Hinojosa: A Reader's Guide* (2001), and in 2008, he co-edited, with Fernando Clemot, *En la Frontera: I Migliori Racconti della Narrativa Chicana* (2008). He co-edited *Life Without Media* (2013) with Joan Cuenca and Eva Comas. Joan Cuenca and Klaus Zilles also coordinated the 6th, 7th, and 8th editions (2011, 2013, 2015) of the International Conference of Communication and Reality. Klaus Zilles writes and publishes on Chicano literature, literature and film, and identity politics in the media.

Index

www.ingramcontent.com/pod-product-compliance
Ingram Content Group UK Ltd.
Pitfield, Milton Keynes, MK11 3LW, UK
UKHW021851100926
8556IPUK00020B/1179

9 781433 131783